SO MUCH TO DO AND SO LITT

You're running a household, juggling schedules, getting dinner on the table, while trying to maintain a sense of calm—and it's no small feat. It's easy to feel overwhelmed by all the daily details and forget that managing your family is the most important job you'll ever have, no matter how many other paid or volunteer positions you hold.

Your job description includes numerous tasks, all of which fall into one of these seven departments.

TIME & SCHEDULING—You're in charge of your family's calendar and daily schedule, making sure each person is at the right place at the right time with the right equipment.

HOME & PROPERTY—You make sure your family's home and yard, your belongings, and your vehicles are maintained and run smoothly.

FOOD—You see that your family's nutritional needs are met—and that mealtimes bring your family together.

FAMILY & FRIENDS—You love and support your kids in countless ways each day, and you also build relationships with other important family members, friends, and neighbors.

FINANCES—You help coordinate your family's budget, bill paying, saving, investing, and charitable giving.

SPECIAL EVENTS—You plan significant occasions like birthdays, holidays, and vacations.

SELF-MANAGEMENT—To ensure you have the energy and stamina to handle all your other responsibilities, you must also care for your body, sharpen your mind, and nourish your spirit.

You're probably managing some of these areas well, but there are others that cause you a lot of frustration. It's that way for every mom—but now you have a trusted resource with solutions to daily dilemmas and answers to your most urgent questions. Kathy Peel, America's Family Manager, is here to help!

THE BUSY MOM'S GUIDE

TO A HAPPY, ORGANIZED HOME

FAST SOLUTIONS TO HUNDREDS OF EVERYDAY DILEMMAS

AMERICA'S FAMILY MANAGER

KATHY PEEL

PICKET
FENCE
PRESS

A FAMILY MANAGER RESOURCE

An Imprint of Tyndale House Publishers, Inc.
Carol Stream, Illinois

Visit Tyndale's exciting Web site at www.tyndale.com

www.familymanager.com

TYNDALE and Tyndale's quill logo are registered trademarks of Tyndale House Publishers, Inc.

Picket Fence Press and the Picket Fence Press logo are trademarks of Family Manager Network, Inc.

The Busy Mom's Guide to a Happy, Organized Home: Fast Solutions to Hundreds of Everyday Dilemmas

Interior designed by Beth Sparkman

Cover designed by Ben Arrowood for RightHandDesign.com

Library of Congress Cataloging-in-Publication Data

Peel, Kathy, date.
   The busy mom's guide to a happy, organized home : fast solutions to hundreds of everyday dilemmas / Kathy Peel.
     p. cm.
   Includes index.
   ISBN-13: 978-1-4143-1619-2 (sc)
   ISBN-10: 1-4143-1619-4 (sc)
   1. Home economics. 2. Life skills—United States. I. Title.
   TX15.P415 2008
   640—dc22   2008006594

Printed in the United States of America

14 13 12 11 10 09

9 8 7 6 5 4

DEDICATION

To Genevieve and Christin

Beautiful brides
and the answers
to our prayers
for John and Joel

Cari

Kerry

Julie

Kari

Gay

Theresa

Becky

Jodi

Mom

Me

CONTENTS

CREATING A HAPPY HOME
STARTS HERE

When you start a new job, most companies provide orientation. You learn where to park your car, where to keep your sack lunch, and what qualifies as acceptable attire for casual Fridays. But when you take on motherhood, the world's most important job, there's no formal orientation—just on-the-job training and trial by fire.

My first few years of motherhood, I feared that if all moms were rated according to their domestic skills and parenting know-how, I would surely be in the remedial group. Boy, did I wish that all the secrets of motherhood and family management were passed down, from mother to mother, in a thick binder, indexed and categorized for every scenario. There were so many things I needed to know, like how to convince a toddler to eat vegetables, when to replace the hoses on our washing machine, and the best time of day to shop for groceries—all of which I had to learn the hard way.

When you take on motherhood, the world's most important job, there's no formal orientation—just on-the-job training and trial by fire.

I certainly could have used such a resource when it was time to enroll our three-year-old in preschool. I did some research and decided on a school that a mom in my neighborhood had raved about. She suggested I arrive early on registration day since classes filled up fast, so on the appointed day I pulled out of my driveway in time to get there 30 minutes before the doors opened. I was sure I'd get a prime parking spot, but as I rounded the corner, I almost hit a snaking line of women, hundreds of women, many of them sitting in lawn chairs, some of them playing cards on top of coolers, all of them stopping to stare at me (or so it seemed). My face turned hot with embarrassment. Oh, how I wished I had known that "early" meant "before dawn."

Since that time, I've collected thousands of tips and motherhood "secrets" that help moms save time and money—and sometimes embarrassment. *The Busy Mom's Guide to a Happy, Organized Home* is the quick-read version of the big binder I dreamed of when I was a young mother. It's for today's moms. Their lives are complex. They work, chauffeur kids to many activities, book vacations, buy birthday gifts, kiss boo-boos, and whip up nutritious meals. They manage their children's educations and social lives, decorate their homes, and provide clean laundry. Armed with cell phones, the Internet, double ovens, grocery stores that deliver, and casual office attire, they are world-class multitaskers, but they are still the most time-strapped generation ever.

Maybe you picked up this book because you can relate. You may count yourself among the 95 percent of moms who, according to AOL, are online two hours every day. You want instant information, so you head to the Web when you need answers. You compare prices, search for coupons, respond to blogs, and solicit advice. Often your research nets too many results. Finding ideas or opinions is easy; knowing which sources to trust isn't.

That's where this book can help. Growing wiser and working smarter is what the Family Manager way of doing things is all about, and it can transform your life. In my own quest to be a good mom and successful manager of my home, I devised the Family Manager system. It's based on the premise that the strategies that run any organization or business well—things like casting vision, creating standard operating procedures, practicing team building, and doing advance work—will help you run your home well. Trust me: These tactics can make your home and life run more smoothly than you ever dreamed. They'll help you order your day and ably oversee the countless tasks that come with your job, including . . .

- creating a place where family members feel good about where they live
- living a balanced, fulfilling life
- knowing what matters most to you and living accordingly
- reducing stress by getting organized and keeping up with housework
- learning to operate as a family team
- encouraging family members to be their personal best and share their skills, resources, and love with family, friends, and community
- planning memorable occasions that strengthen family ties
- appreciating and learning to work with each family member's unique giftedness; helping family members learn to love themselves and others in meaningful ways
- giving each person—including yourself—the room and time to grow in mind, body, and spirit
- having more time for fun and enjoying life

Of course, creating a happy, organized home and being a great mom require more than what is printed on the pages of this book or can be downloaded from the Web. You've got to know what you want for your family, including yourself. In one of those rare moments when the kids aren't tugging at your shirttail and you're not playing beat-the-clock to your next event, I encourage you to fix yourself a cup of tea and take some time to think about what a happy home means to you.

When our boys were young, I wrote the following description of what a happy home meant to me and what I wanted to aim for as our family's manager.

I want my home to be a place where the members know they are valuable, where they feel loved for who they are as unique individuals, where they feel like they belong and can grow in their separate interests. I want our home to be a friendly place for everyone, those of us who can stand clutter and those of us who like everything in its place. There should be a balance in the "common" areas—the family room and kitchen—clean enough to be healthy, messy enough to be happy, so as not to offend either type. Every person's personal space should be his or her own personal space. Their personal belongings are theirs to enjoy, to share, and to take care of.

I want our house to be filled with laughter. I want to have plenty of time to share our daily hurts and joys with each other, but we all have busy schedules. Therefore we designate certain times to spend together. Breakfast in the morning—starting the day off on a positive note—is a must. At least three nights each week I want us to sit down as a family and eat together. We'll share the cooking on those nights, as well as the cleanup, and use the time to talk about each other's worlds. We'll have family meetings to iron things out, talk about schedules, or work on specific projects or problems. Each week we'll go somewhere fun as a family, and we'll plan a fun weekend outing once a month. We'll take two family vacations each year. We'll look forward to growing up and growing old together.

I want to be my best so I can do my best. Therefore, I'll take time to take care of myself as well. I'll work time into my schedule to read books, take classes, learn new skills, and exercise my body; and even if everything else falls apart, I resolve to take time to think about my life.

I admit those are lofty goals, and I certainly haven't achieved them all. But the exercise of getting my dreams down on paper has helped me to remember what's most important and to stay on course over the years. Although moms today face unique challenges when it comes to managing their homes and nurturing their children, many tell me they want the same things I did. Simply put, they want to create a happy, organized home. If you're thinking, *That's what I want too!* keep reading. This book will help you make it happen.

But please do not think that I am telling you exactly how you should run your home. (You'll see in these pages that that's not true.) I do, however, want you to benefit from my experience and avoid learning things by trial and lots of errors like I did. You see, the Family Manager system helped me make our home a good place to be. We maintain a healthy balance of organization and order, flexibility and fun. Our family is a team—even now, after our three boys are grown and two of them are married. We're still committed to working and enjoying the blessings of life together, and to helping each other develop our individual potential. There's no greater blessing on earth, and I want this for you and your family.

Girlfriends, hear this: We play a very powerful role in our families. At some point we all realize that our influence greatly determines our home's environment—certainly the physical aspects, but emotional and spiritual aspects as well. And typically Mom is the glue that holds things together at home. This means that when we personally come "unglued," a whole lot of things begin to crumble.

I pray that this book will be a valuable resource to you—like a trusted friend you can turn to for practical advice, proven solutions, and the inspiration you need to hold things together and create a happy, organized home. For this to happen, you need to understand some things about your very big job as your family's manager.

Getting Down to Business

You oversee an economic institution that includes such services as facility and resource management, meal preparation, child care, education, and transportation, to name a few. Using the strategies and tactics of successful business managers will help you realize your dream for a happy, organized home. Here are the 10 most important things you need to know about your job.

1. Think like a manager. You oversee the most important organization in the world. The Family Manager Creed summarizes your role.

THE FAMILY MANAGER CREED

I oversee the most important organization in the world
Where hundreds of decisions are made daily
Where property and resources are managed
Where health and nutritional needs are determined
Where finances and futures are discussed and debated
Where projects are planned and events are arranged
Where transportation and scheduling are critical
Where team building is a priority
Where careers begin and end
I am a Family Manager

2. Manage by department. To keep from being overwhelmed, you need to develop a way to meet your never-ending Family Manager responsibilities. They can be better managed when categorized in seven distinct departments and supervised accordingly:

TIME & SCHEDULING—managing the family calendar and daily schedule; dispatching the right people to the right place at the right time with the right equipment

HOME & PROPERTY—overseeing the maintenance and care of all your tangible assets, including your belongings, your house and its surroundings, and your vehicles

FOOD—meeting the daily food and nutritional needs of your family

FAMILY & FRIENDS—fulfilling relational responsibilities as a parent and spouse, and with extended family, friends, and neighbors

FINANCES—managing the budget, bill paying, saving, investing, and charitable giving

SPECIAL EVENTS—planning and coordinating occasions that fall outside your normal routine—like birthdays, holidays, vacations, garage sales, family reunions, and celebrations

SELF-MANAGEMENT—caring for your body, sharpening your mind, and nourishing your spirit

3. Know your mission and values. It's important that you take time to consider what's most important to you and your family. Your priorities will help you as you make decisions all day, every day.

4. Cast vision and communicate benefits. Successful managers must inspire and attract employees around a common goal and communicate how that goal affects each person's best interests. It's no different in a family.

5. Build a family team. All good management is about sharing responsibility, helping people find their niches, and empowering them to succeed.

6. Create a base of operations. As your family's manager, you need a "Control Central" from which to supervise your family's comings and goings.

7. Use a Daily Hit List. Selectively choosing each day what you will Do, Delete, and Delegate in each department will help you manage tasks and alleviate stress.

8. Manage according to how you're wired. Family management demands a set of skills that no one person has. There will always be jobs you hate. The trick is learning to work with your strengths and work around areas where you are not gifted and through people who are.

9. Be prepared. It's the Scout motto, but it's also a good motto for Family Managers.

10. Lean on God. He created the family and will give you the wisdom and strength you need to be a great mother, wife, and Family Manager.

In the chapters that follow, you will learn more about these 10 principles. You'll also pick up tips and tactics for each of the seven departments to help you accomplish all the tasks you *have to do* faster and find more time and energy for the things you *want to do*. You will also find helpful checklists and forms.[1] For a bit of quick encouragement when you feel out of control in one of the departments, I invite you to read "The Most Important Things to Remember" at the start of each chapter. It's easy to get overwhelmed by life's details, but I've learned that creating a smoothly running home really comes down to a few key attitudes and actions. Finally, the Web site resource guide and topical index at the end of the book will help you to quickly find information you need to know for your family.

---

[1] Members of the Family Manager Inner Circle can download these interactive forms, as well as a number of others. See http://www.familymanager.com.

Whether you feel like you have all the time you need and things at your home are running fairly well or you're beyond chaos and need all the help you can get, at times every mom needs a few tricks up her sleeve and inspiration to keep going. You can speed-read this book and tag the pages with ideas you want to remember, or you can keep it in a handy place for the days you need some instant advice on how to survive a family road trip or get your kids to do their fair share of housework. Either way, you'll find help for getting on the fast track to a happy, organized home . . . so you can slow down and enjoy the blessings of life.

CHAPTER 1

MANAGING TIME AND SCHEDULING

We can all learn a lesson from attorneys. No doubt you've heard plenty of jokes about lawyers and their billable hours. Actually, the way they see their time—as very valuable—is the way we, as Family Managers, should look at our own time. When you view your time as a commodity, like money, you can look at your days and identify whether you spend too much in one area.

If you constantly feel breathless and behind, this chapter is a good place to begin reading to find ways to restore sanity to your life. Think back on yesterday. Did you lose an hour at the grocery store because you went at a high-traffic time of day? Did you talk too long on the phone with that friend who bends your ear about her problems when you really needed to spend time with your son? Were you late for an appointment because you spent an hour looking for your daughter's ballet shoes because she hadn't put them in their designated place? Can you think of other ways precious minutes slipped through your hands? If so, don't get down on yourself. Recognizing the problem is the first step to solving it.

When you view your time as a commodity, you can look at your days and identify whether you spend too much in one area.

Taking some time to think about how your time is spent every day is an important exercise. It will help you identify your priorities—whether you're living according to yours or someone else's, for whatever reason—and it's the first step necessary for becoming a good manager of the minutes of your day.

Minutes is the key word in that last sentence, because to be a good manager of your family's calendar and daily schedule, you must, like an attorney, see not just the hours but the minutes of your day as valuable. Wouldn't it be helpful if someone invented a way to stop the clock for a full day so we would all have a large, uninterrupted block of time to catch up with everything we're behind on or accomplish a big project? This might make a good story line for a film, but when it comes to reality, we have to catch up and keep up in real time—which for most of us means seeing small bits of time as treasure. You'd be surprised how much you can accomplish when you start using the snippets of time you grab here and there. Granted, you may not be able to scrapbook every age and stage of your 10-year-old daughter's life, but you'll make progress every time you work on a page—which will make you feel better about yourself—and eventually the project will be finished!

It's also important to live in the present as well as the future. That's right, we need to live in two tenses. Here's what I mean.

Living in the present has everything to do with living one day at a time—being prepared for the day's responsibilities, using the minutes of the day wisely, and being alert for and enjoying each day's blessings. Living in the future means thinking ahead about what you want to happen—tomorrow, next week, or next month—and what needs to happen for a goal to be met, using small bits of time along the way to prepare for the future event.

For example, let's say today is Monday and your schedule includes taking your toddler to the pediatrician for a checkup, then dropping him by the house of a friend who said she'd watch him while you do cafeteria duty at your third grader's school. You also have a roofer coming to give you a bid in the afternoon, so when lunch is over you go back to your friend's house, pick up your toddler, go home, and put him down for a nap. You get the mail, check your e-mail, and hope that the roofer is punctual because you can't be late to pick up your third grader. If you're not near the front of the pickup line, you can't get her home in time to have a snack and get her changed into her soccer uniform before your neighbor picks her up for practice.

Let's stop here to look at what has transpired. You definitely needed to be present in the present, giving your full attention to driving, caring for your toddler, listening to the doctor, giving your friend instructions, and making sure you put the right foods on the trays at school.

But let's say you also looked at your calendar this morning and saw that your daughter's Scout troop is having an overnight campout on Friday, and you need to remind her to start gathering the stored camping gear she'll need. You also notice that the annual neighborhood garage sale is two weeks away (you remind yourself how that extra $200 came in handy last year), and you need to start a stash of items you want to sell. And you see that you made a note that Thursday is the last day to sign up for the women's retreat, and you haven't registered yet. You get the picture. We all have to consciously work on today and tomorrow at the same time.

One mom with three closely spaced children (grades one through three) told me it was hard for her to think about tomorrow and the next day because she could barely make it through all she had to do today. She wondered how she could possibly add any future tasks to her already overstuffed days. What she didn't realize—giving birth to three children in three years, who can blame her for responding slowly?—is that by looking ahead and doing what she could to prepare for tomorrow, she could make each "today" go a lot better. When she did start living in two tenses, she noticed big differences in her life.

The Most Important Things to Remember

1. Unless you set and resolve to live by your *own* priorities, you'll wear yourself out trying to meet the demands and expectations of others.

2. You—like everyone else—have 60 minutes in each hour, 24 hours a day. Time is made up of moments, and moments are manageable.

3. The minutes of your days come with a choice: Only you can decide how you'll spend them.

4. Don't let the things that matter least to you rob time from the things that matter most to you.

5. There is no such thing as unimportant time. Each moment is a gift.

6. As you become a better manager of time, you'll begin saving hours. And every hour you save is an hour added to your life.

7. Be flexible. Unexpected events can interrupt the best routines. Bend with the interruption instead of resisting it.

8. When you say yes to something, you're saying no to something else. Don't let it be your family.

9. When you are more efficient at performing the tasks you must do, you have more time for the things that matter most to you.

10. How you carry out each 24-hour day can make the difference between a household in constant uproar and one that hums along smoothly.

Mornings had been nothing short of madness. She refused to make lunches the night before school because there were too many other end-of-the-day tasks to tackle, not to mention helping her kids finish their homework and get in bed at a decent hour. Her routine was to pack lunches in the morning. Yet she felt as if from the moment her feet hit the floor, she was trying to beat the clock. Often she had to make an additional midmorning trip to school to deliver the kids' lunches. (Did I mention this mom's other routine was hitting the snooze button on her alarm three times before getting out of bed?)

She knew that madness is not the best way to start the day. A frazzled mom means frazzled kids. No mom likes sending her kids off without smiles on their faces and sandwiches in their lunch boxes.

Since it was clear that mornings weren't working, she started to experiment. What if she cut up extra veggies for the kids' lunches when cooking dinner? What if she gave her eight-year-old the job of cleaning out the lunch boxes, building and bagging turkey-and-cheese sandwiches (hold the mayo until morning), and storing them in the fridge to pack the next day? And what if her seven-year-old was in charge of readying each lunch box with a napkin, plastic utensils, and a water bottle? This simple change in routine gave her more time in the morning. Having more time in the morning made her relax. Once relaxed she could connect with her kids—instead of yelling at them. She was happier. They were happier. And she even got to have a cup of coffee. She became a staunch believer in living in two tenses, doing what she needed to do today and grabbing a few minutes here and there to make progress toward tomorrow.

Once you start living in two tenses, you realize the importance of protecting your time. When you anticipate future needs while managing those routine yet vital tasks, you naturally want to guard your minutes and spend them on what's most important to you and your family.

Yet even with the best of planning, we all can end up frustrated when projects and people who weren't even on our radar screens take up time we hadn't planned to spend. Being a mom requires flexibility and guarantees interruptions. In many ways our time is not our own, and that's one of the sacrifices and privileges that comes with being a parent. Children—and life events—are predictably unpredictable. Every hour of every day brings events, episodes, and exchanges we cannot control. But some we can. Before we can get a handle on them though, it is imperative that we know what's most important to us. This section will help you organize your day, identify time wasters, take advantage of small chunks of time, and discover new ways of multitasking.

Strategies and Solutions for Time and Scheduling

As a young mom, I collapsed into bed many nights wondering exactly what I'd accomplished that day. In essence, the Family Manager system developed out of my own sense of desperation. Over the years, I discovered three keys to managing my time rather than letting it control me: (1) recognizing and living by my priorities, (2) setting up a Control Central—a base of operations—within my home, and (3) learning how to take back control over the minutes of my day.

STEP 1: LIVE BY YOUR PRIORITIES

Every business leader sets the course for her company. She decides what's most important and establishes guidelines—things like return policies, hours of operation, and employee incentive programs—that reflect the values she considers most important. Running a home and a family should be no different. If you aren't clear on your most important objectives for each of the seven departments, it is likely that you'll end up frustrated and find that life is controlling you, rather than vice versa.

For example, let's say you wanted to take your seven-year-old budding paleontologist to the traveling dinosaur exhibit at a nearby state park, but it's now been shipped to the next state. What happened? Perhaps you believe it's very important to notice and encourage your child's interests, but you've never actually stated that as one of your priorities. So while the day trip to the state park was an option on several Saturdays, catching up on laundry and clearing the week's clutter always seemed more urgent. As a result, you missed the opportunity for an unforgettable day with your child.

Maybe you can relate because you realize that you, too, have not been living by your priorities. All of us face numerous obstacles that keep us from setting priorities and ordering our lives the way we would like. You may relate to the big three I fight in my own life:

1. *Circumstances.* Until we decide it's vitally important that we take an hour or so to go someplace quiet and think about what's important to us, the natural course of life will carry us out of control along a path of minimal accomplishments, meaningless activities, frustration, and mediocrity.

2. *Expectations and pressure from others.* We are all prone to succumb to the agendas of others, appropriate the goals of

What Are Your Priorities?

Imagine yourself years from now taking time to look back on your life. What one or two accomplishments in each of these seven areas would give you the most satisfaction? Remember, there are no right or "exceptional" answers. You don't even need to share this list with anyone else.

The following verbs may prompt your thinking.

advance	contribute	guide
advise	coordinate	illustrate
advocate	create	improve
analyze	deliver	influence
assemble	demonstrate	innovate
balance	develop	introduce
brighten	direct	launch
coach	educate	learn
collaborate	encourage	nurture
collect	engineer	organize
communicate	enhance	schedule
compose	establish	teach
compute	experience	transform
connect	explore	welcome
construct	facilitate	

Time & Scheduling _____

Home & Property _____

Food _____

Friends & Family _____

Finances _____

Special Events _____

Self-Management _____

our culture, and compromise. Let's be honest—peer pressure is not just a teenager's problem. It's a lifelong issue. And it's never too late to start standing on your own and supporting your priorities.

3. *Love of the comfortable.* We tend to arrange life as best we can to avoid pain and to maintain personal comfort. The prob-

lem is that, until we step out of our comfort zones, we experience no significant change for the better, no personal growth, and no relational development. It may be time to sacrifice now for a long-term payoff.

If you want things to change, there's no better time than now to begin incorporating some new tactics and activities into your life that will produce positive change.

First, for each of the seven departments, you need to choose your priorities and decide to live by them. How you spend your time in each department speaks volumes about what your true priorities are—and if you're not spending time the way you'd like, you have to ask whose priorities you're living by.

Maybe you agree that living by priorities is a great idea—but you feel too overwhelmed by life to sit down and figure out what's most important to you. Perhaps you're thinking, *I'm so busy I can't even take time to sort them out, let alone live by them.* I urge you not to fall into this trap.

I suggest you think about one day at a time. You might even want to use a small notebook in which you write your top priorities. Then, as you make choices during the day, simply jot down a few words about the choice you made and how it did or did not fit your stated priorities. You're not doing this to beat yourself up. You're doing it to become conscious of your actions.

Decision-Making Guidelines

Establishing your priorities will give you a yardstick against which to measure the many decisions you must make about how to spend your time and resources. Whether it's a small but important decision like whether to join a Pilates class or ask a neighbor to walk with you three mornings a week, or an important life choice like whether to take a part-time job to ease monthly cash flow or spend more time tutoring a child whose grades are slipping in math and science, these nine steps will help you navigate through the decision and change processes as smoothly as possible.

1. List your options. Just brainstorm and let the ink flow. Don't edit at this point.

2. Think about your choices. Sort your feelings about the options you wrote.

3. Relate your choices to your priorities. What's really most important to you?

4. Think about how your choices will affect other members of your family.

5. Make a decision and a commitment to follow through on it.

6. Help yourself stick to your decision by telling someone what you've decided—become accountable to that person.

7. Be realistic about when you can make the change or start your new habit or action.

8. Launch your new practice as strongly and vigorously as possible. Make it a big deal.

9. Avoid too many changes at once. Whenever you can, plan major life changes—houses, jobs, adding to the people who live at your house—so they do not occur at the same time.

STEP 2: SET UP A BASE OF OPERATIONS WITHIN YOUR HOME

Control Central

Every manager needs a Control Central—be it a desk, a countertop, or an office. In a company, it's the place from which he or she calls the shots. In a home, it's the place from which the Family Manager organizes, tracks the family's schedule, notes changes, responds to messages, makes lists, and keeps all those important papers in their places. By setting up your own Control Central, you can better oversee your family's comings and goings and manage the countless tasks, responsibilities, and decisions that are made every day. In short, by becoming more efficient, you'll save precious moments that can be redirected to your larger priorities.

Here are ideas to consider when setting up your own base of operations:

- Choose a central location in your home. Make sure it has a desk or countertop you can work on. Install a bulletin board in this area, and place a trash can within easy reach. If possible, a filing drawer should be easily accessible.
- Hang a family calendar on an adjacent wall. Record each person's appointments, activities, and important dates.
- Stock Control Central with pens, pencils, a highlighter pen, and some notepads for jotting down ideas and recording phone messages.
- Pull together the following supplies and keep them at Control Central: paper clips, stapler, staples, staple remover, rubber

bands, scissors, tape, and letter opener. Let family members know that these supplies must stay in their new home.

- Put a copy of your local phone directory here, as well as a list of the numbers your family regularly calls. This is also the home for directories from church, school, home-owners associations, clubs, and other groups.
- Keep an ongoing grocery and personal-needs list here so family members will always know where to add items you're running low on.
- Have an easy-access file for takeout menus and coupons.

Family In-Boxes

Purchase stackable in-boxes and label one for each child. Place them near your Control Central. When kids get home from school, have them unload their backpacks right away and put important papers and forms in their in-boxes. Mom or Dad should go through kids' in-boxes each night and review contents, signing and returning any papers that need to go back to school.

Daily Hit List

One of a mom's biggest challenges is remembering all the tasks that need to be done each day. Years ago I designed the Daily Hit List to manage my own daily responsibilities. It's different from other to-do lists because it enables you to categorize your many jobs by each Family Manager department. Using a Daily Hit List will:

- declutter your mind by providing a systematic way to sort through the myriad chores and responsibilities that you face every morning
- clear your perspective, revealing what's trivial and what's priority
- clarify which tasks only you can do and which can be delegated or shared
- improve your memory through the exercise of writing details
- help you remember what steps to take today so whatever's coming tomorrow will run more smoothly

As you begin to use a Daily Hit List, accept that you won't always be able to check off all of the tasks on your list at the end of the day. Move unaccomplished tasks to the next day's list, or delete the ones you deem unimportant for now.

I like to fill out my Daily Hit List early in the morning. Some other moms say that filling it out the night before works best for them. Whatever time you choose, there are three steps for making a Daily Hit List work:

SMART MOVE

Don't overschedule weekends. Plan some free time for activities that refresh you. Block it out on your calendar just as you would an important appointment.

FamilyManager™ DAILY HIT LIST DATE:

HOME & PROPERTY	FOOD	FAMILY & FRIENDS
FINANCES	SPECIAL EVENTS	SELF-MANAGEMENT

6:00 _____

7:00 _____

8:00 _____

9:00 _____

10:00 _____

11:00 _____

Noon _____

1:00 _____

2:00 _____

3:00 _____

4:00 _____

5:00 _____

6:00 _____

7:00 _____

8:00 _____

9:00 _____

Do. Think about and list *everything* that needs to be done. This includes obvious things like preparing meals, putting gas in the car, and depositing money in the bank, as well as other responsibilities such as cleaning, carpooling, and scheduling appointments.

Delegate. Looking at your list, ask yourself, *What can I delegate?* Can a teenager start a load of laundry before he leaves for band practice? Can a younger child fold clothes when she gets home from school? Can your husband start dinner when he arrives home from work? Always delegate according to skills, age, and availability—not gender.

Delete. Once you've delegated, take another look at the list. Are some of the tasks expendable? Do you really need to mop the kitchen floor every day? What is truly unnecessary, at least today?

STEP 3: MAXIMIZE YOUR MOMENTS

The final step in taking control of your schedule is about building some smart and simple time-management techniques into your life. These are things anyone—even the most right-brained, creatively out-of-control of us—can do.

10 Principles of Time Management

1. *Write it down.* Don't trust things to memory. Using lists and checking off completed tasks frees your mind for more important things.

2. *Do it now.* Whenever possible, make this your motto—especially with onerous tasks that could become worse if you put them off.

3. *Have the right tools.* The projects for which we have the tools or resources will be finished before the ones for which we're not prepared. If you schedule some time to organize your child's closet, have on hand various sizes of organizing bins, self-sealing plastic bags, a garbage bag, and boxes to store or give away items.

4. *Believe in buffers.* Anticipate traffic, checkout lines, and children to be slower than you'd like, and adjust your expectations.

5. *Set deadlines.* Deadlines are the best guarantee a job will be done. Jot down on your calendar the time or day you want to have a task completed. If needed, ask a friend or family member to hold you accountable.

☆

SMART MOVE

Life is predictably unpredictable, so always allot a little extra time for tasks. If you think something is going to take you 30 minutes, schedule 40 minutes.

GOOD TO KNOW

An average American spends 27 hours each year sitting at traffic lights.

SMART MOVE

When you get a haircut, manicure, pedicure, or facial, schedule your next appointment as you pay.

SMART MOVE

Take a few minutes during the weekend to organize your work clothes for the week ahead.

6. *Do advance work—don't wait until the last minute.* If you're hosting a big dinner at your home, decide what you can do a week ahead of time, the day before, and so on. Estimate how much time you'll need and when to schedule tasks; anticipate potential time wasters. Then set deadlines for accomplishing goals.

7. *Work with your biological clock.* If you're a morning person, do your most important work then. Schedule tasks that don't demand as much attention and brainpower during lower-energy times of day.

8. *Create boundaries.* Set your priorities, and don't let other people guilt you into crossing them. Give yourself permission to "just say no" to requests that dent time with your family or time spent nourishing yourself. When you say yes to something, you're saying no to something else.

9. *Take charge of your own life and schedule.* Do things on your time. Don't pick up the phone every time it rings—use voice mail or an answering machine. Turn off your "you have mail" computer alert. Answer messages when it's convenient for you.

10. *Don't wait for time to "free up."* If you have a big project to accomplish, schedule work appointments for yourself in 30-minute or one-hour blocks. Be as serious about this time as you would any other appointment. Before you know it, you'll have the project licked.

Scheduling Strategies
Traveling to and from and waiting at appointments can eat hours of valuable time. These tips will help you keep travel and wait time to a minimum.

- Many services and businesses offer online scheduling—a big time-saver.
- Try to schedule the first appointment of the day or the first appointment after lunch. It's less likely you'll have to wait.
- Schedule family members' dental checkups and kids' pediatrician appointments back-to-back so you can make fewer trips.
- Avoid scheduling "maintenance" checkups at the doctor or dentist in May, August, or December—the busiest months of the year for moms.

- Schedule kids' back-to-school or summer-camp physicals well in advance.
- When you make an appointment, write the office or person's phone number on your calendar so you won't have to look it up if plans change. If you've never been to the office or location before, get directions when you make the appointment and take the office's phone number with you when you go.
- If you'll need a babysitter while you're at an appointment, arrange that at the same time.
- Call before you leave for an appointment at your hairdresser or doctor's office. If he or she is running late, use the extra time to get something done.
- Bring along toys or books for small children.
- Always take your calendar with you to an appointment so you can schedule follow-up visits while you're there. You'll have your pick of the schedules, and you won't forget to write the new appointments down.
- If you're running late for an appointment, be courteous and call to let them know you're on your way and when you'll arrive.

Making Phone Time Count

The phone can be your best friend or worst enemy. You decide that by determining whether to view your phone as a tool under your control or as a taskmaster that must be answered every time it rings. Here are some simple ways to save time and make better use of time on the phone.

- Set your cell phone or pager to vibrate instead of ring. Don't let it interrupt what you're accomplishing at the moment—unless a family member is on the line.
- Set time limits on your phone calls and take them only at certain times of day. Keep a watch or timer handy. If you make a call and are asked to hold but can't, don't be afraid to say so.
- Call service businesses on Thursdays or Fridays, when business is slowest. (Their busiest days are Mondays and Tuesdays.) Call during the slower hours. Companies' busiest periods are from 10 a.m. to 2 p.m. and from 5:30 to 7:30 p.m. Schedule repair calls online whenever possible.
- Consider adding a distinctive second ring to your phone line. For a minimal monthly charge, your phone company

☆
SMART MOVE

Use drive time to broach a difficult subject with your child. Sometimes it's less threatening to discuss a sensitive matter when you're both staring out a windshield. Turn down the radio and make comments that build up your child. Ask how you can help him or her move toward a goal or succeed at an undertaking. As you affirm him or her, add a light touch of your hand to your words.

can set up caller ID so you'll know when family members are calling.

- Program the speed-dial features on your home phone and cell phone.
- Cut solicitors short by saying, "Thank you for calling, but I'm not interested."
- Call long-winded friends or family just before lunch or at the end of the day.
- Gently guide nonstop talkers to the point. Remind them that you have only a few minutes to talk, ask them direct questions, or schedule a time when you can talk longer.
- Highlight all numbers you look up in the phone book. They'll be easy to find again.
- Create a family phone book. Keep one at each phone in your house, in your car, and at the office.
- Use a portable phone or headset so you can walk while you talk.
- Store a box of stickers, activity books, and small toys by the phone to distract a small child when you have to make an important call.
- Avoid "phone tag" by making appointments for phone calls. Treat these calls just as you would treat a face-to-face appointment. Put them on your calendar and make notes about what you want to talk about. Think of each as a meeting— because it is. Be prepared with any information you will need before making the call.
- When you need to call someone back at a later date, write the name and phone number on the calendar so you won't have to look them up.
- Use e-mail rather than the phone whenever possible. It's often faster.
- While you're on hold:

  Clean out your purse.
  Purge your coupon file of outdated coupons.
  Organize a drawer.
  Dust a piece of furniture.
  Polish or file your nails.
  Straighten your desk.
  Clean your glasses.
  Tidy your sewing box.
  Organize your wallet.
  Clean out your jewelry box and untangle necklaces.

Memory Joggers

Every day you deal with countless bits of information. While the Daily Hit List will help you stay on top of details, here are 10 other tips for reminding yourself of something you can't afford to forget.

1. Stick a note on the bathroom mirror, on your exit door, or on the car's steering wheel.

2. When you receive schedules for anything from school to soccer to dance class, write the dates and locations *immediately* on your calendar. Use a highlighter pen to make important events stand out.

3. Have a calendar program such as Outlook or the alarm on your PDA or cell phone alert you when you need to remember to leave for a meeting or start the grill for dinner.

4. When you're away from home or the office and remember something you need to do there, call your voice mail or answering machine and leave yourself a message.

5. Carry a small notebook in your purse and/or car. Take a minute to write down pertinent information as soon as you get it.

6. Create your own memory jogger and turn it into a game with your kids. For example, one autumn I was having trouble remembering to shut the garage door when coming home from doing errands. This meant leaves could blow in, causing more work for the boys when they swept it. We put a jar on the counter, and every time I forgot to close the door, I had to deposit a dollar in the jar. My boys got to split the contents.

7. Keep a spiral calendar notebook near your phone and make notes of phone conversations on the day you have them. It keeps you focused on the call, plus having the information and the date you obtained it sometimes comes in handy later.

8. If you are going to a party, write not only the time of the party but also the address on the calendar. Also list anything you'll need to take, such as a gift or a dessert you offered to bring.

9. Keep notepads and pens in convenient locations, such as by each phone and on your nightstand. But don't let your data keeping become paper clutter. Post information on a bulletin board near your Control Central, then act on it, file it, or toss it ASAP.

10. If you keep your car in a locked garage, put clothes for the dry cleaner and videos to be returned on the driver's seat the night before. You won't be able to miss them when you leave in the morning.

Timer tactics

A kitchen timer can help you regulate your schedule and reduce the need to nag. Here are examples:

- If you want to spend only a designated amount of time on a task, set the timer to remind you when the time is up.
- If there's a video game or toy the kids are constantly arguing over, set the kitchen timer for 11 minutes (or whatever length of time you decide), and when the timer dings, the player automatically knows his turn is up.
- Put a kitchen timer in the bathroom and time showers in the morning so you can keep family members moving in and out of the bathroom and out the door on time.
- When you ask your child to do a chore and he nicely asks if he can do it in five minutes, fine. Set the timer so he'll know when five minutes is up.
- Does one of your children love a challenge? Put a kitchen timer in her room. Break the morning routine into five-minute tasks and let her try to beat the clock.
- Create a 10-minute warning. Set the timer in the mornings to go off 10 minutes before walk-out-the-door time.
- If you've got a lot on your mind, as usual, and you don't want to forget that you promised to take a friend to the airport, set the timer to help you remember when it's time to leave for her house.

Planning Ahead

In order to keep a home and family functioning effectively, a Family Manager has to pay attention to the demands of the day but also look ahead to what's coming up. Good family management, as I mentioned earlier, means learning how to live in two tenses. When I made that statement at a Family Manager seminar, a woman in the audience cried out, "I must be doing a great job, because I'm always too tense!" We all welcomed the comic relief but felt her pain.

But it's true. By developing a habit of looking ahead on your calendar, thinking about where you're going and what you want to see happen, then making plans, you'll be ready for most anything—

and you'll avoid a whole lot of headaches in the process. Here are a few ways you do just that:

- On the first of each month, look at your calendar and decide which events you need babysitters for. Arrange for them now.
- Keep your list of babysitters updated and growing. Ask friends and neighbors for referrals so you have plenty of options if your regular sitter has to cancel. (Keep their contact information in your family phone book, along with the hours they are usually available.)
- Mark your calendar, or have your computer alert you, one month before holidays and birthdays. Begin early to plan celebrations and buy presents and decorations.
- Start planning summer vacations and checking into kids' summer camps in February.
- Schedule a time in the summer to have pictures taken of your kids. Enlarge one to give Grandma and Grandpa for Christmas.
- Plan for fun. Collect information and save some money each month for that trip you want to take for your 10th anniversary, three years from now.
- Keep takeout menus in a file at work so you can place an order before you leave and pick it up on your way home.
- Keep an emergency set of clean clothes, underwear, and socks for your child put away for the inevitable day when you have to go someplace and haven't had a chance to do laundry.
- Keep a change of clothes and accessories at the office in case of unplanned meetings or dinner engagements.
- Stock up on sale items even if you won't need them for a month or two.
- When the winter sales hit, buy your kids' coats (a size bigger) for use next year.
- Keep one-dollar bills and quarters on hand. You never know when you'll need them.

Five Minutes Is Worth Its Weight in Gold

Have you come to dread the sight of your to-do list? As a mother whose kids are now grown, I can tell you that the list never gets shorter. (Instead of picking up the kids at school, I'm now picking them up at the airport.) But I still have to find the time to cull bulging closets, reorganize drawers, and purge the freezer of UFOs (unidentified frozen objects). The large blocks of time to

SMART MOVE

Fifty-one percent of mothers plan family vacations. The Family Manager Vacation Packing Checklist can help. (See page 247.)

♡

FROM THE HEART

The secret to effective time management is using small bits of time well. But the idea is not just to do more. It's to create time to do more that matters.

accomplish these tasks are few and far between, but fortunately I've discovered a hidden treasure.

What is that? Five-minute segments. You'd be surprised how much you can accomplish in 300 little seconds, and how many five-minute segments you can grab here and there. Granted, you won't unload the basement of 10 years' worth of clutter in a few minutes, but you'll make progress every time you work on it—which will make you feel better about yourself—and eventually the project *will* be finished!

In five minutes, you can . . .

- Sort through a junk drawer.
- Clean out a couple of shelves in your medicine cabinet.
- Sort children's clothing one drawer or shelf at a time.
- Purge through a basket of magazines and catalogs; toss old ones.
- Remove clutter from one surface area.
- Wipe fingerprints off a few doorjambs and light switches.
- Check the batteries in your smoke detector.
- Throw in a load of wash.
- Fold a load of laundry.
- Sew on a button.
- Empty waste cans and take out the trash.
- Vacuum a room.
- Sweep the front porch.
- Water plants.
- Check the air pressure in your tires, or check the oil.
- Call to make an appointment.
- Sort mail.
- Pay a few bills.
- Answer an e-mail or two.
- Purge your e-mail in-box or clean up computer files, five minutes at a time.
- Add new contact information to your family phone book.
- Make a Daily Hit List (see page 10).
- Put DVDs or CDs back in their cases.
- Pick up some toys or clutter in your family room.
- Do some crunches, push-ups, and leg lifts.
- Take vitamins and drink a big glass of water.
- Moisturize your face.
- Write a thank-you note.
- Pray for friends or read a chapter from the Bible or another inspirational book.

- Rest! Purposely choosing to devote five minutes for personal relaxation and rejuvenation may be the best use of your time.

Multitasking Made Easy

Some time-management gurus don't believe in multitasking. They talk about being "present in the moment"—giving something our whole attention. Maybe that's a reaction from people who once wore themselves out trying to do two or more things at once—and trying to give both equal mental focus. Real multitasking is different: It involves doing things that *don't* require a person's full attention. And there are plenty of tasks that don't deserve our full attention!

Doubling up on tasks lets us spend more time on fun and other things to which we want to give our full attention. Get started by listing tasks that can be done simultaneously. Post the list in a central location. Every time you "catch" someone multitasking, praise and reward him or her! This is a great habit to teach your children.

Two-timing ideas

- Never walk through the house empty-handed. Pick up as you go. If you're going upstairs, take something with you that belongs up there.
- Encourage teenagers to start a load of laundry before tackling their homework. When they stop for a snack, they can move the clothes from the washer to the dryer.
- Have kids strip beds and take linens to the washer before you change the sheets.
- Request that kids fold clothes, sort socks, brush the dog, or reunite a basket of toys with missing parts while they watch cartoons—definitely an activity that does not require full focus!
- Divide and conquer. On a trip to the mall, give each adult or teen a separate list of errands to accomplish.
- Ask young kids to wash patio furniture and bicycles while older ones wash the dog and the car.
- Teach preschoolers to identify colors while they are cleaning, first by picking up the blue toys, then the red, etc.
- Clean the bathroom mirror and shine fixtures while tending your child's bath.
- Put away groceries while you talk on the phone.
- Wash dishes or unload the dishwasher while waiting for the water to boil.
- Hold on to the kitchen counter and do leg lifts while you're waiting for water to boil.

☆

SMART MOVE

Use long drives to talk to your husband about important matters such as goals and priorities for your family. Ask him about his world—what he enjoys most, what's difficult for him, how you can support him.

★

SMART MOVE

While you're waiting
for your food to
be served at a
restaurant, have
everyone in the
family dream aloud
about what they'd
like to see happening
in their lives five
years from now.

- Make a grocery list while you cook dinner. Check the pantry as you go.
- Have kids swish hands and feet around the tub during a bubble bath to loosen a bathtub ring.
- Before you run errands, consider what else you might pick up or drop off on the way.
- Cook two, three, or four meals at once. Clean carrots for tonight's pot roast, afternoon snacks, and tomorrow night's salad.
- Make soup and stew at the same time. Double the recipe and you'll have tonight's dinner and another for the freezer.
- Look through mail-order catalogs while you're on the exercise bike or step machine. Plan purchases; glean gift ideas.
- Bathe the dog while you water the garden.
- Buy two or three of each household staple—deodorant, shampoo, soap—so you won't have to make a special trip again soon.
- During TV commercials, have everyone pick up and put away clutter.
- Steam wrinkles from clothes by hanging the garment in the bathroom while you shower.

Prescription for Procrastination

At times we all need a jump start to get us or to keep us going. But if procrastination is a consistent problem for you, try to understand why you put things off. If you fear doing a poor job, remember that doing your best—not achieving perfection—is your true goal. If you think you "thrive under pressure," consider whether the stress you go through prevents you from doing your best work.

Try one or two of these ideas to help you accomplish a task you've been dreading. Remember, time adds up—24 hours, 1,440 minutes, 86,400 seconds a day—whether we use it or not. A little action now can add up to a big result at the end of the day.

Getting started

- Gear up for a task the night before. If you plan to tackle a project the next morning, set out the supplies or tools you'll need and the clothes you'll wear. Go to bed a little earlier than usual so you'll wake up refreshed and ready to go.
- Make the steps to completing the task tangible. List each one you'll need to accomplish. As you finish each, give yourself the satisfaction of checking it off in red ink!

- Have the right tools available to tackle the project. If you are going to excavate the clutter in the basement, buy plenty of plastic storage bins in various sizes. Save the receipt; you can return the ones you don't use.
- Decide beforehand how you will reward yourself when you complete the job.
- Ask someone you have fun with to help you with the project.
- Speed up your metabolism. Before starting the task, take a brisk, 20-minute walk.
- If all else fails, start a 15-minute rule. Spend 15 minutes every day on something you've been procrastinating about. Before you know it, you'll have the dreaded task licked.

While you're working
- Do the worst part first. The rest will seem easier!
- Put on some peppy music that makes you want to move.
- Listen to a motivational tape.
- Stop and pat yourself on the back when you finish a segment of the task. If you have six drawers to clean out, congratulate yourself each time you conquer one.
- Ask a friend or family member to monitor your progress and encourage you along the way.
- Give yourself the freedom to stop and rest if you need to.
- Visualize how you will benefit from finishing.

Reward yourself!
- Buy a little something to make the task more pleasant. If you dread spending a day in the kitchen cooking and freezing a week's worth of meals, buy yourself a cheery apron or a new pot you've had your eye on.
- Fix yourself a treat to keep you going. On attic clean-out day, put a plate of enticing fruit on a counter or table near the door leading outside to your garbage cans. When you travel to and from the attic, you can grab a bite.
- Post inspirational quotes in your work area. Read them when your motivation starts to wane.

GOOD TO KNOW

In 2006, watching TV was the leisure activity that occupied the most time for both men and women, reports the Bureau of Labor Statistics.

CHAPTER 2

MANAGING YOUR HOME AND PROPERTY

Every home is different. You may walk into one home that is so tidy and clean, you wonder if anyone actually lives there. Then you realize that the children are grown and live away from home. You may walk into another home and, by the toys scattered around the rooms, realize that a preschooler lives there. Still another home may just seem comfortable—some clutter here and there, but it seems to be a somewhat controlled mess: a model airplane halfway finished on a card table, stacks of folded laundry ready for the designated courier to put away, a salt map of South America drying on the kitchen counter.

Despite all the differences in our homes, we probably all share similar desires when it comes to overseeing the Home and Property department: We want to care for our belongings so we can enjoy them as much as possible and so they will last as long as possible. We also want to create, through the decor and furnishings of our homes, a comfortable, welcoming atmosphere for family and friends.

A lot of how you handle this very big part of your Family Manager job has to do with the uniqueness of your family—factors such as how many children you have, their ages, your pets (if any), your home's setting (urban, suburban, or rural), your outside employment, and your standards of cleanliness—and what you've decided is most important in life.

Yet no matter what your home is like, unless you have the luxury of a household staff, maintaining your home and caring for your belongings can eat up huge chunks of time. I've found that a good way to cut back on the amount of time it takes to manage this department—

We want to create a comfortable, welcoming atmosphere for family and friends.

cleaning, organizing, doing laundry, and the like—is to create standard operating procedures (SOPs), which are nothing more than routines that can be the building blocks of efficiency in your home, just as they are in companies.

When you have SOPs like always emptying the dishwasher before going to bed, changing bed linens on the first and fifteenth of the month, or giving your refrigerator a weekly quick-clean the night before trash pickup, you won't waste time deciding when you're going to do what.

Deciding what you want to do and then establishing a smart routine to get the job done will help you follow through on tasks. Routines will also give your children a sense of security because they will know what's expected and what to expect. You'll find that they like not having to hunt for their soccer cleats because they have a designated place to take them off and store them after practice. They'll pick up their toys a little faster before bed because they know that when they finish, you'll snuggle and read a book to them in bed.

Launching time-saving routines at your house involves three simple steps. First you have to identify what you want to change. For example, let's say your dog is shedding so much that by the time you've finished vacuuming, you need to vacuum again. This is starting to get old, so you go to the second step, which is figuring out what you want instead and determining the resources you have to work with. In this case, you'd like to see less dog hair on the floor—and see less of your vacuum cleaner, as well. As far as resources go, hmmm . . . you've got a dog brush and a couple of able-bodied kids.

Okay, now you move to the third step and try a solution—and if it works, you can turn it into a routine. You decide to have your kids take turns giving the dog a good brushing outside every afternoon this week when they get home from school. They cooperate (or face the music; be sure to read pages 154–155) and *voila!* You're vacuuming less and your kids are learning responsibility. Even your dog is happy.

The key to success with any kind of new routine is that little word *step*. A lot of moms get so behind and bogged down they want to change everything—*now!* They overdo, creating a list that covers every cleaning and maintenance task they can think of, and they end up overwhelmed. Remember, Rome and Microsoft weren't built in a day.

The point of SOPs is to make your family's life easier—not to create rigid rules that make home seem more like boot camp. Some moms take housecleaning way too seriously, insisting that the bathroom floor be scrubbed on Tuesdays and the front stairs swept with a wet broom every second Thursday. They need to lighten up and remember that a reasonably clean, fun home is healthier than a squeaky-clean, tense one.

No matter what your current situation, you can make changes that will benefit everyone. But keep in mind that your mission is to enhance efficiency for you and your family—the people who live there 24 hours a day, 7 days a week, 52 weeks a year—not for occasional guests, a nosy neighbor, or your mother-in-law. Having picture-perfect closets is not important. Knowing what

The Most Important Things to Remember

1. People are more important than things.

2. There are no standards but your own. Every family has to decide how clean is clean enough.

3. The more you accumulate, the more you have to clean and maintain—and the more time it takes to do it.

4. When your kids grow up and leave home, they won't remember if the towels were folded in perfect 16-inch squares in the linen closet; they will remember if home was a good place to be and if Mom was a fun person.

5. If you have a choice between taking a family vacation or buying new furniture, go for the vacation. The furniture will end up in a garage sale one day; the memories of the trip will last forever.

6. Everyone who lives under the roof of a home should contribute to its upkeep.

7. If a teenager is an expert at text messaging, he can become an expert at using the washing machine. A man who can program a PDA to remind him of his tee time can program a PDA to remind him to pick up the dry cleaning.

8. Mess causes stress. Getting your home in order will help you get your life in order.

9. There's no such thing as perfection. Giving up trying to make your home perfect is the first step toward making it a good place to be.

10. The choices you make about your home involve a lot more than wall color and window treatments. Home is where human beings develop. It's a place to restore souls, find shelter from outside pressures, grow support for talents, and receive inspiration, comfort, and aid.

you have and being able to find and retrieve things without a cherry picker is.

The truth of the matter is, there's not one right way to manage the Home and Property department. Besides, we all have to change our standards and methods at certain times because people and circumstances are constantly changing. Babies turn into toddlers, and though you once couldn't tolerate a fingerprint on the glass front door, you realize that now you can hardly see through the bottom third of it—and that's okay. Kids grow into teenagers, and when you consider the kinds of trouble some teens get into, you decide to cut your son some slack about cleaning his room before early-morning debate team

No matter what your current situation, you can make changes that will benefit everyone.

practice. Perhaps you go back to work after maternity leave and realize that you're going to need more help with the basics, like weekly cleaning and laundry. Change is inevitable, but the basic goal remains the same: to run your home more efficiently—not run it, or yourself, into the ground. As you read the suggestions about managing your home, keep in mind that they're not intended to be tackled all at once. Your home-care priorities will fluctuate depending on your season of life. So while you want your home to operate smoothly, be sure to give yourself grace along the way.

The Home and Property department encompasses a good deal of territory (literally), so this chapter covers a lot of ground. In it you'll learn valuable organization, storage, and decluttering tips; discover energy-saving cleaning plans and shortcuts; learn how to reduce repair costs and extend the life of your home, car, and other possessions through proper maintenance; and find helpful ideas to use when it's time to redecorate, move, or create a family emergency plan.

Strategies and Solutions for Managing Home and Property

ORGANIZING AND STORAGE BASICS

On a scale of one to ten, what's the pile status at your home? Have stacks of mail and papers overtaken your desk? Are there mounds of outgrown clothes that have multiplied on bedroom floors while waiting to be stored? Do you spend minutes every day looking for items you just know are *somewhere*—you're just not quite sure where? If so, the following six steps will help you bring order to your home and make the most of your storage space.

1. *Inventory your storage space.* Walk slowly around your house, noting all the potential storage space in a notebook. Don't overlook the less obvious places, like under a bed or behind a china cabinet. Also keep track of the items that seem out of place—for instance, those that are far from the spot where you normally use them. The following ideas may help you recognize other potential storage spots in your home:

   - Move a chest of drawers into a closet. You'll free up space in the bedroom and make use of the space under the hanging rods that hold shirts and jackets that don't go all the way to the floor.
   - Use a Peg-Board to organize in a child's room. Lots of different toys can be hung from hooks. You can also use a Peg-Board on a utility room wall to hang utensils.
   - Put stacking vegetable bins under your kitchen sink to get the most use out of this area.
   - Screw hooks into the ceilings of your cabinets and hang coffee mugs by their handles.
   - Put another shelf inside a tall cabinet to elevate some items and create space underneath for others.
   - Hang bath towel racks on the backs of closet doors to hold scarves and belts. Hang a rack on the back of your linen closet door to hold tablecloths and runners.
   - Mount shallow magazine racks on the insides of closet doors to hold children's books, tapes, or CDs.
   - Attach small containers or racks to the inside of cabinet doors for sauce mixes and other small, hard-to-store items.

☆

SMART MOVE

When looking for a place to store an item, think, *Where will I use this?* not, *Where can I put this?*

- Small rolling carts that fit underneath desks or in closets work nicely for storing and easily accessing art supplies or sewing machines and materials.
- Hang a three-tier wire basket from your kitchen ceiling to hold potatoes, onions, peppers, and fruit.
- Store your dining-room table leaves behind the china closet or breakfront. A folding game table might fit behind the couch in the family room. A fold-up easel may hang on the wall behind a child's closet door. Space behind furniture is often overlooked.
- Utilize seldom-used luggage to store things like ski clothes.
- Hang speakers on a wall to free up floor space.
- Convert an old armoire into a cabinet for your TV and electronic equipment.
- Add a to-the-floor dust ruffle to the bottom of a baby crib or child's bed for hidden floor storage.

2. *Get the proper storage tools.* Use inexpensive drawer organizers to keep small items from getting jumbled together. Clear plastic boxes are good for medium-sized items like craft supplies or children's toys. Fifty-five-gallon plastic trash cans are great for storing big things like sports equipment or garden tools.

3. *Store like items together.* Think in categories. Gather all items used for the same kind of project and put them in one spot convenient to the user.

   Examples of things to store together:

   - art and craft supplies
   - auto-care items
   - camera equipment, battery, and charger
   - camping items
   - CDs
   - children's school papers and art
   - china, crystal, and candles
   - cleaning supplies
   - computer software and accessories
   - cosmetics
   - DVDs
   - financial records
   - first-aid necessities
   - flashlights and batteries
   - games

- gardening equipment
- greeting cards/stationery
- hobby supplies
- holiday decorations
- household tools
- kitchen items
- linens
- luggage and travel kits
- medications
- office supplies
- party supplies
- pet supplies
- photos and albums, negatives
- picnic supplies
- seasonal clothing
- sewing supplies
- silver—flatware and serving pieces
- sports equipment
- tax returns and canceled checks
- toys
- trophies
- vacuum accessories
- vases and flower-arranging supplies
- warranties and manuals

4. *Store items as close as possible to the place they are used most often.* Don't simply store things in the first handy or seemingly logical space, which will keep you from getting organized. Think about how you're going to use the object.

5. *Allocate your most accessible space to the items you use most often.* Shelves between eye and waist level are prime storage areas in the kitchen. Don't store your Bundt pan, which you use infrequently, in front of your saucepans, which you use daily.

6. *Make finding as easy as storing.* Use see-through containers whenever possible; when you can't, label the containers. When you stash something in a hurry—and we all do—nonlabeled containers make it that much harder to identify them later.

Attic and Basement

Consider yourself fortunate if you have storage space at the top and/or bottom of your home. Organizing and maximizing the space in your attic or basement may seem like drudgery, but it will pay off for years to come. Follow these steps to better organization.

- Declutter. Lots of stuff tends to end up in the attic or basement because you don't know what else to do with it. If you haven't used something in years, it's probably time to get rid of it. Take anything that can be fixed or used by someone else to a community organization or donation center. I suggest recycling or throwing away the following:

  > old magazines and newspapers
  > receipts and canceled checks older than six years
  > outdated office supplies and equipment
  > mangled holiday decorations and faded wrapping supplies
  > empty boxes and bags
  > outdated furniture you don't want
  > dishes, cookware, and kitchen items you never use
  > high school and/or college essays and notes
  > broken toys and sports gear
  > rusty tools or equipment
  > broken or torn luggage

- Categorize the remaining items into "departments." Your departments might include seasonal decorations, baby furniture, memorabilia, and luggage.
- Purchase inexpensive industrial metal shelving to keep boxes and bins off the floor and safe from bugs, mice, and dirt.
- Avoid using paper or plastic bags for storage. Instead watch for sales on sturdy, see-through plastic bins that can be stacked and moved easily.
- Label all boxes and bins on the top and side for easy identification. Keep an inventory of items stored so you'll know where to find them.
- Use a large plastic bin with a lid for children to save artwork and other items they will treasure when they're older.
- Stash your luggage here, storing smaller suitcases inside larger ones.
- Set up a clothing rack for hanging off-season clothes.
- Baby items that aren't currently being used can be stored together neatly in the old crib.
- Attach a pair of old belts to the rafters in your attic to hold things like skis or a rolled-up rug.

⚠️

CAUTION!

Depending on where you live, various animals can cause havoc in your attic. Squirrels love to nest in insulation. Raccoons and rats like attics as well. They cause damage by chewing on electrical wiring, boxes, books, textiles, and wood, and by leaving droppings. You can try to eradicate pests yourself by scattering mothballs in hard-to-reach recesses or by filling old socks with mothballs or flakes and hanging them near suspected entrances and pathways. Another idea is to soak rags with ammonia and place them in buckets or shallow pans next to entry holes or squirrel nests.

Clothing storage

- Wash or dry-clean garments before storing them, because insects and pests are attracted to dirt left on clothes and fabrics. (Remove starch—silverfish like it.) Hang clothes in canvas garment bags or cardboard clothing boxes with hanging rods from moving companies. You can also install a rod in the attic, hang clothing, then protect it with a clean sheet.
- Don't store clothing in dry-cleaner bags or in garment bags made of synthetic fabrics that don't breathe. Moisture trapped inside can cause mildew. Some plastic bags cause clothes to yellow.
- Store folded clothing in acid-free cardboard boxes (available at home centers, photographic supply stores, and archival supply companies) or in boxes lined with a clean cotton sheet. Place small cedar blocks in boxes to ward off pests.

Not for the attic

These items belong in a storage area that has a more even temperature and humidity level than an attic.

- *Wood furniture.* Changes in humidity and temperature can cause wood to split and crack.
- *Fur and leather.* Heat, fluctuating temperatures, and pests may cause damage.
- *Books.* Mildew, rodents, and changes in moisture can damage old, leather-bound books.
- *Heirloom clothing or formal dresses.* These need a climate-controlled area and should be professionally cleaned and packed.
- *Camera equipment.*
- *Photographs and negatives.*
- *Stuffed toys.* Squirrels, chipmunks, and mice love to chew on these.
- *Rubber and plastic items.* Unless well-insulated, attic temperatures can reach levels that can damage these items.
- *Important original documents.* Birth certificates and your marriage license don't belong in the attic. Instead, keep them in a bank safe-deposit box. Keep copies in a file at home.
- *Wool rugs.* Moths love them.

Basement rules

- Neutralize musty basement odors with activated charcoal or fresh coffee beans in paper bags around the basement.

GOOD TO KNOW

If you're not comfortable giving your house key to cleaning or repair service workers but can't be home to let them in or out, you can purchase a key safe for $40 or less at a hardware store or on the Internet. You control the code and change it as often as you need to.

- Paint the window wells and other basement surfaces white, as it will reflect more outside light.
- Keep a flashlight in a handy place in case of a power failure while you're down there.
- Put a doormat at the foot of the stairs to keep dirt from being tracked to other areas of the house. Or carpet the top step to trap dust you might track in the house.
- Place metal utility shelves at the bottom of the basement stairs to hold overflow from the pantry, such as canned goods, extra paper towels, and toilet paper.
- Always keep boxes off the floor in case of water leakage. If you must use boxes in the basement, place them on top of cement blocks or bricks.
- Store flammable substances, such as oil-based paint and turpentine, well away from the heating system, water heater, or other sources of heat. Never store gasoline in the basement. Gasoline fumes travel and can be ignited by a tiny spark.
- Don't store books and papers in the basement unless they are in moisture-proof containers.

Bathrooms

A disorganized, messy bathroom is the perfect place for humidity, moisture, and bacteria to meet and create a resort for germs—not what you want in a room where people go to get clean. Plus, having an organized bathroom means there's less to clean. The following tips will help:

- Keep bathroom drawers neat and small items accessible with a plastic silverware tray.
- Use plastic totes to store each family member's bathroom items.
- Mount a magazine rack to the wall to hold magazines and other reading material.
- An over-the-door shoe bag on the back of the bathroom or linen-closet door can store hair rollers, brushes, or washcloths.
- Keep the peace by color-coding your towels and washcloths. Assign a color to each family member to reduce sibling squabbles and help uncover the mystery of who "forgot" to hang their towels. Monograms serve the same purpose.
- Store bath toys either in dishpans under the vanity or in a mesh bag that hangs from the shower nozzle so they can drip-dry in the tub.

- Install hooks on the back of the door for hanging bathrobes and damp towels.
- Make sure you have hooks or towel racks that kids can reach.
- Mount vinyl-coated wire racks on the inside of cabinet doors to hold bathroom items.
- Consider buying a wall-mounted hair dryer for easy access and storage.
- Store prescription medicines and over-the-counter remedies on higher shelves, in clearly labeled containers, out of the reach of small children. You can also mount a spice rack on the inside of the linen-closet door to hold medicine bottles.

Children's Bedrooms

Make it as easy as possible for your kids to keep their things organized and their rooms neat. You'll all be happier!

- When storing kids' belongings, put most frequently used items in the lowest, most easily accessible places.
- Divide kids' closets into two parts: one for hanging clothes and one for storing items on shelves. Have two rods on the hanging side: a high rod for out-of-season and seldom-worn clothes and a child-level rod for frequently worn clothes.
- Buy assorted sizes of clear plastic boxes for kids to categorize and store their belongings.
- Make sure children's books are easily accessible. Help them arrange their books by topic or author so they'll have a sense of pride and ownership in a growing library.
- Hang pegs or hooks at child level for jackets, backpacks, and hats.
- Assign most-used items to the easiest-access drawers. For example, if you expect your kids to put on their own socks and shoes each morning, don't put socks in a high drawer children can't reach. For young children, label the front of drawers with details of the contents. (Use pictures for prereaders.) This way they won't have to rummage through drawers to find what they need.
- Don't stuff drawers so full that kids can't remove items without making a mess. Regularly remove outgrown clothes.
- Use drawer organizers to divide socks, tights, and underwear.
- Avoid toy boxes and trunks. Small items sift to the bottom, and you have to empty the contents to find them.

☆

SMART MOVE

Store a stain-removal spray or stick in each bathroom or bedroom so family members can apply it to stains before throwing clothes in the hamper.

☆

SMART MOVE

Consider inaugurating an annual Closet Clearing Day at your house. Designate a specific day, such as the first Saturday in January or the first Monday in October. Put it on the calendar like you would any other occasion.

CAUTION!

Carpeted closets are an ideal environment for moths and carpet beetles, which eat hair, lint, dust, and clothing. A telltale sign of carpet beetles is their shed skins, usually found around carpet edges. After vacuuming, sprinkle laundry borax around carpet edges, and also over padding before new carpet is laid.

SMART MOVE

Turn an ordinary closet into a cedar closet by installing cedar particleboard on the walls and ceiling. Put weather stripping around the door to keep the scent in. If the scent is fading in an existing cedar closet, rub the walls with fine sandpaper.

Master Bedroom

If your own bedroom is disorganized, chances are you could use the space in your closets and drawers more efficiently. The following tips will help you maximize this space and make your room a more comfortable refuge for you.

Closets

- Hang work, play, and dressy clothes in their respective categories, giving prime placement to the kind of clothes you wear most often.
- Group the same types of clothing within each category: shirts with shirts, skirts with skirts, and so on.
- Replace all wire hangers with plastic tubular hangers that don't misshape clothes or create rust marks.
- Keep empty hangers at the end of a rod so you'll always have one handy.
- Hang nicer knits and special-occasion clothes on padded hangers.
- If you have trouble remembering what goes with what, post a list of possible outfits, including accessories, on the inside of your closet door.
- Don't keep clothing that is the wrong size or color, is out of style, or has permanent stains or irreparable tears. If they're in good condition, give them away. Otherwise, throw them away. (Keep a large paper shopping bag in each closet to collect clothes to be donated.)
- Keep clothes to be mended in a designated place.
- Store off-season clothes in another closet, or put a sheet around them and hang them in the back of your closet.
- Use an over-the-door shoe organizer to store socks, hosiery, small purses, and gloves.
- Keep only the few pairs of shoes you wear regularly on the floor. Store the others in transparent boxes on a shelf above the clothing rod. Roll up magazines and put them in boots to keep them in an upright position.
- Keep a small step stool in your closet to reach higher shelves.
- Have one clear plastic box or a basket to hold unmatched socks whose mates may show up one day. Keep another box for panty hose with runs that you can still wear under pants. (Avoid frustration by keeping them separate from good hosiery.)
- Hang a small mesh laundry bag to collect soiled delicates. Tie it up and toss it into the washer with other clothes.

- Keep a laundry bag handy for clothes to go to the dry cleaner.
- Use a tie rack for belts, scarves, leotards, lingerie, and ribbons.
- Put a cup hook on an inside closet wall to hold a small pair of scissors to clip loose threads and price tags.
- Keep a small wastebasket in your closet for tags, cleaner bags, and pocket or purse debris.
- Fill a small basket with last-minute fix-up items: a lint brush or roller, a pincushion, safety pins, and a roll of masking tape (for emergency hem repairs when you don't have time to change clothes).

Drawers

Jammed drawers can be counted on to produce frustration. The following tips will help you get this storage space under control.

- When cleaning a drawer, remove the contents, then vacuum the inside using a handheld vacuum or the dusting brush or crevice tool on your vacuum cleaner. (If you want to suck up only the dust—and not small items that have fallen to the bottom of the drawer—cover the nozzle of your vacuum hose with a section of panty hose held in place with a rubber band.) Wipe out the drawer with a damp cloth or premoistened disinfectant wipe.
- Stack clothing only two or three layers high and arrange so that the most delicate items are at the top of the stack and durable items are at the bottom. Leave at least one inch between the top edge of the drawer and the top of the contents.
- You can avoid wrinkles by placing clothes in drawers in certain ways. Fold clothes across their width. Creases fall out more quickly than when folded lengthwise. If you store skirts and pants in a drawer, roll them around plastic bags or tissue paper to prevent creasing.
- Don't put overly heavy objects in a drawer. The weight will put extra strain on the bottom of the drawer.

Home Office

Whether you use a desk, a countertop, or a room for your home office, the following suggestions will help you keep your supplies organized. (For more tips, see "Home-office sanity savers," pages 207–208.)

- Place only the most frequently used items in your desk drawers, grouping similar items together.

GOOD TO KNOW

Large sprigs of rosemary are good for moth control. They work better if closet doors are kept closed.

SMART MOVE

Use a silicone spray or put soap on drawer runners if a drawer sticks.

☆

SMART MOVE

Buy a label maker at an office-supply store. You can label shelves, notebooks, kids' belongings, and more.

⚠

CAUTION!

According to the
Federal Trade
Commission's
Identity Theft Survey
Report, each year
approximately
10 million American
consumers discover
that their personal
information has
been used to open
fraudulent bank,
credit card, or utility
accounts, or used
to commit other
crimes.

Family Manager Filing System

A logical way to store papers is to categorize them by the seven Family Manager departments.

Time & Scheduling. Tips and articles on time management, last year's calendar, public transportation schedules.

Home & Property. Decorating ideas, sanitation and recycling information, auto information, dream house pictures and plans, gardening information, household inventory, appraisals, receipts for all home improvements, additions, and repairs.

Food. Nutritional information, takeout menus, party menus, caterers, centerpiece inspirations, recipes.

Family & Friends. Assign each family member a file-folder color and store the following in each person's files: birth certificate, immunization records, school history/ report cards, résumés, hobby and sports information, prescriptions for eyeglasses and contacts, pet records. If you have young children, the Missing Children Center in Tampa, Florida, recommends keeping a home identification file on each child to assist law enforcement officials in the event of a child abduction. The file should include a complete set of fingerprints as well as dental information.

Finances. Banking (checking and savings) records, spare checks, loan papers, insurance, receipts for purchases, mortgage or rental papers, tax information, investments, organizations to which you pay annual dues, retirement information, health insurance information.

Special Events. Travel, vacation research, maps and tourist information, garage-sale records (what worked and what didn't work last time you held one), birthday party and holiday ideas, holiday greeting-card list, family reunion research, rental company brochures.

Self-Management. Personal interests and hobbies, personal medical records, weight loss tips, beauty and wardrobe information, community or church volunteer work.

- Keep a "desk junk" drawer or basket for miscellaneous things that tend to accumulate. Empty and organize it at least once a month.
- Store empty file folders near your desk or filing cabinet so you can create new files as soon as you have paperwork or items related to a new subject.
- Don't overload electrical outlets. A surge protector power strip will allow you to plug in your various computer components and protect the system from power surges. Set computers and laptops on a stable surface, out of direct sunlight, with plenty of ventilation around them.
- Avoid the nightmare of losing your work by regularly backing up your files on your hard drive. Keep an external storage device with your backed-up computer content at an alternate site.

Organize your desk

When things have gotten out of control at your desk or work area, set aside a few minutes, grab a large trash container, and throw away the following items:

- business cards you don't need
- last season's catalogs
- magazines and journals more than two months old
- junk mail
- pens that don't write and pencils with bad erasers
- school papers you or your kids don't need
- expired coupons
- old sticky notes
- articles you clipped or copied but don't have time to read
- recipes you don't have time to try

Paper piles

Conquer paper piles with this seven-step excavation plan.

1. Put all the papers you need to deal with or file in one place. Get a wastebasket or recycle box, portable paper shredder if you have it, file folders, labels, pens, and a stapler.

2. Start with the paper on top: Decide if it's valuable and necessary. If not, toss or recycle it. (Or shred it if it includes account numbers, your home address, or other identifying information.) If it's worth keeping, move to step 3.

☆ **SMART MOVE**

Turn a pile of papers over before you go through them, so that the oldest papers are on top. You'll see progress faster because typically you can throw away many of the older papers.

☆ **SMART MOVE**

Shred anything you don't need that has your Social Security number, account number, birth date, or maiden name on it.

☺

FUN FOR KIDS

Let young children organize a lower cabinet for their own plastic cups and dishes.

☆

SMART MOVES

• Place bay leaves or a few pieces of mint gum on pantry and cupboard shelves to help keep them bug free. A bay leaf in your flour can help prevent weevils.

• Discourage ants by washing down any area they might enter with full-strength white vinegar or boric acid. Or mix equal parts red pepper and sugar; sprinkle where ants travel.

3. Choose a file heading for it, label the folder, and file the paper. You can use some of the headings listed in the sidebar "Family Manager Filing System" on page 36.

4. If two or more papers belong together, staple them. Don't use paper clips. They get caught on each other and fall off easily.

5. Pick up the next piece of paper and follow the same procedure, either creating a new file or placing it in one you've already created. Consolidate as much as you can.

6. When you've finished with all your papers, sort the files according to the Family Manager departments, then alphabetize the files within the departments. Place files in a file drawer or carton.

7. Purge regularly. Each time you refer to a file, thumb through it and discard any papers that are no longer necessary.

Kitchen

The kitchen is the hub of the home. A lot of traffic flows through this room, so keeping it organized is essential. If that doesn't describe it now, carve out a couple of hours to rethink and reorganize your kitchen. The time you invest now will pay off in the long run.

• Keep only the glasses you use regularly in prime storage space. Store glassware and cups upside down to prevent dust and discourage insects.
• Store extraneous pots and pans, bowls, casseroles, and dishes in a high, seldom-used cabinet. Keep only items used at least weekly in prime storage.
• Use only clear-glass or plastic containers for storing food in your refrigerator so you always know what you're saving.
• Use lazy Susans on deep shelves or in corner cabinets.
• Hang a foil, wrap, and bag organizer inside a cabinet or pantry door.
• Give away space-taking cookbooks you never use. Cut out favorite recipes and file them in inexpensive photo albums.
• Store canned goods by category with labels facing forward so you can see what's on hand at a glance.
• Store spices alphabetically or group them by use: baking spices, pasta spices, etc. Stair-step spice racks to help you see what you have on hand with one glance. You can also hang spice racks inside pantry doors.

- Add another shelf inside a tall cabinet to elevate some items and create space underneath for others.
- Do not store food near heating ducts, furnaces, hot-water pipes, or other heat sources. Most foods store best in cool, dry places at a temperature of 40 to 60 degrees.
- Rotate food and supplies. Place new items behind old ones. If you buy in bulk, be sure to label all containers. Indicate the contents and date of purchase.
- Discard all bulged or leaking cans—without tasting the product.
- If you have partially used containers of the same items, check their expiration dates. If they're still good and have approximately the same expiration dates, combine them.
- Save only five grocery bags at a time. Don't let them multiply between the counter and refrigerator or in the pantry.
- Save search time by labeling the shelves in your freezer: Breads and Quick Meals, Vegetables and Fruits, Desserts and Beverages, and Meat.
- Keep silverware within arm's length of the dishwasher.
- Store table accessories—napkins, dinnerware, place mats, salt and pepper shakers—so they're in a place that has easy access to the dinner table.
- Keep cooking utensils and hot pads where you can reach them without moving from the stove. But don't place hot pads too close to heating elements or burners. Lay long, thin objects such as ladles and spatulas so they all face the same way and don't get jumbled. Or keep them in a container on the countertop.
- Have only one junk drawer, and keep it under control. When you have an extra five minutes, like when you're waiting for water to boil or popcorn to pop, declutter it a little at a time.

Laundry Area

Life's too short to spend more time than necessary in the laundry room. Organizing this area will make the work speedier and more pleasant. (For more ideas on laundry and clothing care, see page 71.)

- Stock your laundry area with detergent, bleach, stain remover, fabric softener, soap for hand-washables, starch, a zipper mesh bag for delicates, a measuring cup, an old toothbrush for stubborn stains, hangers, laundry baskets, and ironing supplies.

CAUTION!

Avoid storing spices on top of the stove; this interferes with cleaning, and heat can affect the spices' quality.

SMART MOVE

Put each family member in charge of putting away his or her own laundry. Children as young as five can put away their own socks. As they grow, they can begin putting away other things. By the time they are 12, they can do most of their own laundry, start to finish. It is a matter of teaching them and working with them patiently as they learn to do it correctly.

GOOD TO KNOW

According to the U.S. Department of Energy, the average U.S. household does seven loads of wash per week.

- For the benefit of all family members, write down and post directions near your washing machine on how to wash different types of clothing.
- Attach a magnetic caddy to the side of the washing machine for items found in pockets and buttons that come off in the wash.
- Have a small trash can nearby for dryer lint and litter from pockets.
- Prethread some needles and keep them handy in a pincushion for instant repairs.
- Keep a container for orphan socks in your laundry area.

Work Centers

Create work centers to store all the necessary items for a task in one place. Work centers help abolish clutter, make sensible storage, and keep you working smarter, not harder, since you don't have to spend time hunting for something you need to complete a project. Here are ideas for work centers to create in your home.

Mail Center. A Mail Center can be used to organize your mail every day. Keep a trash can or recycling container close by so you can toss junk mail immediately. Use magazine storage boxes to sort items. You might label one for each family member, one for bills, another for magazines and catalogs, or whatever makes sense for your family. Depending on the space available in your home, your Control Central area might also be the place for mail sorting and bill paying.

Kids' Arts and Crafts Center. Devote a shelf, a plastic crate, or a storage bin near the kids' play area to stack construction paper, sketch pads, glue, glitter, scissors, markers, crayons, pipe cleaners, and pom-poms. (A shower curtain makes an excellent drop cloth for messy projects.)

Gift-Wrap Center. Designate a large drawer, plastic crate, or part of a cabinet to store everything you need for wrapping (wrapping paper, tape, scissors, ribbon, etc.). Keep a few generic gifts for adults and children on hand too. Stock this center with blank cards, as well as greeting cards for birthdays, anniversaries, holidays, graduations, engagements, weddings, babies, confirmations, deaths, and retirements.

Bill Pay Center. Stock a drawer or plastic bin with pens, stamps, envelopes, return-address labels, and a calculator for paying bills. If you pay some of your bills online, put these items near your computer so you can do everything at the same time.

Study Center. Having a designated space for homework gives a child a sense of routine. Each child needs his or her own area in which to do homework. If they don't have desks, designate a specific area (such as the dining-room table) where each child can work. Store everything your children need in one spot so they don't waste time scavenging for highlighters or binder paper. Keep office supplies, such as construction, lined, and plain paper; different colors of felt pens and pencils; folders for reports; and poster board on hand for homework projects.

Baking Center. Kitchen space can be divided into work centers. Think of your kitchen in terms of the tasks you perform (chopping, baking, and lunch making) and arrange it accordingly. When possible, each kitchen center should revolve around a major appliance, some storage space, and a work surface. Store equipment and food near the center where they'll be used—baking goods and utensils near the mixer, dishes near the dishwasher.

Garage

If bikes, yard tools, and sporting equipment have taken over space in the garage once occupied by your car, it's time to reclaim this territory and organize it for optimum usage.

- Group like items together—sporting equipment, tools, gardening tools.
- Put utility shelves on one wall for storing things like gardening supplies, insecticides, paint, and auto-maintenance supplies. (Be sure to put poisonous products on a high shelf or lock them up.) Assign lower shelves to family members for their work boots and sports equipment.
- Hang inexpensive kitchen cabinets on the walls for storage. Put Peg-Board on walls for hanging storage.
- "Brand" your tools by painting your initial on them in a bright color. This way, when neighbors borrow something, your brand will remind them to get it back to you.
- Install large hooks to store garden hoses inside during winter months.
- Use clear, labeled storage containers so you don't have to dump the contents each time you need something. Jelly or baby-food jars can hold different kinds of screws, nails, and washers.
- Use silverware sorters to hold things like twine, scissors, and box cutters.

Garage Safety Inspection Checklist

❑ Is the circuit breaker box well marked?

❑ If you have young children, are electrical outlets covered?

❑ Are cabinets containing toxic chemicals locked?

❑ Is a fire extinguisher easily accessible?

❑ Are windows and doors secured against break-ins?

❑ Are there signs of rodent activity?

❑ Are lawn mowers and other cutting machines in good repair, with necessary guards?

❑ Are products that have safety packaging properly closed?

❑ Is gasoline stored in approved, clearly labeled containers?

❑ Is scrap wood, sawdust, or other waste lying around on the garage floor?

❑ Are solvents and paints in sealed and labeled metal containers and stored away from heat sources, such as your furnace or water heater?

❑ Do any electrical power tools have frayed cords or bad plugs?

❑ Are electrical power tools unplugged and stored when not in use?

- Store paintbrushes in coffee cans, brush end up, or hang them from a Peg-Board.
- Clip loose sheets of sandpaper to a clipboard and hang it from a wall hook.
- Store single-edged razor blades in a block of Styrofoam. (Keep up high out of kids' reach.)
- Think "up high." Hang bicycles and other sports equipment from the garage ceiling. If you have rafters, put boards across them to make a ministorage loft over part of the garage. (This is a particularly good place to store things you need only seasonally—outdoor holiday decorations, snow shovels, or lawn furniture.)
- Use large plastic trash cans with lids for potting soils, compost

materials, and fertilizers. Keep them sealed, away from children's toys and equipment, and away from water. Don't store fertilizer and gasoline close to each other.

- Keep a trash can on the driver's side of the garage so car debris can be easily tossed.
- Paint parking spaces on your garage floor for tricycles, skateboards, wagons, and scooters.
- Install an inexpensive shop light above your primary work area.
- Hang a tennis ball from the ceiling, positioning it so that it rests against your windshield when you've pulled far enough into your garage.
- Designate a special "fix-it" shelf or area for broken tools and other items that need to be fixed.

CLUTTER

A house becomes a haven when it inspires easy living. Ridding your home of needless clutter and organizing the things you use and care about will help make your home an enjoyable place for all. Use these strategies to bring clutter under control.

Declutter in a Day

- Schedule a day when you can do a whole-house clutter sweep. This way you'll save on start-up/knockdown time.
- Schedule the Salvation Army or another charity to come to your house soon after your decluttering day. This gives you a deadline.
- Dress so you can put all your energy into the job. Wear comfortable clothes and sneakers.
- Be prepared. You'll need several types of containers: boxes labeled "Give Away," "Garage Sale," and "Store," plastic storage bins (the see-through kind are best), and a large plastic garbage bag for every room. If you think you'll be distracted by things you don't know what to do with, put them in a box too. Label the box "Questionable" and give yourself a deadline for deciding where those difficult items will end up. Also have a small box to collect safety pins and buttons, a shoe-size box for random photos you find, and another box or a piggy bank for coins.
- Start with the most cluttered room in your house. Work your way methodically around the room. Remove clutter from shelves, bookcases, drawers, tabletops, floors, and walls.

☆

SMART MOVE

If it's hard for you to toss things, ask a friend to help you attack your clutter for a day, and then return the favor for her. The time will pass faster when you're working together, the work will get done more quickly, and she'll be more objective about your clutter. After you both have cleared your homes of clutter, you can encourage each other and keep each other accountable. Or schedule a Family Manager Coach to help you.

GOOD TO KNOW

Ten minutes a day looking for misplaced items wastes 60 hours a year.

- Toss or give away as much as possible. Be ruthless with things like gift boxes, grocery sacks, old magazines and catalogs, and craft materials you saved but haven't used. Weed out games your family doesn't play and books you'll never read.
- Don't allow nonemergencies to interrupt your clutter-clearing time. Eliminate all distractions. Turn on your answering machine, turn off the TV, and put on some peppy music. If you find the umbrella your friend left three months ago, don't call her now to tell her about it.

Clutter Combat Rules

Once you've decluttered, follow these guidelines to prevent clutter from taking over your home again.

In-and-out rule. Establish an in-and-out rule. Every time a new item comes into the house, show an old item the door.

Put it up, not down. Make this your family motto: "Put it up, not down." Start the routine of returning everything you get out back to where it belongs.

Save photos, not objects. You want to hold on to the memories—not things that clutter valuable storage space. For example, take a photo of your son in his Scout uniform. When he outgrows it, keep the photo and give away the uniform.

Designate a key place. Have a specific basket, bowl, cup hook, or key hanger for family members' keys.

Set destroy dates. Limit the time you keep newspapers, magazines, and catalogs you intend to read. Assign yourself a "to read" basket, and empty it once a week. When a new catalog arrives, toss out the old one.

Eliminate and concentrate. Eliminate what you don't want, need, or use. *Concentrate* on what you use, need, and care about. For every underused item in your house, ask these Clutter Control questions:

- When is the last time it was used? worn? played with?
- Does it deserve space in our home? If it wasn't here, what would be here instead?
- Are there memories attached to it? (If so, remember you may be able to capture the memory with a photo of the item.)
- What will I do with it? Fix it, sell it, store it, toss it, or donate it?

Conquer Paper Clutter
Preventing paper piles
Use the ideas below to create clutter-free zones throughout your home.

- Flat surfaces, such as kitchen countertops, the dining-room table, and side tables, are magnets for paper clutter. Try to catch yourself before you put papers on the closest flat surface, and ask, *Where do these papers go? Do I need them?* If not, toss them.
- Keep your dining-room and kitchen tables set to discourage family members from piling their stuff on them.
- Designate specific places for papers and train yourself and your family members to put papers where they belong now, not later. For example, invitations should go on the bulletin board at your Control Central, and current school papers go in your child's in-box; you should also have certain places for things like coupons and receipts.
- Create a Paper Clutter Jail for papers that family members leave out. Have them post bond to retrieve their papers.

Mail and newspapers
- Set up a Mail Center—a place to sort your mail every day (see page 40).
- Don't let newspapers pile up. Yesterday's news is old, so toss it.

Magazines and catalogs
- If you've let your magazines get out of control, schedule a time to get them organized. Put it on your calendar.
- Before you start, get the supplies ready that you'll need to do the job efficiently: boxes, scissors, file folders and labels or label maker, and plastic sleeves or magnetic photo pages— whichever you use for your recipe compendium. Designate some of the boxes for magazines worthy of donating to a school, nursing home, or hospital. Use others for magazines to be recycled or thrown away.
- Go from room to room and gather all magazines and catalogs. If there's an article in a magazine you want to read but haven't gotten around to, cut out the article and put it in a file labeled "To Read." If there are recipes you want to save, cut them out and place in your recipe box or notebook, or scan them into your computer. Cut out coupons and put them in a file; deal with them another time.
- Clip address labels from catalogs you don't want. Return the labels to the company that sent them and ask to be taken off

GOOD TO KNOW

The U.S. Postal Service processes and delivers almost 703 million pieces of mail each day.

SMART MOVE

Use a clean dustpan as a toy scoop to pick up toys with multiple small pieces.

the mailing list. If you get duplicate issues of a catalog you enjoy receiving, send the company the duplicate label and ask to have the extra listing deleted.

- When you finish, immediately load the boxes in your car and give yourself 24 hours to get them where they need to go.
- Set destroy deadlines for all those magazines and catalogs you've been intending to read but never have. If you haven't gotten around to reading an issue from two months ago, skim it and cut out articles you really want to read, then throw it away. Give yourself a couple of weeks to scan dated news magazines, clip stories for kids' reports or future reading, then toss.
- Visit http://www.stopthejunkmail.com to reduce the amount of junk mail you receive. For $20 a year, you can get your name off thousands of mailing lists used by telemarketers, junk mailers, direct marketers, and databases.

Diminish piles a little at a time

If conquering the paper piles in your home feels like an overwhelming task, try doing it a little at a time. You'll eventually get the task licked.

- Excavate piles of paper five minutes at a time. Create a "To Be Filed" box for important papers you need to save. When you have a five-minute block of time, file a few of the papers from the box into your filing system.
- Practice double-timing when you're watching television. Grab some empty files and your label maker, a trash sack, and a pile of papers you need to deal with. Shrink the pile while you're watching a movie.

Clutter Combat Tactics for Children

Kids' bedrooms breed clutter. By establishing guidelines like the ones below, you'll teach your children valuable lessons about taking good care of their possessions.

Room rules

Establish "room rules" for kids, such as:

1. Do not take food into the bedrooms.

2. Keep all dirty clothes in a basket or hamper.

3. Do not leave dangerous items—such as balls, plastic building pieces, and roller skates—on the floor.

4. Put away toys no longer being played with before getting out something new.

5. Clean up the room before going to bed.

If your efforts to get your kids to control their clutter seem to be going nowhere, try one or two of the following ideas.

Swine Fine. Create a Swine Fine jar to help children learn responsibility. If they don't pick up their belongings, call out "Swine fine!" and require them to deposit a designated amount of money in your jar.

Clutter Contest. Play the "Clutter Be Gone" game. Give each family member a plastic trash bag. Walk through your house and see how much clutter you can each collect in 15 minutes. The winner is the person with the most clutter in his or her bag when time is up.

Clutter Jail. Train family members to pick up their things by creating Clutter Jail. If something is left out, it goes into the Clutter Jail (a box or laundry basket will do) and can't be reclaimed until Sunday night when the family member pays a fine to cover handling charges.

Filing system. Buy each child a filing box or crate. Help set up files for things like schoolwork, pictures, awards and certificates, personal mail and cards, stories, articles for future reports, and hobby brochures.

Children's artwork. Here's a plan for all those countless works of art your children bring home from school. Purchase clear plastic storage bins; label one per child. Once a drawing or painting has been displayed on the refrigerator or bulletin board for a few days, store it in the appropriate bin. Keep the bins easily accessible in a cupboard or nearby closet. At the end of the school year, have each child pick a few favorites to save in a memorabilia box that you store in your attic or basement.

Even better, scan your children's artwork into your computer and use them as your screen savers. This way their masterpieces are "stored" in a safe place, and they will love seeing some of them on your screen. Best of all, you'll have less paper clutter to deal with.

CLEANING

Cleaning in Manageable Chunks

Few moms have a large block of time to do a complete deep-cleaning and get all rooms spotless at the same time. Here's a plan for cleaning a little bit at a time. Each day tackle three or four 10-minute tasks and

☆
SMART MOVE

Keep a box of disposable gloves handy. This way if the baby starts crying when you're in the middle of a messy cleaning job, you can pull them off and pick up your baby with clean hands.

one bigger chore (on days when you have the time) to keep up with this dreaded responsibility.

10-minute tasks

Living areas
- Clean glass, mirrors, TV, computer screens, and tabletops.
- Dust tabletops, shelves, pictures, or mantel. (Now's a good time to cut down on knickknacks. They're too time consuming to clean, and you'll have to put them away anyway if you have crawling babies or toddlers. Keep a dust rag handy to quickly dust and store them away a few at a time.)
- Remove the books from one shelf on a bookcase, dust the books and shelf, and replace them.
- Use a wide, soft-bristled paintbrush to remove dust from blinds and the pleats in lamp shades.
- Clean the dust off broad-leaved plants by using damp socks on your hands.
- Spot-clean sofa cushions and throw pillows. Use a masking-tape lint roller to quickly pick up pet hair.
- Polish one or two pieces of wood furniture.
- Damp-mop the floor in a room.
- De-web light fixtures and dust the ceiling fan.
- Wipe off switch plates.
- Spot-clean doors and molding.

Bedrooms
- Clean mirrors, glass, and tabletops.
- Strip bed and throw linens in the washing machine. Keep linens moving through the washing and drying cycles when you have a few minutes here and there.
- Dust part of your bedroom and spot-clean picture frames.
- Clean switch plates and doorknobs with all-purpose cleaner and a cleaning rag.
- Dust furniture and windowsills.
- Vacuum or dust-mop floors/carpets.

Bathrooms
- Spray and wipe faucets and mirror with glass cleaner.
- Wipe off windowsills, towel racks, and scale.
- Sweep or vacuum floor, then damp-mop.
- Use a clean sponge mop to wash the tub and wall tiles in the bathroom. This will prevent back strain.
- Straighten a shelf or two in the linen closet.

☆ SMART MOVE

An average of 40 pounds of dust comes into a home each year. Put doormats on the outside and inside of all your doors to help trap dust.

⚠ CAUTION!

Don't dry-dust. It stirs up dust and sends it someplace else. Use a static-cling duster that captures dust particles or pretreated dust cloths. If neither is available, use a damp rag.

Seven-Minute Nightly Sprint

Start a seven-minute nightly cleanup routine. Some time after dinner and before bedtime, set the kitchen timer for seven minutes. Put on some music and have family members pick up and put up for seven minutes. Throw away today's paper, plump the sofa pillows, fold the throws, pick up the day's clutter. In seven minutes someone can even vacuum one room, clean the sink and mirror in a bathroom, or do a little dusting. If you start a routine of doing this every night, you'll be amazed at how you can do a better job of staying on top of housework and clutter.

List some tasks your family could accomplish in seven minutes each night that would help keep up with housecleaning and clutter.

_____

_____

_____

_____

Kitchen

- Purge your pantry of food you never use, one shelf at a time.
- Clean the outside of large appliances—one at a time.
- Shine the outside of small appliances—two at a time.
- Wipe kitchen counters and backsplash.
- Spray the inside of your microwave with a plant mister, then turn the microwave on high for a few seconds. Allow it to sit for a minute or two, then wipe with a clean cloth. You can also clean the microwave by nuking a few tablespoons of baking soda in a cup of water. Wipe up the mist with a paper towel. Use a toothbrush to scrub stubborn stains.
- Dust sills or wash curtains—one window at a time.
- Wipe off countertops.
- Wash and disinfect trash can.

- Sweep or vacuum floor.
- Clean out one section or shelf in a drawer or cabinet.
- Damp-mop floor.
- Clean off one shelf in the refrigerator.

One-hour cleaning tasks

When you have more time to spend on housework, it pays to do some of the deep-cleaning projects listed below.

- Clean your stovetop and replace aluminum drip pans under burners; wash the stove knobs with mild soap, warm water, and a toothbrush.
- Move large appliances and clean beneath them with a vacuum. Pay particular attention to the coils.
- Remove items stored on top of your refrigerator. Spray it with all-purpose cleaner and let the grease and dirt "marinate" while you empty the refrigerator drip pan and vacuum the coils. Then wipe the top clean with paper towels and cover with plastic wrap. (Moisten the surface slightly so the plastic wrap will stay put.) That way you'll never have to clean up there again. You can just peel off and replace the dirty wrap periodically. A one-hour task will take just 10 minutes next time.
- Wash woodwork.
- Clean light fixtures and doorknobs. Carefully remove plastic panels from florescent light boxes. Wash them with warm, soapy water.
- Clean the bathroom vent fan. Dirt and lint buildup inside bathroom vent fans can impair efficiency, encourage mildew growth, and shorten the life of the unit—so don't skip this task. To clean, remove the vent cover and wipe the inside with a rag. Use an old toothbrush to clean the fan blades. As with any electric fixture, don't use water to clean.
- Clean and straighten the linen closet.
- Clean the fireplace hearth and remove ashes.

Clean while you sleep

If you start some cleaning tasks before bed, they'll be done the next morning.

- Line a white bathroom sink with paper towels soaked in laundry bleach. In the morning, toss out the towels and admire your white sink. (Do not let bleach touch metal drain fitting, and do not use bleach on colored porcelain sinks, as it will fade the color.)

☆

SMART MOVE

Here's another way to clean blinds: Wearing a pair of cotton work gloves, dip one hand into a solution of all-purpose household cleaner and water. Use the fingers of that hand to wash the slats. Wipe them dry with the other hand.

- To clean residue from the bottom of a vase or thermos, simply fill it with water and drop in an Alka-Seltzer tablet. Rinse it out the next morning.
- Give your toilet an overnight soaking of white vinegar each week. By morning, it will be completely disinfected. Just flush clean.
- Clean out clogged drains. Pour ½ cup each of baking soda and salt down the drain. Follow with a cup of boiling water and let it sit overnight. Flush with hot tap water the next morning.
- Spray your oven with cleaner in the evening and let it do its job. You can also remove tough stains from the bottom of your oven by spreading automatic dishwasher soap or baking soda and covering it with wet paper towels. Wipe clean the next day.
- Fill your teakettle with equal parts vinegar and water. Bring to a boil, turn off the heat, and let it stand overnight. This will remove lime deposits left behind by hard water.
- Got a broiler pan or burner trays that are caked with grease? Put them in a plastic bag along with a cup of ammonia. There's no need to cover the pan or tray, because the fumes do the work. Seal the bag, put it outside overnight, and wash with soap and water the next morning.
- Clean oil stains on cement floors overnight. Make a paste of automatic dishwasher detergent and hot water. Scrub mixture onto the spot and let it work overnight; rinse with water. Repeat the process if necessary. Or sprinkle oil spots with cat litter. Leave overnight and sweep away the next morning.

One-Day Clean Sweep Plan

When you need to do a whole-house cleaning, two are better than one. Barter with a friend who would like to get her house clean too. She comes to your house for your cleaning day, and you return the favor. Here's a plan to get it done.

Morning: tackle living areas and bedrooms

- Strip bed linens. Begin washing. Keep laundry moving from washer to dryer every 30 minutes.
- Begin vacuuming. Moving from room to room, use brush attachment to vacuum cobwebs from ceilings and corners. Use upholstery attachment to clean sofas and chairs.
- Dust furniture and bookshelves with a treated dust cloth that attracts dust. Use a damp cloth to wipe fingerprints from around doorknobs and light switches.

- Clean mirrors and any glass furniture tops.
- Vacuum floors.

Early afternoon: tackle the kitchen

- Vacuum the ceiling and corners, fan blades, and light fixtures with brush attachment.
- Vacuum refrigerator coils and front grill.
- Wipe off refrigerator shelves.
- Clean inside the microwave. (Bring a cup of water to a boil so it will steam up the interior and loosen gunk. Wipe off walls and tray with a damp cloth.)
- Wipe off stove top and finish cleaning the oven. Replace drip pans.
- Wipe down countertops, backsplash, and the outside of all appliances.
- Take out the trash and disinfect the trash can.
- Wipe off woodwork, and drawer and cabinet handles.
- Clean the floor.

Late afternoon: clean bathrooms

- Launder throw rugs.
- Vacuum the ceiling and corners, light fixtures, windowsills, and baseboards.
- Spray shower, tub, and toilet with heavy-duty cleaner. (Be sure to open a window or turn on the exhaust fan first.) Let solutions go to work.
- Use one sponge to wipe the shower and/or tub and another sponge to rinse clean.
- Wipe the outside of the toilet clean, then throw the sponges in the wash.
- Clean the inside of the toilet with a bowl brush.
- Wipe off woodwork and switch plates.
- Clean the mirror and shine chrome with all-purpose cleaner.
- Wipe off the bathroom scale and knickknacks.
- When surfaces are dry, vacuum the floor to remove hair.
- Mop floor (sponge mop is best) with heavy-duty disinfectant.
- To remove a stubborn bathtub ring, moisten a sponge with undiluted white vinegar and rub. (In the future, use bubble bath to help eliminate ring around the tub.)

Shortcuts and Smarter Cleaning

- Spray fabric guard on anything prone to stains—sofas, chairs, kids' comforters, tablecloths, tennis shoes.

- Before vacuuming, always check to be sure the disposable vacuum cleaner bag is secured tightly into the base of the vacuum. If it's not, the vacuum will likely throw out as much dust as it takes up.
- Never allow the vacuum cleaner bag to reach the bursting point. It could weaken the suction and cause the bag to leak dust.
- Change or clean the furnace and the air-conditioning filters at least once a month (depending on the season). If the filter is gray when you remove it, you should be replacing it even more often. A clean filter will prevent fried or frozen dirt from being blasted around the house.
- Be sure doors and windows fit snugly in their frames. If they don't, add weather stripping to keep dirt and allergens at bay.
- Paint basement and garage floors with a concrete sealer to keep concrete dust down.
- Use dark-colored throw rugs just inside the entryways to your house, at the kitchen sink, and anywhere else with heavy traffic patterns. They show less dirt and won't need to be washed as often as light-colored ones.
- Use drawer dividers to corral various items. Make sure the dividers are at least half the height of the drawer, or items will still tend to jumble together.
- The next time you paint interior walls, select a finish (such as semigloss) that is durable and easy to clean.
- Put pet dishes on vinyl place mats.
- Confine art projects involving crayons, finger paints, glue, and other messy mediums to a plastic craft table. Use an old shower curtain as a drop cloth beneath the table to protect your floor.
- Wipe your TV screen with a fabric softener sheet. This will help cut down on static electricity, which attracts dust.
- Train your kids to take off their shoes as soon as they come in from outside. If your house has an entryway or mudroom with space for a shoe rack, purchase one. Store indoor shoes or slippers on one side of the rack and leave the other side open for street shoes.
- When buying new furniture, carpeting, or rugs, remember that texture and subtle patterns show less dirt than smooth, solid-color fabrics.
- Use pump soap dispensers instead of bar soap to wash hands. You don't have to deal with cleaning built-up scum in soap dishes.

GOOD TO KNOW

Many toy companies replace lost pieces for a small fee. For example, check out Customer Service at http://www.hasbro.com to order replacements for games including Battleship, Hi Ho Cherry O, Lite Brite, and Scrabble.

- Apply car wax to glass shower doors every two to three months for easier cleaning.
- Keep a masking-tape lint roller easily accessible to quickly pick up pet hair from furniture.
- Windows are less likely to streak if you clean them on a cloudy day. Direct sunshine causes them to dry faster and unevenly. Clean windows using newspaper (instead of paper towels). Newsprint makes glass really sparkle.
- Wipe windows horizontally on the inside and vertically on the outside. As you clean the glass, you'll be able to easily spot whether any streaks are on the inside or outside.
- Wash walls from the bottom up. Drips are easier to clean from already-washed walls.
- Keep a package of pretreated dust cloths in the closet of each bedroom. Dust whenever you have a spare minute or two.
- Glue felt pads on the bottoms of vases, table lamps, and other heavy metal accessories to prevent scratching of wood furniture.
- Apply spot remover from the edge to the center of a stain so it won't spread.
- Never spray glass cleaner directly on framed paintings or prints. The liquid can leak through the frame at the edges and damage the artwork. Instead, spray the cleaner on a cloth and rub glass gently using a circular motion. Avoid cleaning mirrors with water, which can trickle down behind the glass and damage the silvering. Instead, clean with rubbing alcohol on a soft rag.
- Be alert for natural housework opportunities. If the kids splash water all over the bathroom floor, that's a great time to mop it. On a rainy day, take your houseplants outside and pull off dead leaves—let the rain water them.

Kitchen cleaning shortcuts
- Clean drips from pots and cookware right away; wipe countertop spills as soon as they occur.
- Keep fresh vegetables in plastic bags with holes that allow air to circulate. If the vegetables go bad, you can lift them out of the fridge with a lot less mess.
- Line crisper drawers with paper towels so you don't have to clean the drawer—just toss the dirty towel and replace with a clean one every two weeks or so.
- Spray the egg compartments in your refrigerator with cooking spray. No more stuck, broken eggs.

- Slip plastic lids, such as those from coffee cans, under sticky items (like jam, jelly, or honey) in your refrigerator or pantry.
- Always turn on your oven exhaust fan when cooking.
- Before working with messy foods, such as dipping fish or chicken in bread crumbs or peeling potatoes, cover the countertop or sink with waxed paper or a ripped-open brown grocery bag to catch the mess. When finished, wad up the paper and throw it away.
- Place a piece of waxed paper in the bottom of your microwave to catch spills.
- Your first step in cooking or baking should always be to fill the sink with warm, soapy water. Toss bowls and utensils in the water as you finish using them.
- Use less elbow grease. Soak grimy pans in warm, soapy water while you eat. After the meal, messy pots and pans will be much easier to clean. For really greasy cookware, use automatic dishwasher detergent instead of regular dish soap.
- Don't dirty extra dishes. Grate cheese on a paper towel or a piece of waxed paper. Mix dressing directly in the salad bowl. The same holds true for casseroles. Put them together in the pan you plan to bake them in. Marinate chicken or steaks in zip-top plastic bags instead of bowls or pans.
- After using your blender, fill it partway with warm water, add a squirt of dishwashing liquid, and then run the appliance for a few seconds. Rinse it out, then turn it over and allow it to dry on a towel.
- Keep a plastic windshield ice scraper in the kitchen to gently pry dried-on foods from the floor and countertop.
- Clean out your refrigerator the night before trash pickup each week.
- Keep a few clean trash liners at the bottom of your kitchen garbage can. When it's time to empty the can, a fresh liner is readily available.

Bathroom time-savers

- The best time to clean the bathroom is right after taking a shower, when the steam has loosened the grime.
- As they finish their baths, encourage kids to swish their hands and feet around the waterline to loosen bathtub ring before they let the water out.
- Install a handheld showerhead so you can rinse the tub when you're finished showering.

⚠ CAUTION!

When using heavy-duty cleaners in the bathroom, be sure to open a window or turn on the exhaust fan.

- Turn on the exhaust fan when taking a shower to draw out excess moisture and prevent mildew.
- Keep a toilet brush in a caddy next to the toilet. Train family members to give it a frequent swish.
- Keep a box of disposable gloves underneath the bathroom sink for unpleasant cleaning tasks.
- Allow cleansers a chance to work. Instead of rushing to wipe up tile cleaner as soon as you apply it, move on to another task for a few minutes.
- Remove mold from bathroom tile by soaking a cotton ball in bleach. Press it into the yucky area and allow it to sit for a few minutes.
- Wrap a terry-cloth rag around a screwdriver to clean out shower door tracks. Spray generously with all-purpose cleaner and make several passes along the track.
- Before mopping the bathroom floor, vacuum around your tub (which should be dry), toilet, and sink to remove lint and hair.

Eliminating Smells and Odors

When selecting fragrances for your house, choose softer, more neutral scents in the living areas. Reserve any stronger aromas for your bedroom, bathroom, dresser drawers, and closets. If you use fragrance in your kitchen and bathrooms, make sure it isn't covering up an odor that requires prompt attention. Don't use fragrances in the dining room when you're serving food.

- Eradicate bad smells immediately by checking all the likely places: bottoms of trash cans, athletic shoes and equipment, the laundry hamper, the litter box, the dog bed, or the mildewed shower stall in the basement. Be vigilant in finding the source.
- Always line garbage cans with a plastic bag. Spray the can with a pleasant-smelling disinfectant each time you empty it, or put a couple of fabric-softener sheets in the bottom before you replace the bag. Twice a month, wash the can with a disinfectant cleaner and hot, sudsy water, then let it air-dry before placing a bag inside.
- Keep drains odor free by pouring three tablespoons of baking soda into the drain once a week and running very hot tap water over it for one minute.
- Eliminate odors from garbage disposals by grinding chopped-up citrus rinds and flushing the disposal with hot water.
- Always drain any liquids from cans, containers, and serving

pieces into the sink to keep the garbage bag relatively dry. Empty the bag often.

- Boil a few slices of lemon in a pan of water for 20 minutes to clear the air of burned food odors.
- When frying foods, place a small bowl of white vinegar next to the stove to combat odor.
- Freshen your dishwasher by sprinkling baking soda under the bottom rack in between loads.
- Keep an open box of baking soda in the refrigerator to absorb smells. (Write the date on the box; replace it every two to three months.)
- Keep the bathroom door closed but open a window for fresh air. In windowless bathrooms, use a bathroom spray that is effective but not overpowering.
- Sprinkle baking soda liberally into smelly shoes. Let them stand overnight, and then shake them out before wearing.
- Banish really smelly shoes to the great outdoors.
- Transfer washed clothes to the dryer promptly. If clothes sit in the washer overnight, run a rinse cycle before drying to eliminate any possibility of mildew.
- To neutralize carpet odors, sprinkle baking soda over your carpet, wait 15 minutes, then vacuum thoroughly.

Children and Housework

Many moms feel guilty about asking their kids to help around the house. Believe me, you do them a favor when you involve them in family maintenance. You are teaching them life skills—like running the vacuum cleaner—they are going to need. But you're also teaching them teamwork and collaboration skills that will serve them in any walk of life. Delegating also helps balance responsibilities and workloads in relationships. And it builds on the idea that your home belongs to everyone; therefore, each person has a role in taking care of it. The following list (which continues on page 61) includes jobs that are appropriate for various age levels.

Preschoolers can . . .
- make a bed with a comforter
- fold towels and washcloths
- put away clothes in drawers
- hang clothes on hooks
- put dirty clothes in hampers or laundry baskets
- help feed animals
- pick up toys

☆

SMART MOVE

Plant a lemon verbena shrub near a window to bring a lovely fragrance inside.

FamilyManager™

Who's Responsible for What?

1. Home and Property

❏ Picking up clutter _____

❏ Cleaning the kitchen _____

❏ Cleaning bathrooms _____

❏ Cleaning the family room _____

❏ Sweeping/mopping/waxing floors _____

❏ Dusting _____

❏ Vacuuming _____

❏ Making beds _____

❏ Changing sheets _____

❏ Doing laundry _____

❏ Taking clothes to dry cleaner _____

❏ Mending _____

❏ Shopping for clothing and accessories _____

❏ Shopping for household items _____

❏ Organizing closets and drawers _____

❏ Organizing garage, attic, basement _____

❏ Collecting and taking out trash _____

❏ Recycling _____

❏ Performing household repairs and maintenance _____

❏ Contacting repair services _____

❏ Decorating _____

❏ Yard work _____

❏ Maintaining outdoor furniture and equipment _____

❏ Car maintenance _____

❏ Watering plants _____

❏ Cleaning carpets _____

❏ Washing windows _____

2. Food and Meals

❏ Meal planning _____

❏ Creating a grocery list _____

❏ Shopping for groceries _____

❏ Making breakfast _____

❏ Making lunches _____

❏ Cooking dinner _____

❏ Cleaning up after meals _____

❏ Making sack lunches _____
❏ Planning and orchestrating dinner parties _____
❏ Keeping up with coupons _____
❏ Feeding the baby or young children _____
❏ Organizing the pantry _____
❏ Planning and taking food to special functions _____

3. Family and Friends

❏ Caring for small children _____
❏ Arranging for child care _____
❏ Managing school transportation _____
❏ Bathing the kids _____
❏ Reading to the kids _____
❏ Putting the kids to bed _____
❏ Researching and registering kids for activities _____
❏ Transporting kids to lessons, practices, etc. _____
❏ Helping with homework _____
❏ Purchasing school supplies _____
❏ Teaching kids right and wrong _____
❏ Disciplining kids _____
❏ Planning creative activities for kids _____
❏ Monitoring television, music, and the Internet _____
❏ Scheduling play days _____
❏ Teaching manners and social skills _____
❏ Taking kids to the doctor and dentist _____
❏ Overseeing college testing/application process _____
❏ Traveling to visit potential colleges _____
❏ Arranging family outings _____
❏ Arranging date nights with spouse _____
❏ Caring for aging parents and in-laws _____
❏ Keeping up with extended family _____
❏ Buying presents for relatives and friends _____
❏ Sending greeting cards _____
❏ Writing thank-you notes _____
❏ Caring for pets _____
❏ Overseeing relationships with neighbors _____

4. Money and Finances

❏ Periodically reviewing family's financial priorities _____
❏ Organizing bills _____
❏ Paying bills _____
❏ Balancing bank account _____
❏ Selecting appropriate investments _____
❏ Establishing credit _____
❏ Creating budget _____
❏ Researching and buying insurance _____

❑   Working with attorney to update will   _____

❑   Creating saving plans for big things like college   _____

❑   Shopping for best deals   _____

❑   Filing health insurance claims   _____

❑   Keeping up with receipts   _____

❑   Keeping home office supplies stocked   _____

❑   Dispersing children's allowances   _____

❑   Selecting appropriate charities   _____

❑   Organizing tax information and filing return   _____

5.   Special Events

❑   Planning and coordinating birthday celebrations   _____

❑   Planning and coordinating Thanksgiving and Christmas _____

❑   Planning and coordinating other holidays and celebrations

       such as Valentine's, Easter, Fourth of July, graduation,

       baby showers, and family reunions   _____

❑   Decorating for holidays   _____

❑   Organizing neighborhood activities   _____

❑   Planning and orchestrating vacations   _____

❑   Planning and overseeing garages sales   _____

❑   Buying gifts   _____

❑   Keeping gift-wrapping center stocked   _____

❑   Planning weekend outings   _____

6.   Time and Scheduling

❑   Overseeing family calendar   _____

❑   Making dental and doctor appointments   _____

❑   Scheduling after-school activities   _____

❑   Coordinating car pools and rides for family members _____

❑   Orchestrating morning schedule   _____

❑   Doing advance work for future events   _____

❑   Helping children manage time   _____

❑   Securing babysitters   _____

❑   Overseeing evening schedule   _____

❑   Dealing with bedtimes and curfews   _____

❑   Responding to invitations   _____

7.   Self-Management

❑   Taking care of yourself—physically, spiritually,

       mentally, and emotionally   _____

8.   Other

❑   _____   _____

❑   _____   _____

❑   _____   _____

❑   _____   _____

❑   _____   _____

- wipe off baseboards, windowsills, and wooden shutters, using an old pair of socks on their hands
- empty light wastebaskets
- wipe off the front of large appliances using a spray bottle of water and a sponge
- help wipe up spills
- dry unbreakable dishes
- sweep with a child-size broom
- bring in the newspaper
- pick up litter in the yard

Kindergartners can . . .
- vacuum small areas with a lightweight, handheld vacuum
- sweep the porch or other small areas with a dustpan and a broom
- clean bathroom sinks
- hang up the towels after their baths
- store bath toys
- help in kitchen—stirring, tearing lettuce, and putting refrigerated rolls on pans
- set the table with napkins and silverware
- clear dishes from the table
- help load the dishwasher
- straighten plastic dishes in a lower cabinet
- straighten pots and pans
- sort family members' clean laundry
- put away their own laundry
- help rake the yard and pull weeds
- dust furniture
- shine windows (that you've washed) with a clean blackboard eraser
- strip linens from beds
- straighten books on a bookshelf
- put game and puzzle pieces in correct storage containers
- brush upholstered furniture with a lint brush to remove pet hair
- be responsible for having a tidy room

Younger elementary kids can . . .
- make their beds
- take out the garbage
- sweep the stairs and walkways
- clean out the car
- vacuum their own room

FROM THE HEART

Don't think your children are so busy with school and activities that they don't have time to help with housework. According to a 2007 report by Harris Interactive, American children ages eight to eighteen play 13.5 hours of video games per week. Boys average 17 hours per week, and girls average 9 hours per week.

- sort and straighten toys
- fold and put away laundry
- empty the dishwasher
- feed and care for pets
- set and clear the table (if using plastic dishes and nonbreakable drinking cups)
- sort clothes for washing
- help with yard work
- clean off outdoor furniture
- wash outside toys and equipment
- help wash the car

Older elementary kids can . . .
- clean bathroom mirrors
- vacuum
- clean toilets
- clean countertops and the kitchen sink
- mop small-area floors
- use the washer and dryer
- wash, dry, and put away dishes
- fold laundry and put it away
- pull weeds
- rake leaves
- shovel snow
- clean pet areas
- take out trash
- clean cobwebs and dust in high places with a cobweb pole (To make one, put one thick cotton sock inside another and slip them over the end of a yardstick, securing with a rubber band.)
- help straighten garage
- sweep garage

Teenagers can . . .
- wash windows
- mend clothes
- wash the car
- change linens
- do their own laundry
- iron
- clean bathtubs/shower stalls
- polish furniture and dust lamp shades
- empty the vacuum cleaner bag
- straighten and organize linens

- clean tiles and toilet with disinfectant
- clean out the refrigerator
- defrost the freezer
- clean the stove and oven
- polish silverware
- clean out and organize the attic, basement, and garage
- mow the lawn and trim the yard
- clean light fixtures
- change lightbulbs
- wax the car

ALL YOUR STUFF

Appliances
Shopping smart
Discovering that a burner on your stove no longer works or that your refrigerator doesn't keep things really cold like it once did creates a dilemma: Should you get it fixed or buy a new home appliance? The following tips will help you decide.

1. Sometimes it pays to have an appliance repaired; other times, it doesn't. A new unit can pay for itself in energy savings, and depending on the problem, repair work can cost as much as a new unit.

2. Do your research. Talk to friends about their experiences with various brands, and check the Internet for product evaluations.

3. Decide what capacity or size you need and what special features you want.

4. Measure the space where the appliance will "live." And don't forget to measure the door and hallway clearance available when your appliance is delivered.

5. Ask the dealer to show you the care manual for the appliance you are interested in. Look it over before you buy, and be sure special cleaning products aren't required.

6. Ask about the warranty. Find out what is covered and for how long. If the salesclerk asks if you'd like to buy an extended warranty, consider:

   - Most products don't break down that often, and those that do may well be covered by the original warranty.
   - What are the terms of the manufacturer's warranty? If it covers labor and parts for a number of years, you

GOOD TO KNOW

Keep your refrigerator temperature between 36 and 38 degrees. Freezers should be maintained at a temperature of 0 or below.

Time to Replace Your Appliance?

The age of an appliance helps determine its longevity. According to the National Association of the Remodeling Industry (NARI) and Sears Home Central, here are average life spans of some of the appliances in your home:

- *Washing machine: 13 years*
- *Dryer: 13 years*
- *Refrigerator: 15+ years*
- *Stove (gas or electric): 17–20 years*
- *Microwave oven: 16 years*
- *Furnace: 15–30 years*
- *Water heater: under 12 years*
- *Room air conditioner: 12–15 years*
- *Central air conditioner: 11 years*
- *Basic sewing machine: 24 years*
- *Dishwasher: 10 years*
- *Garage door opener: 10 years*

Remember, these are just averages, and every appliance is different. Some can live long past their life expectancies.

really don't need a second policy. Divide the cost by the number of months that type of appliance is expected to run. Sometimes good warranties cost just a few dollars a month and are worth the investment, especially if the plan allows unlimited service calls.

- Check out the *Consumer Reports* ratings for the item in question. Usually you can learn the expected life span of the product, which you can compare to the length of the warranty. If the item is likely to last a very long time, consider purchasing the extra warranty.
- If you decide to go with the extended warranty, check the terms and conditions carefully. Find out if the repair is paid directly by the company or if you're required to file a claim first. What's the average length of time for processing a claim? How high is the deductible?

Fridge and Freezer Facts

Before shopping for a refrigerator or freezer, consider taking the following steps to be sure you purchase the right appliance—and are able to install and maintain it properly.

- A family of two needs 12 cubic feet of food storage. Add an extra two cubic feet for each additional family member. Add more if you entertain guests regularly.
- A family of two needs four cubic feet of freezer space. Add two cubic feet for each additional person. Increase the freezer space if you stock frozen products or shop infrequently.
- Analyze your shopping and cooking habits before deciding which refrigerator to buy. If you shop more often and eat more fresh than frozen food, you'll want proportionally more refrigerator than freezer space.
- A top-and-bottom fridge/freezer configuration offers the most storage flexibility. Side-by-side models have more total storage space, but it's often difficult to store large items—pizzas, boxed pies and cakes, family-size containers of pasta dishes such as lasagna—in them. One advantage of the side-by-side model is it's easier to see what you have on hand at a glance since it isn't as deep as the top-and-bottom style (less digging is required).
- If possible, place your refrigerator away from heat sources like stoves and even sunlight. Extra heat will cause it to work harder to stay cool.
- If it's not already, put your refrigerator on coasters so you can easily move it to clean behind it.

GOOD TO KNOW

If the electricity goes out, frozen food will last about 48 hours, as long as you don't open the freezer.

SMART MOVE

Attach a magnetic dry-erase board on the side or front of your refrigerator. Keep a running list of leftovers and the date you saved them.

- Ask the salesperson if there are any less expensive warranties available—he or she may only be offering you the most expensive option. Realize that you can always shop around—contact the warranty company directly to see if they have a better deal.

7. Ask about delivery charges and service availability.

Getting to know your new appliance
- Once an appliance is in your home, try each feature and control. Most defects show up during the first few uses.
- Read and follow all manufacturer's instructions.
- Use a separate, grounded electrical circuit for each major appliance.
- Use a three-ring binder or accordion file to keep all your appliance manuals together. This makes them easily accessible, plus it's a good selling point if you put your house on the market. Read the manuals to find out what kind of maintenance is required to keep appliances performing at their maximum. On each booklet, jot down the date and store where the purchase was made, as well as the salesperson's name. Staple your receipt to the booklet. Refer to this record when deciding whether to keep or toss an aging appliance.
- Buy the best washing-machine hoses you can afford. Inspect the ones you have, since after three years the rubber ones tend to be more brittle and prone to breaking. Stainless steel mesh hoses are best. (Turn off the taps to your washing machine when you leave for an extended period of time.)
- Clean the lint trap on your dryer before every load. Heavy lint buildup can cause a fire.
- If your refrigerator has wire shelves, buy sheets of acrylic or plastic at a home-and-garden store or a hardware store. Cut the sheets to fit on the wire shelves. This will help prevent smaller items from tipping over. Cleaning will be easier too.
- Clean your refrigerator's condenser coils quarterly—more often if you have a dog or cat. Clean underneath the unit once a month. (Be sure to unplug the unit before cleaning.)
- Keep your refrigerator's door seal clean. These seals often need to be replaced because of excessive mildew, which can be expensive. Clean the door seal with soap and water—never with bleach, which can cause it to become brittle and crack.

Bedding
At least every decade, invest in a new mattress and pillow. Your body will appreciate the fresh support, and you'll sleep better—an important benefit for busy moms.

Pillows
Good pillows help keep your spine and head aligned in the same way as when you are standing. When purchasing a pillow, make sure you buy one that offers the support you need, as well as the

softness, thickness, and firmness you consider comfortable. The different types include:

- Down: Filled with fine goose or duck down feathers, the fluffy feathers next to the body of the bird that keep it warm. These supply spectacular comfort, last a long time, and offer adjustability. But they're also usually expensive and need to be fluffed frequently. They may cause allergic reactions in some people.
- Down-and-feather mix: Soft but not luxurious since the quills of the feathers, which serve to give mass to the pillow, sometimes poke through the cloth. These pillows offer the comfort and resilience of down along with feathery support. If you can't afford down, the mix is a less expensive alternative.
- Feather: Goose feathers are the best; ducks are second. These may cause problems for folks with allergies.
- Synthetic fiber: Long lasting and relatively inexpensive. Generally, these polyester-puffed pillows last as long and are as comfortable as down. If allergies are a concern, these are a great alternative.
- Latex: Less expensive, more resistant to mildew and dust mites than other types of pillows.
- Foam rubber: Inexpensive and hypoallergenic. You can sculpt these to match your comfort level. Because these are extra firm, people who like sinking into their pillows won't like these.
- Buckwheat hulls: Moldable. But these are usually smaller than regular pillows, and they can be noisy and irritating.

Comforters and duvets

Comforters can be filled with cotton, down, silk, wool, or hypo-allergenic synthetics; they do not have removable covers. Duvet comforters are made to be encased in a duvet cover, which can be taken off for cleaning or changed with the season or when you redecorate.

- Choose wisely. Unless you are allergic to it, consider a down comforter; if cared for, it will last 8 to 10 years, according to manufacturers. (Ours is 10 years old and still looks great.) Goose down is your best choice because goose feathers fluff better.
- Buy a thick comforter. Try to get one with a fill of 600 to 700.
- Cover carefully. Your duvet shell should be made of ticking. Make sure down filling doesn't bunch up in places.
- Clean regularly. If your comforter is not machine washable, dry-clean it every now and then, according to how much it's used and if it shows dirt.

GOOD TO KNOW

Pillow sizes:
- Standard (20x26 inches)
- Queen (20x30 inches)
- King (20x36 inches)

Sheets

- Keep only two sets of linens for each bed and give the rest away.
- *Thread count* describes how many threads are woven into each square inch of sheet. The higher the thread count, the more comfy the bed linens. Muslin sheets have a thread count of 140 to 180; percale, 180 and up. Choose sheets with a thread count of at least 200.
- Be aware that sheets with a thread count of 300 to 400 feel great but don't last quite as long.
- Sheets made of a 50/50 blend of cotton and polyester tend to be stiff. A blend of 60 percent cotton with 40 percent polyester offers more softness.
- If you live in a cold-weather climate, consider buying silk satin sheets, which will keep you warmer. They're expensive, though, and must be dry-cleaned.
- If you live in a hot-weather climate, try linen sheets. They're expensive but they last. Another breathable fabric for sheets is cotton jersey knit—the same material T-shirts are made of. But beware of deep-colored jerseys—they often fade.

Mattress matters

- Flip your mattress once a year to extend its wear.
- Invest in an extra-thick mattress pad to add as much as three years of use.
- When purchasing a new mattress, always check out the lesser known brands. You may get as much comfort and wear from these as from the "super deluxe" mattresses, and you'll save at least 25 percent.
- The coils in a bed maintain its shape. Expect a good king-size mattress to have at least 450 coils; queen size, 375; full size, 300.
- Be brave: Lie down on every mattress you're considering buying, and roll around on it. Just sitting on it won't tell you anything about comfort. If it sways or you hear creaks, keep looking.
- Beware of the temptation to buy an extra-thick mattress. If it's three to five inches thicker than your old mattress, you'll have to buy new sheets—an added expense.

Books and Bookshelves

Good books are like good friends. There is something soothing about pulling an old book off the shelf and reading a favorite passage. The tips below will help you care for treasured, older books and make space for new ones.

Create a Book Log

If you often loan out books, keep a log so you can keep track of where they go when you loan them out.

BOOKS BORROWED

Title	Loaned to	Date	Returned

- When you start to organize your books, don't pull all of them out at once. Instead, designate a different shelf for each type of book and shuffle the volumes around as you go. Each section will develop as you work.
- Group your books into categories—by subject matter, by the author's last name, or by types: paperbacks and hardcovers, tall and short books. If you shelve according to subject matter, try alphabetizing the books within the section by title or author. Choose a sorting method that makes the books you use easiest to find.
- Store kids' coloring books, activity books, and sheet music in magazine storage boxes.
- Prevent mildew by rubbing oil of clove on wood bookshelves. Rub it in thoroughly so that it won't stain book covers. If you have bookshelves with doors, open them to air out the books once in a while.
- Store books in dry places but not near a radiator or heating vent. Heat can crack book bindings.

★

SMART MOVE

Put a long extension cord on your vacuum to save steps and reduce time spent plugging in and replugging in.

- Combat humidity by putting small packets of moisture absorber near places that may become damp.
- Put bookplates or address labels in your books.
- If you have a book that is especially meaningful to you, consider having it leather bound.

Carpet Care

- Buy a good vacuum cleaner, but be wise about it. You don't need dozens of extra attachments. You need a round brush, a crevice tool, and a four-inch upholstery brush. Test how heavy the vacuum cleaner is and how hard it is to push before you buy it.
- Vacuum at least twice a week—and high-traffic areas more often. Once dirt is allowed to sink deep into the fibers, the carpet tends to wear out more quickly.
- Clean spills immediately. The longer they sit, the better the chance of a permanent stain.
- When cleaning spilled liquid, use only a white cloth, because colored cloths can bleed and make the stain worse.
- Spritz a stain with a little cold water to help dilute it, then blot it. Repeat this process until the stain is gone.
- Keep stains wet. If you can't remove a stain yourself, douse it with club soda or keep it moist by misting with cold water until it can be professionally cleaned. A dry stain is harder to get out.
- Rent a rug shampooer or have your carpet professionally cleaned at least once a year. Be wary of carpet-cleaning specials. Ask if the company charges for extras—like spot removal and other basics that should come in the package deal. (Be sure your professional carpet cleaner is experienced, as well as bonded or insured, before you agree to the service.)
- Before shampooing, give the room a good vacuuming. Slip a sandwich bag under each leg of the furniture to prevent water damage when shampooing the carpet. Be careful not to overwet the carpet, as this can separate the backing and seams or cause shrinkage and discoloration.
- To remove dents in the carpet made by heavy furniture, place ice cubes on the marks, about two inches apart. As they melt, the moisture is absorbed, causing the carpet fibers to plump up.
- If a carpet thread is loose, snip it level with the pile. If you try to pull out the thread, you risk unraveling part of the carpet.

Clothing Care and Laundry
Washing
- Treat stains promptly, before they set. Store a stain-removal spray or a stain stick in each bathroom.
- Dab a little club soda on a stain to temporarily keep it from setting.
- Wash all pieces of an outfit at the same time. If they fade, they'll do so evenly.
- Turn knits wrong-side out to avoid snags and pilling.
- Use suggested amounts of detergent recommended by the washer's manufacturer. Too much detergent can weaken fibers; too little won't remove stains.
- Use bleach only on white and colorfast washables; always read fabric and bleach labels.
- If your water supply has a high iron content, be wary of using chlorine bleach, which can draw out the iron and deposit it as spots on clothes.
- Don't overdry clothes. Too much heat can weaken fabrics.

Ironing
- If you iron clothes using steam, use only distilled water to avoid stains.
- Turn silks inside out before ironing them.
- Avoid creating shine on wools and dark colors by turning them inside out before ironing or by using a pressing cloth or ironing shield on top of the clothing.
- To avoid crushing a fabric's nap, place a thick towel underneath the garment and press the wrong side.
- If you spot a stain, don't iron the garment. Heat will make the stain permanent.

General clothing care
- Help buttons stay on longer by coating the center of each one with clear nail polish. Use dental floss instead of thread to secure buttons onto overcoats.
- Hang clothing on wooden or plastic hangers instead of wire hangers.
- Use contoured suit hangers for coats, jackets, and suits.
- After wearing a suit, brush it with a natural-bristle clothes brush and then hang it out overnight to air. This will stretch time between dry cleanings. (Frequent dry-cleaning weakens fibers.)

DO-IT-YOURSELF DECORATING

Decorating your dwelling is one way of reflecting the uniqueness of your family. For some, choosing paint, fabric, and furniture is fun. Others view decorating as an expensive necessity. They buy new wallpaper because the old is peeling off the walls and a sofa because they need a place to sit.

Whether decorating is fun or frustrating for you, it's important to do some research and make well-thought-out choices since decorating mistakes can be costly. The steps below will allow you to confidently transform any room.

Six Steps to Decorating on Your Own

1. *Survey your home and family.* Ask yourself the following questions to get a better understanding of how your home is used before you start buying furniture and painting walls.

   - How large is your family? What are the ages of each family member?
   - How long will each person live in the house with you?
   - How long do you plan to stay in the house?
   - How often is each entry door used?
   - Where does everyone sleep?
   - How many people use each bathroom?
   - Where do individuals go when they need to spend time alone?
   - Where is food consumed? In the kitchen? In the dining room? In front of the TV?
   - How many clothes, linen, and coat closets do you have?
   - Is there room for more than just cars in the garage?
   - Is there storage space in the basement or attic?

   Address specific space and furniture needs with the questions below:

   - Where does your family gather for leisure activities?
   - Do you have or need an all-purpose family room or area to play board games and watch television?
   - How often do you entertain, and what is your style— casual buffets or dining-room sit-down dinners?
   - Is a media center, laundry area, play space, or home office required? What about a workshop, exercise room, or playroom?

- Does your family require storage for books, sports equipment, electronic equipment, or collectibles?
- How much electronic equipment—TV, CD player, speakers, video games, PC—do you have? How often is each used? Where is each stored?
- What kinds of tables would be helpful or enhancing: end tables; coffee tables; nightstands; a game table for board games, cards, puzzles, and hobbies?

2. *Create an inventory.* Make a list of what you have now: existing furniture, lighting, art, and all the accessories. Note what you plan to keep and what you'd like to replace. Take photographs of the items you're keeping to simplify shopping for coordinating pieces later.

    Now for the fun part—making up the dream list of pieces and/or accessories you'd like to add. Be sure to prioritize your list to determine which purchases are most important. This process helps ensure that you purchase items in a methodical manner and helps minimize expensive impulse buying.

3. *Start a resource/idea book.* Buy a binder with pockets or a loose-leaf notebook with tab dividers and a box of plastic insert sheets. Use it to store product literature, magazine clippings, paint chips, and fabric swatches. Give each room or project its own section in the notebook. Have one page at the beginning for names, phone numbers, and comments about recommended professionals, craftspeople, and service companies, and tips from friends.

    Whenever you see a photo of a room or a piece of furniture you like, clip it from the magazine and put it in your notebook. After you've collected 20 or so, spread them out and look for similarities. You may see Oriental rugs in many of the room photos you like. Or perhaps you've amassed a pile of clippings showing French provincial furniture, or you note that buttery yellow walls keep appearing. Continue adding things you like to your notebook, and periodically cull items that no longer interest you. The result is your personal style guide.

4. *Create a room-decorating envelope.* Put samples of all your existing materials for each room in large, separate envelopes. Include the drapery and upholstery fabrics, carpet swatches, and room measurements. If you can't get a small cutting of your carpet, buy a spool of thread that's close to the color or

SMART MOVE

If you're too busy to shop, are unsure of your "eye" for color or fabric, or don't enjoy the process, working with a professional decorator is probably a good move. Designers charge either a flat fee for the project or an hourly rate. Most also take a percentage of the cost of goods you order through them. Ask friends for references, and interview several candidates to find the designing style and personal demeanor that make you feel most comfortable. Don't hire anyone who makes you feel intimidated or pushed into decisions.

take a photograph of the rug. Be sure to include the furniture photos from your "to keep" list in each corresponding envelope. On the back of each photo, record the dimensions of each piece. When it's time to shop, take the envelopes along with you.

5. *Shop widely and wisely.* With the decorating envelopes in hand, visit furniture, decorating, and fabric stores, as well as tag sales, local and online auctions, and flea markets. Note what you like and what things cost so you can plan a budget. If the house you're in now isn't the one you plan to live in forever, invest only in furnishings that can move with you. Look for furniture and fabrics that will work anywhere—go for neutral colors and avoid trendy looks. Another way to ensure that new acquisitions will work in future homes is to decorate using colors you've liked consistently over the years.

6. *Take the $100 test.* Before making a purchase over $100, always ask yourself how long you think you'll keep the item. If your answer is less than three or four years, don't buy it. Be patient. As painful as waiting can be, it's always worth it. New products constantly come on the market, and your tastes are likely to change. You may find a lamp or an accessory that you like even better in the next store or catalog. When you can, shop sales. Furniture is expensive, and getting something you love for less is a great feeling.

Decorating Tips from Professionals
Arranging a room

- Before deciding where to place furniture, determine the focal point of your room—a fireplace, a tall piece of furniture, a bookcase wall, or windows with a great view—and plan the seating from there.
- If the room you're decorating is small, don't be tempted to use smaller-scaled furniture to fit more pieces in the room. It will look cluttered. Instead, use fewer pieces of normal-sized furniture.
- Don't crowd a room with too much furniture. Let the space "breathe," especially at all the corners.
- In rooms with low ceilings, staining, carpeting, or painting the floors a darker color than the walls will make the room feel bigger.
- Add warmth to your kitchen by using as many organic materials as possible: wood, tile, cork, baskets, terra-cotta pots.

- Wallpaper with vertical stripes will make the ceiling of any room appear higher.

Furniture selection

- Keep your room from becoming too "leggy" by striking a balance between upholstered furniture and pieces with exposed legs.
- The sofa is one of the most important pieces of furniture you can buy. If your room is large, an 84-inch sofa that seats three people is ideal.
- Every chair and sofa requires a corresponding table or flat surface for books, magazines, drinks, and food.
- Place a coffee table 18 inches in front of your sofa, and allow another 18 inches between the ends of the sofa and other furniture to allow ample walking space.
- Avoid a glass coffee table or one with sharp corners if you have small children, a clumsy spouse, or elderly relatives living with you or visiting often.
- End tables don't have to match, but both should be about the same height—26 to 30 inches. A one-inch difference between the heights of two tables is not noticeable.
- Placing a stool in the kitchen will promote conversations there. The standard heights for stools are 24 and 30 inches, so choose the height that works best for you.

Window treatments

- Almost all windows look more finished with some sort of shade, curtain, or drape.
- Pretty tea towels and sheets can be turned into lovely curtains for a kitchen or bedroom.
- For bedroom windows in sunny rooms, consider a roll-down blackout shade behind the curtains so you can sleep undisturbed.
- Valances above the curtains, made of the same fabric, create a formal, finished look around the window.
- Swags, pull-backs, tassels, and fancy-looking curtain rods are relatively inexpensive ways to dress up windows.
- Curtains made of horizontally lined fabric that falls to the floor makes ceilings appear taller and rooms appear bigger.

Lighting types and uses

There are three basic types of lighting: general, task, and accent lights. A good lighting plan incorporates all three types and takes into consideration the function and style of each type. Here's a brief course in how to use lighting.

- General lighting replaces sunlight and provides overall illumination to help you see and walk safely through your home. Ceiling or wall-mounted fixtures, chandeliers, recessed lights, and track lights are examples of general lighting.
- Task lighting provides special lighting for reading, working on the computer, or paying bills. Task lights should be free of glare and shadows and be bright enough to prevent eye strain. Pendant lighting, bedside lamps, table lamps, and some track lighting are examples.
- Accent lights provide visual interest or dramatic focus and add mood and character to a room. This type of lighting can spotlight plants and art or highlight the texture of a wall or drapery. Examples are pinspots, floor canisters, under-shelf lighting, and torchères (tall floor lamps that uplight a ceiling).
- In the family room, arrange lighting so each seating area is bright enough for reading.
- You can achieve a warm glow in your dining room or hallway using wall sconces.
- Three-way bulbs and dimmer switches give you easy-to-change lighting options. With one flick, a bright living room can be converted to an inviting place for coffee and conversation.
- Colored lightbulbs can be used to create different types of light. Incandescent bulbs add a warming yellow cast, while cool fluorescent lights lend a slightly gray tone. Halogen bulbs show true colors. Pink lightbulbs provide softer lighting than standard white bulbs.

Mirrors and wall hangings

- Suspend a mirror between two windows to add light and space to a room. If hung at the end of a hallway, a mirror will give the illusion of continuing space.
- Place a favorite painting or mirror in your entrance hall so you and everyone else can enjoy it coming and going. Be sure to double hang (use two hooks instead of one) your picture or mirror so it will remain stable when the door is slammed.
- Before you hang a mirror, check to see what it will reflect. You don't want to see the inside of bathrooms, the driveway next door, or a dark corner of the living room.
- A counter-to-ceiling mirror will make a bathroom seem bigger.

- Hang pictures at eye level. Sixty inches from the floor to the center of the picture is about right.

Floor coverings

- Use a colorful rug as a welcome mat inside your front door. Make sure the background is a medium color so dirt won't show.
- Buy the most expensive carpet you can afford for high-traffic areas such as stairs, corridors, and family rooms. Cheap carpet wears quickly, and because it has to be replaced more often, it eventually costs as much or more than higher-priced options.
- Less expensive carpet is acceptable in bedrooms since there is less wear. With careful care and regular cleaning, carpets and rugs can last at least 10 years.
- Large area rugs and Oriental carpets immediately warm a room, but dark background colors make rooms feel smaller.
- A cotton dhurrie rug, a flat woven rug from India, will add color to a hallway or small bedroom.
- Natural fiber carpets, like sisal, jute, and coir, have rough textures, so they should be used only in rooms where people are unlikely to walk barefoot. If you have young children, avoid sisal rugs. Their natural fibers are itchy on little feet, and they are difficult to clean.

Painting

One gallon of paint normally covers about 400 square feet. To calculate the number of gallons you need, multiply the total wall length by the ceiling height. For example, if you have a 12x12 room (48 feet of walls) with an 8-foot ceiling, you have 48 feet times 8 feet or 384 square feet of wall space to paint. So you'd buy one gallon. Assuming there are doors and windows in the room and you are able to achieve your desired results in one coat, you will even have a little left over for touch-up later. It's always good to have at least a pint left over for touch-up.

Generally, it is best to use flat paint on walls, but use semigloss on walls that may get dirty. You can wash walls painted with semigloss, but the downside of semigloss is that it shows the flaws in a wall. Use enamel paint on doors, woodwork, and windowsills.

Selecting a color

Most paint stores and large building supply stores have sophisticated paint-matching systems. If you want to match an existing color, take a piece of trim, a cabinet door, or something else with the color you want to match. If the paint you want to match is in a can, you can paint a small amount on a piece of white cardboard, let it dry, and take that in to match.

If you are selecting a new color, be sure to take home several paint samples in the general color range you desire from the paint store. The lighting in your home can make a major difference in how a color appears. Hold the "paint chip" on the surface you will paint and observe it there. Then make your choice.

Even though some paint brands claim to cover in one coat, you will invariably need additional coats of paint if you are making major shade or color changes—light to dark or dark to light. If in doubt, ask for advice in the paint store.

Tips from painting pros

- Begin by moving furniture away from the walls and covering the floor and furniture with cloths or inexpensive plastic tarps. Protect windows and windowsills with newspaper.
- Remove all hardware and switch plates; don't try to paint around them. Put them back up when the paint is completely dry.
- Prepare your walls before you begin. Repair nail holes with spackling paste, using a putty knife to fill the hole and scrape away excess. Before it dries, rub the area with a rag to wipe away excess. Fill all cracks with acrylic caulk. Use as little as possible, then smooth and remove excess with your finger.
- If you are using multiple gallons of paint for a room, mix them all together in a five-gallon bucket (available from your paint store). Even though the shade is calibrated, one can of paint will vary slightly from another. By mixing them together, you eliminate shade changes.
- Paint the ceiling first and then walls. Next paint the trim: crown molding, windowsills, window frames, doors, and door frames. Paint baseboards last.
- Using a three- or four-inch brush, begin by painting at least a three- to four-inch border of paint (called "cutting in") around your ceiling or wall and around all woodwork. Then use a roller to complete your work.
- Consider using a five-gallon bucket and paint grid when rolling, rather than a roller pan. It makes the job much easier.
- When using a brush, paint from a smaller paint bucket rather than from the paint can. Pour what you think you'll need for the next hour—up to about two inches—and reseal the paint can.
- Always thoroughly reseal the lid on a can of paint after you use it to prevent the paint from drying out and to avoid a big mess if the can tips over.

- Even though great advances have been made in water-based enamel paints, nothing beats the look and durability of oil-based enamel paint for your trim.
- When repainting, never paint latex enamel over oil-based enamel. It will not adhere properly and could peel prematurely.
- Good brushes produce superior results, especially for trim work. To avoid cleaning a brush used in oil-based paints every day, you can wrap it in aluminum foil or use a plastic bag to seal the brush and put it in the freezer until you are ready to paint again (within the next few days).
- Dip the tip of the brush into the paint only about an inch and drag off any excess on the edge of your paint bucket.
- When you take a break, leave the brush in the paint to keep it from drying out.
- When it's time to clean your brushes, do so thoroughly. If you are using oil-based paint, be sure you are in a well-ventilated area away from flames. Hang rags out to dry rather than throwing them in a container, which creates a fire hazard. Brush bristles with a wire brush, smooth, and set aside to dry. Once they're dry, store brushes flat so bristles will not be bent and damaged.

YOUR HOME'S STRUCTURE

General Maintenance
Common (and sometimes deadly) home maintenance mistakes
Although we can't always predict or prevent sudden emergencies, knowing what to do and not to do in certain situations can keep a bad situation from becoming worse. Here are 23 common domestic disasters and what to do about them.

1. *Failing to respect electricity.* Make sure you flip the breaker or remove the proper fuse before attempting to repair anything electrical. Don't overload circuits. A frequently blown breaker is a sign of overload or other trouble; flickering lights can indicate a problem and a potential fire hazard. In either case, call an electrician.

2. *Failing to have your heating system checked yearly.* Carbon monoxide is an odorless gas released when anything burns. Even small amounts can cause headaches and illness, and if allowed to build up, carbon monoxide can be a deadly killer. Have your heating system checked yearly by a heating professional before cold weather sets in, and

GOOD TO KNOW

Paint dries best when the temperature is between 60 degrees and 70 degrees. If there's a chance of rain or if it's really humid, wait for drier weather.

GOOD TO KNOW

If you call a repair technician to come to your home on a weekend or evening, you will probably be charged more. Also, if a technician starts a job and doesn't finish until after five o'clock, you could pay overtime rates. Ask about weekend and overtime rates when you call about scheduling.

install carbon monoxide detectors in strategic locations in your house, including your bedrooms. You should also keep one in the basement or wherever your furnace is located, though it should be at least 25 feet away from it. Also, detectors should not be installed within one foot of the ceiling or at wall intersections, where there is little or no air movement.

3. *Failing to check for radon.* Radon is a colorless, odorless substance that is the second-leading cause of lung cancer in the United States. The EPA estimates that one out of 15 U.S. homes has unhealthy levels of radon. Radon test kits are available at hardware and home-maintenance stores for less than $25. If the test indicates that your home has dangerously high radon levels, you should contact local or state EPA authorities for recommendations of what to do. You can also call the National Safety Council's radon hotline at 1-800-SOS-RADON. Generally, curing a radon problem is not a major expense.

4. *Failing to look for and fix water leaks.* Even a small amount of dripping water can do big damage over time to visible things like drywall, cabinets, and flooring, as well as unseen structural supports such as wall studs and floor joists. Damp areas caused by water leaks promote the growth of mold and mildew. A leaky dishwasher or washing-machine connection, drainpipe, faucet cutoff valve, toilet, or shower drain can eventually cost you thousands of repair dollars. Moisture also attracts insect pests.

5. *Waiting too long to paint your house.* When you see small cracks, exposed wood, or strips of paint hanging off your house, it's past time to paint. The longer you wait, the more water is penetrating wood surfaces. Not only does water damage the wood over time, it also exacerbates the cracking and peeling of paint.

6. *Failing to prepare surfaces before painting.* For paint to do its job, it has to adhere to the surface and seal out moisture. Before painting, scrape and/or sand all loose paint from the surface, even if you have used a power washer. Repair any damage and prime with a coat of primer or paint. Don't paint over rust buildup or rotten wood. Never prime or paint wet wood.

Flu or Carbon Monoxide Poisoning?

Symptoms of carbon monoxide poisoning are similar to influenza, so it's easy to misdiagnose the problem. Be aware that the highest incidence of carbon monoxide poisoning occurs during flu season—also the heating season.

If you experience the following symptoms and they disappear once you leave the house, suspect carbon monoxide poisoning.

- headache
- dizziness or weakness
- bright cherry-red lips
- shortness of breath
- flushed skin
- nausea or vomiting

7. *Putting poor-quality padding underneath new carpet.* This can greatly reduce the life of the carpet. And never keep really dirty padding under new carpet. The soil and stains can seep up and spot the new carpet, as well as cause odors.

8. *Overcleaning sinks, tubs, and toilet seats.* Too much scrubbing with abrasive cleaners wears off the finish. Use non-abrasive cleaners.

9. *Counting on unreliable warranties.* An extended or aftermarket warranty is only as good as the company behind it. Stick with well-known companies—and read the fine print.

10. *Failing to follow manufacturer's maintenance procedures.* Not maintaining almost anything according to the manufacturer's instructions will void the warranty. Be careful about trying to repair an appliance yourself. Not only might this be hazardous, but it can void the warranty.

11. *Not putting enough insulation in your attic.* More heat is lost through inadequate roof insulation than through any other part of the home. Lost heat translates into higher heating bills.

⚠

CAUTION!

Never close the
fireplace damper
while live coals are
still burning.

12. *Spending too much on plumbing.* If you have a leaky kitchen or bathroom faucet, instead of buying a new one (which may be expensive and not match the room and original fixtures), take the leaky valve cartridge to a local plumbing store. Chances are a 59-cent washer will do the job. If not, the plumbing store should be able to replace the whole valve for less than $10.

13. *Failing to keep things clean.* Dirt and dust are often unseen enemies that cause damage and malfunction. For example, dirt in the carpet breaks down fibers. Dust that collects on refrigerator coils causes the refrigeration system to over-work, shortening the life of the refrigerator. Dust is a major reason CD players skip.

14. *Failing to change air-conditioning/heating system filters.* Forgetting to clean permanent filters or replace disposable ones monthly not only reduces efficiency but over time will cause dirty, unsightly buildup to occur around vents.

15. *Not having your chimney cleaned.* Creosote buildup can occur in all chimneys that burn solid fuel, presenting a major fire hazard. There is also the potential of carbon monoxide poisoning. Have your chimney cleaned each year in the spring.

16. *Failing to keep gutters free of debris.* Clogged gutters can cause water to go places you don't want it to go, causing damage to the wood trim and roof of your house.

17. *Not trimming back trees and bushes from your roof.* Over-hanging limbs can cause debris buildup and eventually cause damage to the roof.

18. *Failing to prepare for freezing temperatures.* An eight-inch crack in a water pipe can spray 250 gallons of water a day, causing thousands of dollars of damage. Just a little mainte-nance can prevent this. Remove and store hoses, and cover outside faucets and exposed pipes to protect them from extreme temperatures. Open cabinet doors underneath sinks and allow both hot and cold water faucets to drip slightly. Close foundation vents to keep pipes from freezing under the house. In extreme environments, use heat tape or thermal cables on water pipes susceptible to freezing. Seal any leaks that allow cold air to rush in on pipes. If you are going to be out of town, ask a friend to check your home regularly, and never set your thermostat lower than 55 degrees.

19. *Not knowing how to shut off the water to your house.* Just in case the worst happens, everyone in the family needs to know how to shut off the water. Water to a specific sink or toilet can be turned off by turning the water valve under the toilet or sink clockwise. It's also a good idea to purchase a water meter key at a hardware store, keep it in a handy place, and know how to use it to open and lift the meter plate and shut off the main water valve to your home.

20. *Failing to inspect dark, out-of-the-way spaces.* Check your attic and crawl space twice a year. Take your flashlight and shine it in out-of-the-way areas for water leaks, nesting animals, or anything unusual. Small problems unobserved can cause big problems if left unchecked.

21. *Failing to keep things out of direct sunlight.* UV rays not only damage your eyes, they also cause damage to items inside your home. Carpets and wood floors fade, and whites yellow in direct sunlight. Consider installing shades in windows with a western exposure.

22. *Failing to replace your washing-machine hoses every two years.* These cause millions of dollars of damage each year. You can replace old hoses with new metal-clad ones, which have a longer life. But don't fail to check them regularly, and shut off the hot and cold water supply when you leave on vacation.

23. *Caulking incorrectly.* Before applying new tub caulk, fill the tub with water and get in. The weight will open the gap around the tub to its widest so you can apply enough caulk. Use a damp rag wrapped around your forefinger to smooth the caulk in place. Wipe off excess caulk from the rag frequently. Leave the water in the tub for a day before draining.

Quarterly Maintenance
First quarter (January, February, March)
- Plan any major remodeling or repair projects. Start getting bids from contractors and schedule work. This is a great time of year for indoor painting or repair projects. Usually less construction work goes on during winter months, so contractors are often available.
- Check your plumbing system for leaks.
- Inspect ceramic tile grout around tubs or showers. Caulk as needed.

- Clean mineral deposits from inside the dishwasher by pouring a gallon of white vinegar in the bottom of the dishwasher and running through a wash cycle.
- Tackle indoor painting jobs.
- Repair hairline cracks in walls, which often appear during the winter, with spackling paste.
- Check for wasps' nests and remove them while the insects are dormant.
- Repair, reglue, or replace wallpaper as needed.
- Vacuum dust from coils beneath refrigerator. (This will increase energy efficiency by 6 percent.) Make a note to do this three more times at regular intervals this year.
- Replace heating-system filters. (Check your manual and note on your calendar how often this should be done. For some, every month is appropriate.) Write the date of the replacement on the filter.
- Do an attic and basement safety check. Make sure trash or unwanted clutter isn't accumulating. Look for evidence of frayed wiring. See that your circuit-breaker box is well marked. Make certain no paint or flammable liquids are stored near the furnace or water heater.
- If you have a septic system, make a note on your calendar to treat it once a month. Ask a local hardware store for products available in your area.

Second quarter (April, May, June)
- Check your attic for roof leaks. On a rainy day, use a flashlight to locate water drips and spots. Hire a roofing contractor to repair or replace any broken, bent, or missing shingles or tiles.
- Clear leaves and debris from gutters, downspouts, and window wells.
- Check the attic and crawl space for water leaks, nesting animals, or anything unusual.
- Inspect both the exterior and the interior of your home for carpenter ants and termites. Clear dirt or debris from the foundation to prevent insects from getting into your structure. Call an exterminator if necessary.
- Hire a chimney sweep to clean soot, remove birds' nests, and inspect for cracks.
- Shut off the furnace pilot light for the summer.
- Change the air-conditioner filters now and several other times during the cooling season. If your filter is permanent, clean according to manufacturer's instructions. If you have room

units, vacuum the evaporator coils behind the front grill of window units. A professional should service central air systems.

- Check air-conditioner condensate drain to make sure it is clear.
- Service and clean your lawn mower and garden tools.
- Remove any new wasps' nests on or around your house in the evening just before dark, when wasps and their kin are less likely to attack.
- Open foundation vents if your house's foundation is pier and beam.
- Put peel-and-apply weather stripping around windows and doors to reduce air leakage and cut utility bills.
- Check the grading of your yard and landscaping for settling or erosion. Spread new soil if necessary.
- Move surplus firewood away from the foundation of the house. Firewood often attracts termites during warm weather, so store it away from any structures.
- Trim any branches near a heat pump or air-conditioner condenser so they don't obstruct airflow or tangle the fan.
- Make sure windows open smoothly. Give the garage-door hardware a squirt of lightweight oil.
- Check for damage to exterior wood trim. Look for water stains, new cracks, blistering paint, warping, and soft places—which can mean dry rot. Repair as needed.
- Check fences and decks for damage, and repair as needed.
- Test smoke detectors.
- Apply lawn fertilizer with preemergent to kill weeds before they germinate.

Third quarter (July, August, September)

- Replace washing-machine hoses every other year.
- Have carpets cleaned by a professional, or rent a steam cleaner and do it yourself.
- Clean out and organize your garage.
- Pressure-wash driveways, walkways, and house exterior.
- Pressure-wash and reseal your wood deck. This removes dirt and extends the beauty and life of your deck.
- Trim back any branches or shrubs two feet from your roof.
- Service your snowblower.
- Clean your clothes-dryer exhaust vent. Check the flapper door on the outside exhaust vent and remove any lint buildup with a vacuum. If the vent is flexible, check for kinks and patch any small holes with duct tape.
- Unscrew the aerator from the end of each faucet, wash them

SMART MOVE

Sharpen garden scissors by cutting through several thicknesses of aluminum foil.

carefully, and then replace. This will help with low water pressure that often occurs in the late summer.
- Caulk all joints and cracks around posts, columns, doors, and windows.
- Scrape, prime, and spot-paint any minor blistered, cracked, or peeling paint. If you discover a lot of problem areas, consider repainting the entire exterior.

Fourth quarter (October, November, December)
- Replace heating-system filters; have the system professionally serviced and checked for carbon-monoxide leaks.
- Drain outdoor plumbing; store hoses. Cover outside faucets and exposed pipes to protect them from extreme temperatures.
- Rake leaves.
- Build a compost pile.
- Check fire extinguishers and smoke detectors.
- Clear leaves and debris from gutters, downspouts, and window wells.
- Add insulation to your attic if necessary.
- Check attic and crawl space for water leaks, nesting animals, or anything unusual.
- Insulate any exposed water pipes inside the house.
- Cover any delicate plants before hard freezes.
- Take out window air conditioners or cover the outside of units to prevent rusting.
- Close or cover foundation vents before the first freeze.
- Cover attic turbine vents on your roof.
- Winterize your lawn mower: Clean it, change the oil, and drain the gasoline from the tank.
- Weather-strip leaky windows and doors, or put on storm windows, if needed.
- Check your electrical system. Be sure bathroom, garage, and outdoor circuits are grounded and protected by ground-fault breakers.
- Wrap plants that need protection before cold weather sets in.

Building and Remodeling
Whether you are repairing damage to your home, updating a bathroom, or building a new home, the biggest decision you will make is choosing the contractor. Be aware that professional repair people and home-improvement contractors rank high on the complaint list of the Better Business Bureau. Here are tips to help you make a wise decision.

- Ask friends for recommendations. Be leery of contractors who make unsolicited visits or calls.
- Ask recommended contractors for a list of their recent projects, along with the names and numbers of home owners you can call for references. Drive by to see the homes. If home owners are around, say hello and explain that you're checking the work of a recommended contractor. Ask if they are satisfied with their home. Have they had any problems? Were problems corrected quickly? Would they call this service person again or purchase another home from this builder?
- Shop around. Obtain estimates from at least three contractors. Don't let anyone pressure you into making a quick decision, even if a discount is offered. Questions to ask:

    How long have you been in business?
    How long will the job take?
    How much will it cost, and what is included in this figure?
    How many workers will you use?
    What grade of materials will you use?
    Do you have liability insurance? workers' compensation?
    Do you belong to the local builders association (one that is affiliated with the National Association of Home Builders)?
    What kind of energy features do you install?
    What kind of warranty do you offer on your projects? (Ask for a written copy.)
    Who will haul away the trash?
    Who will correct problems with major appliances—and whom do I call if something goes wrong?

- Deal with licensed professionals only. Contact your state government's licensing board to confirm a contractor's home-improvement license. Check with the Better Business Bureau to see if a particular contractor has had complaints filed against him or her.
- Check the contract carefully. Ask someone experienced in building to go over your contract with you. It should include:

    a complete definition of the job to be done
    a description of the grade of materials that will be used, along with their cost
    the cost of labor
    subcontractors' names
    starting and completion dates
    payment schedule/financing details

☆
SMART MOVE

Before you remodel or add on to your house, check local zoning laws and any subdivision or neighborhood association bylaws to see if there are regulations you must abide by.

warranty agreements
cleanup responsibility

- Protect your funds. Don't pay anything until both parties have signed a written contract. Never use cash, and never pay an advance of more than one-third of the total contract. And make sure you're completely happy with the job before you pay the final balance.

Building your dream house

- Begin collecting ideas you like and don't like about other homes. Clip photos from magazines that show ideas— architectural styles, appliances, fixtures, colors—you would like to incorporate into your dream home.
- Determine how many bedrooms and bathrooms you'll want. How big of a living room would suit you? Do you need an office, an exercise area, or a hobby space? Do you want extra storage space? Consider how much upkeep you can handle, inside and out.
- Evaluate your property needs. How much maintenance do you want to do? What about location? What areas are convenient to transportation, shopping, schools, or other places of interest to you?
- Attend open houses and home shows. You can examine model houses as well as find potential builders.
- Study all of a model home's construction features: the grade of carpet, cabinets, trim, and paint. Ask lots of questions, and make sure you get specific answers. Keep notes of discussions with potential contractors.
- Remember that more expensive does not necessarily mean better quality.

MOVING

Getting Ready for Your Move
Six weeks before

- Get at least three bids from professional movers. Ask friends or the Better Business Bureau for recommendations. If possible, visit the moving companies' locations. If they don't have helpful staff, clean and well-maintained trucks, and quality storage facilities, scratch them off your list.
- Decide if you want to have the moving company pack your belongings or if you want to pack them yourself. If you pay them to pack, they will be liable for broken crystal, chipped furniture, etc. Ask for a breakdown of the cost difference

between their packing everything and their packing some fragile items while you pack everything else. If you do pack yourself, use lots of high-quality packing materials.

- If you decide to buy full-replacement-value insurance on your belongings, determine the replacement value of everything you own.
- Get a signed copy of the bid you accept. Make sure the price is guaranteed, or determine if there are any conditions.
- Make a checklist of everything you need to do before and after the move. Start collecting boxes.
- Talk with your kids about the move. Let them voice fears and expectations.
- If you haven't done so already, plan a trip to hunt for housing in your new city. Take the whole family if you can.

Four weeks before

- Designate a room on each floor of your house with enough space to serve as your packing room. Keep all your packing materials—boxes, two pairs of scissors, wrapping materials, tape, felt-tip markers—in that room.
- Pack the packing room first; then, one room at a time, start packing the things you won't need in the next few weeks. Even if you pack only three boxes a day, they really add up over time.
- Eliminate everything you don't want to move—and don't want to pay to have moved. Start boxes for charity or a garage sale.
- Put plastic trash bags in every room. If you always have one nearby, you won't be tempted to pack things you really should toss.
- Arrange to transfer funds to a new bank and establish credit.
- Arrange for insurance for your new home or apartment.
- Arrange transfer of your children's school records.
- Arrange with doctors, dentists, and eye doctors to have your records and prescriptions transferred or to take them with you. Make sure you have enough prescription medicine to get through a week in a new city.
- Notify the post office of your move and fill out change-of-address cards.
- Order address labels for your new home. You can use these to leave your new address with friends or businesses.
- Contact utilities, insurance agencies, and other businesses you regularly deal with and let them know you're moving.
- Check on auto licensing and insurance requirements if you're moving to a new state.

FUN FOR KIDS

Ease the pain of moving. Have a farewell party for your children and their friends. Let kids decorate moving boxes with sponges, brushes, fingerprints, and footprints. Let their friends help them pack their toys and books.

SMART MOVE

Give your child's teacher your new address and enough stamps and envelopes so he or she can have each former classmate write a letter to your child after you've gone.

- Close local charge accounts.
- If you planned a garage sale, have it now.
- Use up canned goods, frozen foods, and other household supplies. Buy small quantities when you run out of something.
- If you're flying to your new city, buy plane tickets and reserve hotel rooms.

Two weeks before
- Arrange to connect utilities at your new home.
- Make family farewell visits to parks and other favorite sites.
- Have an informal going-away party: an open house or a potluck. Keep arrangements simple so you can spend time with friends.
- Let your kids see their friends often.
- If you're driving to your new city, have the car serviced.
- Take pets to the vet. Make sure ID and rabies tags are securely attached to their collars. If your pet will be flying, get the required certificate from your vet for the airlines.
- Return any items you've borrowed from friends and take books back to the library. Collect all items remaining at the repair shop, dry cleaner, and gym or club lockers.
- Arrange for a cleaning service to clean your home after you've moved out.

Three days before
- Pack suitcases with clothing and personal items you'll need on your first day in your new home.
- In a special carton, place items you'll need the first hours in your new home—soap, toilet paper, towels, paper plates, plastic utensils, coffee, cooking pots, sheets, pillows, etc. Mark the carton "Load Last—Unload First."
- Label any boxes you do not want to be loaded on the truck.
- If you haven't made arrangements with your mover to do this, take down shelves, mirrors, TV antenna or satellite dish, and any other installed items you're taking with you. (Be sure not to take items that the home buyer is expecting to keep, per your contract.)
- Make activity packs for the kids to play with on the drive or the plane, or at their new home. Include a favorite stuffed animal or blanket, healthy snacks, and moist towelettes.
- Reserve a babysitter's services for moving day. See if a close family friend or relative can take younger kids somewhere for part of the day.
- Get traveler's checks and cash.

- Make sure drawers don't contain any spillable or breakable products.
- Dispose of all flammables. Many towns have a designated hazardous materials drop-off place at a recycling center or fire station. (Check the Web site of your local government to learn specifics.)
- Empty the fridge and freezer at least 24 hours before you move out of your home.
- Arrange for accommodations for the night before the moving truck comes: at home with everything packed, with friends or family, or in a hotel.
- Put together a small tool kit. You'll need this often as you unpack.
- Verify packers' or movers' arrival time. Confirm your truck reservation and when you'll pick it up.

The day before
- Get ready for packers. Be around so packers can ask questions.
- If you're packing yourself, finish it all well before your truck comes. Packing dishes and other last-minute items will consume most of a day. Double-check closets, the garage, the attic, and the basement for forgotten items.
- Finish packing personal belongings. Leave out an alarm clock.
- Plan a simple breakfast for the next morning.

Moving day
- Be available to answer movers' questions and sign forms. Make sure everything is loaded and the truck driver has your new home's address.
- When the truck is loaded, pack the phone and other last-minute items.
- Do one last check: Are windows closed and locked? Has anything been left behind? Are the furnace and lights turned off? Have you arranged to disconnect or transfer utilities? Leave a note for the new residents, along with any extra house keys, with your new address and phone number.

Tips as You Pack or Unpack
- Label boxes by the importance of their contents:

  1=essentials
  2=necessary but not essential
  3=low priority

- Newsprint leaves ink; try wrapping items in unprinted newsprint, available from moving companies, instead.
- Consider placing color-coded stickers on the boxes to indicate which room its items belong in. Keep a list of what color indicates what room.
- Small plastic bags are handy to hold screws, picture hooks, and other small parts. Tape them securely to the inside of drawers so you can find them easily once you're in your new home.
- Pack light; that is, try not to make boxes heavier than 45 pounds. Using lots of smaller boxes and fewer big ones helps.
- Pack items like TVs, DVD players, and computers in their original boxes whenever possible.
- Label boxes boldly on all sides so you won't have to move them around to know what's in them.
- Use wide packing tape with its own dispenser to make your job easier. When you seal a box, make sure the tape extends at least halfway down each side.
- Put a layer of crumpled paper at the bottom of each box, with additional cushioning in the middle and on top.
- Don't pack breakable items with heavy items.
- Write "Fragile" on the outside of boxes holding delicate items.
- If a box must be kept right side up, write clearly on the outside of the box "This end up," with an arrow.
- Once at your new home, don't let everyone randomly choose boxes to unpack. Plan who should handle what room, and set a few ground rules, such as, Empty a box completely before you start another.
- Arrange furniture before unpacking boxes.
- Put the kitchen, bedrooms, and bathrooms together first; you'll need them throughout the unpacking process.

SAFETY

Household Emergencies

We can't prevent sudden emergencies, but good preparation and a little know-how can keep a bad situation from becoming worse.

Grease fire. Never throw water on a grease fire. If the fire is small enough, turn off the burner and smother the flames with a lid or damp towel. Baking soda also will douse flames, so keep a box handy. Store a fire extinguisher (chemical or foam, not water based) in the kitchen where it can easily be grabbed—not in the cabinet space above a burning stove. (Check extinguishers regularly, following the manufacturer's instructions to make sure nozzles aren't clogged and pressure is sufficient.) Stand six feet from the flames when spraying a fire extinguisher.

Electrical fire. Unplug the appliance and use a fire extinguisher (chemical or foam, not water based) to douse flames. Or smother the appliance in a heavy blanket or rug. Never throw water on a burning appliance.

Overflowing toilet. Turn the stop valve clockwise underneath the toilet to shut off water. Bail out half of the water with a cup and bucket. Use a plunger to open a clogged toilet. (Put petroleum jelly on the lip of the plunger, which helps stabilize its position on the drain hole, then place the plunger securely over the bowl's drain hole and pump the plunger up and down.) If plunging doesn't work, try a toilet auger (also called a snake) to loosen the blockage. Most rental companies rent augers by the hour.

Burst pipe. Shut off the water supply either at the stop valve (underneath the sink) or at the main shutoff valve, which is usually located in the basement, crawl space, or utility room near the water meter. (Find out where it is before an emergency arises.) Call a plumber. Turn off the water heater to prevent overheating and cracking. If possible, seal the crack in the pipe with a rag or waterproof tape. Keep a bucket under it. Close the doors to the room where the pipe has burst, and stuff towels under the door to keep water from running out. If ceiling plaster is bulging, move furniture and carpets out from under it and place a bucket under the area. Pierce the bulge to let the accumulated water out. This will limit damage to one area.

Frozen water pipe. When you turn on a faucet in subfreezing weather only to get trickling water or none at all, ice has built up inside pipes. Shut off the main water valve. Apply heat to the frozen pipe with a hair dryer or heat lamp, working backward from the faucet toward the frozen area. Keep the faucet turned on to release pressure from thawing water. Turn on the main water valve again.

Flooded basement. Never step into standing water in a basement. Even if you can see that there's no danger of electrical shock from cords plugged into outlets, you may have forgotten about a hidden electrical outlet that's now underwater. First, call the power company and ask them to turn off the gas and electricity to your house. Bail out water with buckets, or soak it up with a mop or a wet-dry vacuum. If the water is more than an inch or so deep, rent a submersible electric pump from a rental company or call a plumber.

Once the standing water has been drained, place fans in opposite sides of the room to dry it out.

Burst washing-machine hose. Turn off the water faucet connected to the hose behind the washing machine. (Be cautious about any electrical appliances that are standing in water.)

Move any furniture or rugs that could be damaged, then mop up the water or remove it with a wet-dry vacuum. If water has seeped into carpeted rooms, pull the carpet and pad back and dry with a fan. Replace washing-machine hose.

Sink clog. Bail out water into a bucket. Boil a large pot of water and pour it down the drain. If this fails, position a plunger over the drain and push it down forcefully three times. Repeat if necessary. If the blockage is in the U-bend pipe, place a bucket underneath the bend and unscrew the U-bend. Carefully poke a piece of wire up the pipe until you free the clog. If this doesn't work, try using a plumber's snake.

Water heater leak. Shut off the water-supply valve to your water heater. If it doesn't have one or you can't locate it, turn off the main water supply to your house. Switch off the gas or electricity supply to the water heater, and call a plumber.

Jammed garbage disposal. Push the reset button on the bottom of the unit. If it still won't work, turn off the power to the unit. Then use a wooden spoon or broom handle to move the blades back and forth to dislodge the object. Never put your hand inside the unit.

Gas leaks. Extinguish all fires, cigarettes, and other open flames, and open as many windows as possible. If you smell a strong gas odor, get everyone out of the house immediately. Call the emergency service number of your utility company from a neighbor's house. Cut off the supply of gas to the house by turning off the valve beside the gas meter. If the odor is faint, check pilot lights to see if one has gone out. If so, wait for the gas smell to diminish and then relight. If you can't find the source of the odor, call for emergency service.

No electricity. Check to see if all the lights in your neighborhood are off. If only your house is without power, turn the main switch at the top of your breaker box off and then back on. (The breaker box, sometimes called a service panel, is usually in the basement or utility room.) If the panel has round glass fuses, pull the handle attached to the main fuse completely out of the panel. You may need to replace old fuses with new ones. Never touch the panel if the floor around it is damp or if your hands are wet.

Keep Your Drain Clean and Clear

Avoid the unpleasant task of unplugging drains:

- Pour boiling water down the drain on a weekly basis.
- Clear your sink drain once a month. Pour ½ cup of baking soda down the drain followed by a cup of vinegar. Let it sit for a few minutes and then run the hot water. This will also help keep the sink from smelling.
- Place a strainer over the drain to stop big bits of food from descending into the pipes.
- Never pour coffee grounds or grease down the drain.

Shut off and unplug all appliances and electronics; they might draw a rush of electrical current when power is restored and could cause damage to fuses and circuitry. Switch on appliances and lights one at a time.

No phone line. Check with neighbors to see if their phones are also out of service. If they're not, and if your home was built after 1982, there may be a diagnostic jack in a box near the location where the phone line comes into your home. Plug a phone into this jack; if you get a dial tone, the problem is inside the house. Check your accessories—cordless phone, answering machine, modem—to see if they are functioning properly. If the phone works without an accessory on the line, the problem probably is in the accessory. If it doesn't, you'll need to contact your phone company to arrange a service call.

Loss of heat. For gas heat, check to see if the pilot light is burning. If not, relight it, following the manufacturer's directions. For electric heat, check for a blown fuse or a tripped circuit breaker. Call a repair person, if necessary. To keep your home as warm as possible, shut exterior doors and close all curtains and shades, except those that allow direct sunlight in.

Be Prepared for Disaster

Natural disasters—hurricanes, floods, wildfires, tornadoes, earthquakes—strike suddenly. Taking the necessary steps to prepare ahead can make a life-or-death difference for your family.

☆

SMART MOVE

Purchase and install
these products:
- smoke detectors
  and batteries
  (at least one
  detector for
  every level in
  the home)
- carbon monoxide
  detectors
- fire extinguishers
- escape ladders
- fireproof safe
- outlet protectors
- fireplace screens

- Twice a year, designate the days you adjust your clocks for daylight saving time and then back to standard time as Home Safety Day. Change the batteries in your smoke detectors and see that fire extinguishers and flashlights are in working order.
- Make an inventory of all your possessions, and keep a copy in a safe place away from your home. Take several photos of any valuable items.
- Make sure every adult, teen, and older child knows how to turn off the water, gas, and electricity at the main switches.
- Keep the following emergency phone numbers handy in case of a crisis:

  emergency services (fire, police, and ambulance)
  nearest hospital
  physician, dentist, and pharmacist
  poison control center
  emergency numbers for gas, electric, and water companies
  neighbors
  immediate family
  taxi
  veterinarian
  insurance companies

- Call your local American Red Cross chapter or Emergency Management Office and ask which disasters they suggest you be prepared for in your area. Do they have any free booklets they can send you? Ask how you would be warned of an emergency, and learn your community's evacuation routes. Ask about special assistance for elderly or disabled persons.
- Discuss with your spouse and children how you would respond to various disasters—fire, severe weather, and other emergencies.
- Identify the safest places in your house in case of a tornado or an earthquake.
- Instruct family members to turn on the radio for emergency instructions. Be sure you keep working batteries in one or more radios.
- Outline escape routes from each room of your home.
- Pick two meeting places: a place near your home in case of a fire and a place outside your neighborhood in case you cannot return home after a disaster.
- Practice emergency evacuation drills with all household members.

- Designate one out-of-state and one local friend or relative for family members to call if you are separated by disaster.
- Learn first aid and CPR.
- Keep family records in a waterproof and fireproof container.
- Post emergency telephone numbers near telephones.
- Teach children how and when to call 911.

Family emergency communication plan
Develop a family plan in which responsibilities are shared and you work as a team.

- Complete and carry the Family Communication Card, provided online by the U.S. Department of Homeland Security at http://www.ready.gov/kids/_downloads/familyplan.pdf.
- Post emergency numbers by every phone.
- Decide on a place to meet if you're separated from your family.
- Have an out-of-state contact. Call this person after the emergency to let them know how and where you are.
- Know emergency response plans for your workplace and your children's school or day-care center.
- Know the medications taken by family members.

Prepare
- Understand your community's warning signals (what they sound like, what they mean, and what actions you should take when they are activated).
- Have working flashlights on every floor, and know where to find them.
- Prepare an emergency supply kit for your family (see page 98).
- Have a plan to care for your pets. Animals are not allowed inside emergency shelters (service animals are the exception).
- Have your family's special needs and health insurance information handy.
- Learn basic first aid. Classes are offered by various community organizations.

Practice
- Test your children's knowledge of the plan every six months.
- Conduct emergency evacuation drills.
- Replace stored water every three months and stored foods every six months.
- Install smoke detectors throughout your home and change the batteries once a year.

⚠

CAUTION!

Candles are
responsible for
about 23,600
residential fires in
the United States
each year.

Emergency supply kits

An emergency may limit your access to food, water, heat, and other
necessities. Keep a stock of emergency supplies on hand that will
last for at least three days. Replace your emergency supply of water
and food when they reach their expiration dates. When you change
your clocks for daylight saving time each year, update your kit,
which should include the following:

- battery-powered radio and flashlight, with extra batteries
- bottled drinking water (one gallon per person per day)
- canned or packaged foods that do not require refrigeration or
  cooking (enough for three meals per person)
- plastic eating utensils and dishes
- nonelectrical can opener and utility knife
- paper towels, toilet paper, soap, detergent, laundry bleach
  (unscented)
- plastic sheeting and duct tape for creating shelter
- blanket or sleeping bag for each family member
- change of clothing and an extra pair of shoes for each person
- basic tools (wrench, hammer, screwdriver, scissors)
- signal flare, matches, whistle
- cell phone and extra battery
- fire extinguisher
- extra set of car keys
- cash or traveler's checks
- important phone numbers and information
- first-aid kit and manual
- prescription and nonprescription medicines
- special foods needed by family members
- formula, baby food, diapers, wipes, and bottles
- denture needs, extra eyeglasses, contact lenses and supplies
- plastic garbage bags

Pet emergency kit
- identification collar
- rabies tag
- pet carrier or cage
- leash
- medications
- newspaper
- litter
- trash bags for waste
- veterinary records
  (necessary if your pet has to go to an animal shelter)

Fire Safety

According to the National Fire Prevention Association, in 2006 someone died in a fire about every 162 minutes, and someone was injured every 32 minutes. Taking the following steps will decrease the risk of fire in your home—or guide you should a fire occur.

- Test smoke detectors monthly. Change batteries yearly.
- Check pilot lights regularly.
- Clean accumulated kitchen grease.
- Keep pot and pan handles pointed toward the back of the range top.
- Teach your children that fire is a tool, not a toy.
- Post the fire department number on or near every telephone.
- Store flammable liquids in properly labeled, tightly closed nonglass containers. Keep them away from heaters, furnaces, water heaters, ranges, and all gas appliances. Make sure they are out of the reach of children.
- Ensure that no one smokes in bed.
- Keep lighters and matches out of the reach of children.
- Do not place or store pot holders, plastic utensils, or towels on the range.
- The storage area above the range should be free of flammable and combustible items.
- Portable heaters should be operated at least three feet from upholstered furniture, drapes, bedding, and other combustible materials.
- Check and clean chimneys annually.
- Plan your escape route and an alternate route. Practice both plans with your family.
- Know the location, type, and purpose of your fire extinguisher.
- Examine your extinguisher for any signs of damage or tampering.
- Know how to use your extinguisher.
- Make sure your kitchen fire extinguisher is ABC rated.

Crimeproof Your Home

- Replace hollow entryway doors with sturdy ones made of fiberglass, wood, or steel.
- Install dead-bolt locks, either the single-cylinder type, which turns with a key on the outside and a lever on the inside, or the double-cylinder type, which requires keys on both sides. The double-cylinder locks are best if a door contains glass. A burglar may break the glass, but he won't be able to turn the dead bolt without a key.

⚠ CAUTION!

As a result of home fires each year, about 4,000 people are killed and property loss exceeds $4 billion.

Burglar Deterrents

Taking the following precautions will help protect your home and property.

- Avoid the most obvious hiding places for valuables: under mattresses, in nightstands, in jewelry boxes, on dressers, in underwear drawers.
- Consider sliding your jewelry box into a hall closet or bathroom cupboard (not the medicine cabinet). Store cash in a container you use for hobby materials, such as a knitting tote bag. Tuck jewelry, wrapped carefully in foil, in the freezer.
- Install a few fake wall outlets in out-of-the-way places and store treasures there. Also useful: false books, hollow cleaning-product cans.
- Few burglars want to sort through a basement—consider hiding items there.

⚠️ **CAUTION!**

If you come home and notice that your house has been broken into and burglarized, leave immediately. Call the police on a cell phone or from a neighbor's house. Once the police arrive, you can go into the house and begin to take inventory of what is missing. Call your insurance company when you have a complete list of what has been stolen.

- Lock all doors and windows every night and whenever you leave your home. Most burglaries occur during workday hours.
- Make sure your door's hinges are on the inside. Pins in hinges on the outside are easy for a thief to remove with a screwdriver.
- Install a security system that includes sensors on all doors, motion sensors in the master bedroom and living room, and a loud siren.
- "Advertise" your alarm by displaying security-system decals on doors and windows.
- If you don't have a security system, try battery-operated units with motion detectors and alarms. These can hang from doorknobs or sit on tables.
- Make sure your doors have peepholes, and use them before opening your home to a stranger.
- If a stranger knocks and asks to speak with you, ask him to show ID before you open the door.
- Don't hide a key in the usual places: under the doormat, on top of the door frame, in the mailbox, in a flowerpot. Give a spare to a nearby neighbor or relative instead.

- "Case" your own house for burglary: What unprotected entry points do you see?
- Better yet, call in the experts. Many police departments provide free security inspections for residents.
- Mark your possessions. Operation ID is a nationally sponsored program that makes personal property identifiable in the event of a burglary. Contact your local police department about how to sign up for this service.
- Get together with a few neighbors and create a Neighborhood Watch program. Remember to include residents in apartments and condos.
- Keep trees and shrubs trimmed so your yard is easily visible to neighbors and doesn't provide cover for thieves. Be on the lookout for easy access to the second floor from tall trees close to windows.
- Plant bushes with thorns under your windows.
- If someone asks to use your telephone, make the call for him or her rather than letting a stranger into your home.
- Make sure your doors and main-floor and basement windows are well lit. Consider using motion-detector lights or lights that come on automatically when it's dark.
- Make sure your windows have locks.
- Lock your garage door.
- Don't leave major-appliance or electronic boxes on the curb after a purchase. These alert thieves to your latest buys. Break down the boxes and tie them so the wording doesn't show on the outside. If possible, dispose of them at a nearby recycling facility.
- Keep an eye on appliance repairmen and cleaning people when they are in your home.
- If you have sliding-glass doors, install bolt locks on them.
- Don't put your home address on luggage; use a business address.
- Call the police if you notice any suspicious cars or people in your neighborhood.
- Lock up ladders and tools burglars may use to break into your home.
- Display a "Beware of Dog" sign whether or not you have a dog.
- Leave curtains open a little; a closed-up house signals it's empty.
- Teach your kids not to tell strangers their parents aren't home; instead, they should say you're busy.
- Close curtains at night.
- Don't put your address on your key chain.

CAUTION!

A burglar enters a home in the United States every 14 seconds, and 38 percent of robberies are committed with firearms.

When you leave town

Have the post office hold your mail when you're away; don't let a bulging mailbox signal your absence. You can take care of this in person or online at http://www.usps.com. (Ideally, you should make this request a few days before you leave town to ensure the service begins the day you leave.)

- Stop delivery of newspapers when you're away, or ask someone to pick them up for you.
- Ask a neighbor to pick up any packages that are delivered while you're away and to remove solicitations and takeout menus left on your front door.
- Hire a teenager to mow the lawn or shovel the snow while you're gone.
- Before you leave, put your TV, lights, and stereo on timers. Set them to go on and off at different times, just as they would if you were home.
- Leave a car in your driveway when you're away. Let a friend use the car or move it occasionally to make it look like you're home.

Home Inventory

To determine the replacement value of your home, insurance agents recommend creating a videotape inventory of your possessions—room by room—so any claim for theft, fire, or flooding is readily backed up with visual documentation. Include all items you own—furniture, electronics, jewelry, and clothing. When in doubt, film it.

- Open all your closets, cupboards, and drawers, and don't be shy about pointing out special features or the value of certain items. Include all those possessions in the basement, attic, storeroom, or laundry area. Take focused close-ups of smaller items for better identification. Also, film the outside of your home; include the landscaping, decks, toolsheds, and outdoor furniture.
- Keep receipts or other written proof of the value of items in your home, in addition to the videotape. Record written descriptions, including all the relevant information about items.
- Consider having expensive items—jewelry, furs, collections, silverware—appraised so you'll have written proof of their value.
- Never consider a home inventory complete. Every time you buy something, film it, file the receipt, and add it to the inventory.
- Store copies of this invaluable inventory in a safe-deposit box, with an insurance agent, or at the home of a close friend.

CAR CARE BASICS

Experts say it's possible to actually double the life of your car by sticking to a regular maintenance plan. In addition to the maintenance services outlined in your owner's manual, the following recommendations will help you keep your car running trouble free.

- Change your oil and filter every three months or 3,000 miles. (Some new engines are built to go 5,000 miles or more between changes. Check your manual and discuss the intervals with your mechanic.) When you change the oil, make sure the radiator and coolant tanks are full too.
- Regularly check tire pressure when tires are cool—in the morning or before a long trip. Check your owner's manual for the correct pressure.
- Don't overload your car. This has the same effect as driving on underinflated tires. Both cause excess wear and may lead to a flat. ("Peeling out" also hurts tires, potentially erasing hundreds of miles of tread life.)
- Have your tires balanced and rotated about every six months or 6,000 miles.
- Have engine hoses and belts checked and adjusted periodically. Replace them as needed.
- If a belt squeaks when starting your car, get it adjusted as soon as possible. A broken belt can lead to further damage and a lot of inconvenience.
- Have your coolant (antifreeze) checked before summer heat and winter cold.
- Tune up your car according to the recommendations in your owner's manual.
- Never drive when your car is overheated.
- Find a reliable mechanic you can trust. Having the same technician get to know you and your car can prevent a lot of expensive problems.

When Should You Call Your Mechanic?

In addition to battery, engine, brake, or other warnings that light up on the dashboard, be alert to the onset of any of the following trouble signs; report them to a mechanic as soon as possible.

- Difficulty starting
- Unusual vibrations
- Brake-pedal softness or hardness; brake noise
- Unfamiliar engine noise

GOOD TO KNOW

American passenger vehicles average about 12,000 miles per year, according to the Environmental Protection Agency.

- Engine roughness and loss of power
- Stalling at traffic lights
- Steering wheel pulls to the left or right while driving
- Uneven tire wear
- A ride that is noticeably less comfortable
- Clutch chatter or slipping
- Exhaust-system roar; rust holes in the muffler
- Horn failure
- A gauge that shows an abnormal reading
- Fluid leakage on the pavement beneath a parked car

  - Green or yellow spots could be coolant. You may have a bad water pump or a leak in the radiator or heater hoses.
  - Red spots are usually caused by transmission fluid. You may need new transmission seals.
  - Black or dark-colored slippery fluid is oil. You may have an engine leak.
  - If you see an oily liquid with very little color, this is probably brake fluid, and you should have your brake system checked immediately. (Warning: Don't ever get even a little bit of brake fluid on your car. It will eat away the finish.)
  - Water leakage is probably just condensation from your air conditioner and not a problem.

How to Find a Good Mechanic

Ask friends or neighbors for recommendations of a good car-repair facility. Don't rely on coupons to find a good mechanic. Just because a garage offers a discount doesn't mean it will best serve your needs.

- When choosing a shop, look for a neat, well-organized facility with cars in the parking lot equal in value to your own. The staff should be courteous and helpful as well. Look for any evidence of mechanic training, such as certificates posted on the walls. Ask the shop for the names of a few customers, and call them for references.
- Before you take your car to a mechanic (or to your dealership's service department), read your warranty. Find out what's covered and for how long. Some parts are covered past the average three-year or 36,000-mile agreement.
- Clean your car before you take it in. When you show you care about your own vehicle, there's a good chance the mechanics will care more about it too.
- Don't try to fake advanced knowledge of engine repair, but do

know the basics. The best way to start is to read the owner's manual.

- Once you choose a repair shop, have them complete a minor job first. If you're pleased, they can handle more complicated repairs later.
- If you are not pleased with the service you received at a shop, don't just rush to another one. Instead, discuss the problem with the manager or owner and give the business a chance to solve the problem. Reputable shops value customer feedback.

Car Cash Savers

- You may not need to buy higher-octane gas. Use the lowest-octane gas that does not cause your engine to knock when you accelerate.
- Fill up before the light comes on. Make it a habit to fill up when the tank is half empty. It is safer and allows you to stop when you are passing a station with the best price.
- Do not top off your fuel tank. Gas can expand in your tank and overflow.
- Turn on your air conditioner in warm weather. You'll actually use more fuel by rolling down the windows, especially on long trips at high speeds.
- Don't drag around extra weight in your trunk, and if you have a detachable roof rack, remove it unless you're using it. Your car will use fuel more efficiently.
- Make sure your tires are filled properly. As much as 2 percent of your fuel can be wasted if your tires are not fully inflated.
- Avoid long periods of idling. Restarting actually uses less fuel than idling for more than a minute.
- Change your air filter regularly. Gas mileage sinks when the filter is dirty.
- Save as much as 17 percent of your fuel by driving 55 mph instead of 65 mph.

CHAPTER 3

MANAGING THE FOOD DEPARTMENT

The kitchen is the heart of the home. Whether small or large, filled with handsome appliances or hand-me-downs that barely work, it's always the most crowded room in the house. Apart from the cooking that goes on there, the kitchen is where family bonding happens. It's where loved ones gather, traditions are forged, homework problems are solved, and memories are made.

Admittedly, I'm not much of a cook, but the nourishment my family receives in our kitchen isn't just for their bodies. It's also food for the soul. When my boys were growing up, the kitchen was the go-to place for Mom and Dad (Bill's a better cook than I am—and he enjoys it more too). The kids knew where to find us at the end of the day, ready to dish out words of wisdom along with extra helpings of chicken-in-the-blankets—one of their favorites. They often told us about what was going on at school and other things on their minds as they sat at the bar, drinking a glass of milk or peeling potatoes.

The kitchen is where family bonding happens.

. . . .

It's important to think about what goes on in your kitchen and what you'd like to have happen there, because food helps create the atmosphere of your home. What "feel" do you want to create—a fun coffee shop–like environment, for instance, or a well-oiled machine where family members are fed healthy meals in an efficient manner? What do you eat and when; how do you buy and prepare it; and who does what? How we act around food, how we talk about it, as well as what we serve and when and under what circumstances we eat—whether we stand in the kitchen and wolf it down, eat in front of the TV on trays, or sit down to a nicely set table—says a lot about our families and the attitudes about food our children will take with them into life.

As the Family Manager, you are creating a place where food can bring out the best in your diners—even if you don't consider yourself a wonderful cook. No matter what your culinary acumen, now and then it's good to evaluate the food and meal routines in your home and decide whether you need to make some adjustments. Maybe you or other family members have been wanting to shed a few pounds. Maybe you're concerned about the amount of fat you're eating. Maybe you've been eating out and on the run too often. Even if you are entirely satisfied with what you eat and the way you eat it, maybe it's time to reassess who does what.

Food also has a lot to do with traditions and your family legacies. Favorite recipes passed down from one generation to another draw a family closer—whether you always make Grandma's potato salad on the Fourth of July or Aunt Betty's peppermint fudge at Christmas.

Good food also helps to keep kids at home. When they know there's good food and enough of it to share, your kids will want to invite their friends to your house. When our boys were growing up, Bill and I made sure they knew that they could invite their friends over to hang out and raid the pantry. Some of these friends were linebacker-size (Bill called them Raiders of the Lost Fork), so having them hang out at our house may sound like a mixed blessing. But trust me, it's better for your grocery bill to be a little higher and the music a little louder if the kids are at your house, because you know where they are and what they're doing.

Good food helps to keep kids at home.

When our oldest son, John, hit adolescence, Bill and I worried—as many parents do—about where he and his friends would go after football games and school dances. There were not many alcohol- and trouble-free places to hang out. We decided this problem might be an opportunity in disguise and hit on what became a fun Friday-night routine. After games or parties, we invited the kids to congregate at our house. Bill donned his chef's apron and fixed his famous midnight breakfasts. Sometimes we served pancakes with seasonal toppings, and other times we made scrambled-egg burritos the kids could stuff with their favorite Tex-Mex fixings. We planned some of these get-togethers in advance and decorated according to the event's theme. Others were spur of the moment. The point was that our kids knew there would be food on hand and their friends were welcome.

I think most moms would agree that the Food department is one of the most labor intensive of the seven. There's the planning of meals, the shopping for the food, the prep work, the cooking, the serving, and of course, the cleanup. Multiply this by three, not counting snacks and entertaining, and you've got yourself an average day. At times the tasks in this or any department can seem overwhelming, and when they do, it's a good idea to step back, breathe deeply, and ask God to adjust your perspective.

Not long ago my friend Ann got her perspective realigned at the grocery store. She was shopping with her four closely spaced children. The baby was strapped to her in a carrier, the toddler and

The Most Important Things to Remember

1. Your entire day runs more smoothly when you effectively manage the Food department.

2. You oversee around 1,095 meals per year—snacks and parties not included—which means you think about, shop for, and prepare a whole lot of food.

3. Developing a good strategy for handling meals is a worthwhile endeavor and will get you in and out of the kitchen faster.

4. What your family eats and drinks greatly influences the health of each member.

5. It is not necessary to be a gourmet cook to adequately feed and nourish your family.

6. Your attitude is as important as the ingredients in your meals.

7. Food and teamwork go hand in hand, perhaps more naturally than any other area of family management. Eating and cooking together builds bonds.

8. When meals are planned in advance, with all the food and ingredients on hand, everyone tends to relax and feel calmer.

9. There is more to eating than good food. The ambience—where and how you set your table or trays, or organize your picnic—can make your meal a more pleasant experience and help define your family culture.

10. Reclaim the family dinner hour. Decide to eat together certain nights each week—and then don't let anything disrupt these plans.

the preschooler were in the cart, and the kindergartner—I mean "helper"—was running down the aisles. Her plan was to grab what she needed (only what she needed) and get home as fast as possible. Good plan, since there wasn't much room in the cart for food.

Between warning her son to "stop bugging your sister," keeping an eye on her wandering assistant, and searching the shelves for deals, she noticed an older woman watching her. The woman was alone (translation: carefree) and smiling—not the least bit annoyed by my friend's cart full of chaos. "I'd give anything to be in your shoes again," she told her reassuringly. "One day you'll long for the time when you had all four in tow. Treasure every minute."

Sometimes it's funny how God answers our prayers in unexpected ways. This was one of those aha moments for Ann as she looked up and whispered, "Thank You." Her tension dissolved as she remembered that shopping with four young kids is difficult, but it's also a source of tremendous joy.

Whether you relish every moment in the kitchen or dread the daily question "What's for dinner?" the time-saving, efficiency-enhancing hints in this section will help you gain a little time to relax and enjoy the bonds forged and memories sealed in the heart of your home.

Strategies and Solutions for Managing Menus and Meals

MENU PLANNING

- Get the whole family involved in menu planning. Schedule a brainstorming meeting to discuss favorite meals and foods. Remind everybody of the basic ground rules of brainstorming before you start.

  There are no stupid or wrong ideas. Every food mentioned goes on the list.

  No negative comments should be made about another person's suggestions.

  As with any other meeting, only one person talks at a time.

- Write a family menu of various meal choices. Every Sunday night, let each family member "order" the meal for one night that week. Post the resulting weekly menu on the refrigerator door. The first parent home knows what to start for dinner. If you have a motivated teenager in the house, enlist his or her help on dinnertime prep as well.

- Create three weeks' worth of dinner menus and keep them simple. After three weeks, begin reusing the weekly menus again. You can vary things a bit; for instance, you don't have to have roast chicken every third Thursday. Have it on Monday in the fourth week instead. This basic meal plan can carry you throughout a year, making allowances and changes for seasons—such as using the fresh fruits and vegetables available at that time of year and the foods your family especially likes to eat during each season.

- Tap your friends for their meal-planning secrets. Host a menu-planning party and invite two or three friends. Talk about how you each plan menus, share recipes, and address specific problems—like nine-year-olds and vegetables or teenagers and junk food.

- Have a basic repertoire of five or six dinner main courses that you can vary by switching around seasonings. For instance, one week you might sauce boneless chicken breasts with crushed tomatoes, grated mozzarella, and grated Parmesan; another week season them with white wine, lemon juice, and thyme; and a third week, brush them with a mixture of

FUN FOR KIDS

Establish a weekly "Kids in the Kitchen" night. Let your children use simple cookbooks to create a menu for dinner. With appropriate supervision, they could try a different combination of recipes every week. They'll use reading and math skills to follow recipes. They can exercise creativity by making menus and place mats with the name or logo of their "restaurant."

FUN FOR KIDS

Invent a new flavor of ice cream. Begin with a plain flavor and add nuts, chocolate chips, crumbled candy bars, crushed cookies, chocolate-coated candies, or peanut butter. Brainstorm together about what you'll call it.

Dijon mustard and honey. An Italian pizza crust (one brand is Boboli) could be topped one night with goat cheese, chopped black olives, canned artichokes, and chopped fresh herbs; the next week topped with caramelized onions; and a third week topped with cubes of leftover chicken, fontina cheese, grape tomatoes, and fresh mint.

- Develop a repertoire of five meals you can prepare in less than 30 minutes. Always keep the ingredients on hand.
- Don't feel like you have to reinvent the wheel every week. Some of the best family traditions revolve around food. Maybe Dad grills hamburgers every Saturday night. Maybe Sunday night is always breakfast-for-dinner night. Maybe Tuesday is pasta night every week.
- Have "planned-overs." Whenever possible, double or triple a recipe and freeze the leftovers for a quick meal on a busy night. Do this regularly and you'll find you spend a lot less time cooking. Leftovers from one night's roast chicken can be turned into chicken potpie, tacos, stir-fry, salad, or sandwiches on another night. Make enough pasta one night so you'll have extras for another evening. Serve with tomato sauce one night, then toss with sautéed garlic, the juice of one lemon, and a can of undrained chopped clams on another night.
- Try an alternating cooking arrangement. Your husband cooks on Mondays and Wednesdays; you cook on Tuesdays and Thursdays; you eat out or order pizza on Fridays; and you're flexible about Saturdays and Sundays. If you have teenagers, they can help create the schedule as well.
- Start a dinner co-op. You cook and deliver dinner for everyone in the co-op one day a week. In return, dinner is delivered to your door four days a week. Find four other moms who have similar family sizes, cooking abilities, and lifestyles. Arrange a time to meet to talk about food preferences, food allergies, cooking days, menus, and delivery times. Next, purchase sealable, microwavable, dishwasher-safe container sets. Each set should include an entrée container, two side dishes, and a salad bowl. Each family needs to purchase four complete sets. This way, when it's her turn to cook, each mom will have four sets for the food she delivers to the other moms.
- Team with a coworker. You both cook double portions of what you're fixing for dinner on Monday and Wednesday nights, then take the extra portion in a cooler to the office the following day. That relieves you both from having to cook on Tuesday and Thursday nights. Again, this works best if

you and your colleague have similar family sizes, tastes, and nutritional preferences. You also must have a refrigerator at work to store the food in during the day.

MEALS

Dinnertime

This may be the most important time of the day for your family—perhaps the only chance you'll all have to sit together and talk. It pays to make the most of this meal. The following tips may help.

1. Make eating together a priority. Decide with your spouse how many nights your family will eat together each week. Agree that this is a priority, even if your kids protest.

2. Beware of the "whining hour." If you have small children, have some light, healthy snacks to tide them over until dinnertime. If you work outside the home, try to arrange your dinner-prep time so you don't have to start cooking the moment you walk in the door at night. If you can devote the first 15 or 20 minutes exclusively to your child, whether to read a story, check homework, or just cuddle, she'll probably be less clingy in the long run and go back to her own activities when you start on dinner. On really stressful days, try to plan a meal that will require little time that evening; for instance, you might use your slow cooker or microwave a frozen casserole.

3. Don't let complicated recipes and menus limit the time your family can sit around the dinner table and talk about the day. It's more important to eat together than to serve elaborate meals.

4. Predetermine and post menus. With tight schedules and double-parent burnout at the end of the day, the last thing you need is disorder and dissension over what to fix for dinner.

5. Assign everyone a meal-related job. Cooking and working cooperatively with other family members teach kids responsibility and important skills they'll use the rest of their lives. Even young children can learn early on that they're part of the family team. A three-year-old can help set the table, tear lettuce, wash vegetables, or just play with "cooking" toys while parents and older siblings prepare dinner. Kids eight and older can be responsible for clearing the table and loading the dishwasher. You may want to have two children

FROM THE HEART

Eating together is an unparalleled opportunity for family discussion of issues both large and small, and the passing on of values. Encourage conversation by not allowing TV and phone calls during dinner.

SMART MOVE

Think of your kitchen as a classroom. Elementary-age kids can learn that one cup does not mean a coffee cup and a teaspoon is not just any spoon from the drawer. When we double or halve recipes, we can teach math skills. And dinner-prep time is the perfect time to teach children about the safe use of appliances and equipment.

alternate nights, and if one is busy on a particular night with a practice or a babysitting job, he can switch kitchen duties with a sibling.

6. Be prepared. Keep an ongoing grocery list in a prominent spot in the kitchen so everyone can record needs. When you're preparing dinner, have one family member check on staples and add to the list. Create a routine: When someone opens the last bottle or package of an item, he or she immediately adds it to the list.

7. Create a user-friendly kitchen. Designate a low cabinet where kids can organize plastic cups and dishes. (If you have young children, put safety catches on cabinets that store dangerous things.) Keep table accessories—napkins, dinnerware, place mats, salt and pepper shakers—easily accessible to the dinner table.

8. Clean as you go. After you've used an ingredient in your recipe, immediately return it to its place and toss all wrappers and scraps. This saves time and keeps you from forgetting whether you added that pinch of salt. Fill your sink with warm water and soap while cooking. Soak pots, pans, and utensils while you're eating for easier cleanup later.

9. Focus on your family. Cut off the outside world and break the "I have to answer the phone" habit. Let your answering machine or voice-mail service take charge of calls. Showing interest in a child's world is a great way for parents to express their love and promote bonding. To get quality conversations started, ask a question such as "What was one interesting thing that happened today?" or "What made you feel happy today?"

10. Create a pleasant dining atmosphere. Don't reserve ambience for guests or celebrations; serve it with every meal. Adding ambience doesn't have to be time consuming or expensive. Use cloth napkins and pretty place mats, light candles (store them in the refrigerator so they'll burn longer), and turn off the TV. Replace background noise with pleasant music.

11. Think (and talk) positively. Ban critical words and arguing. Avoid disciplinary discussions that could be handled another time. Dinner is not the time to talk about who's not doing chores or problems at school.

12. Show appreciation. Compliment everyone who helped with the meal. And when it comes to cleaning, remember that it's more important for your family to work as a team than for the kitchen to be spotless. Praise team members for their effort. "You did an excellent job of washing the dishes, but please try to remember to clean out the sink after you've finished."

13. Start and finish together. Make sure everyone who is at home is seated at the beginning of the meal. Say a prayer of thanksgiving before you begin. And even though kids may complain, you're teaching good manners by having them remain at the table until everyone is excused.

14. Plan an ethnic night. Come up with a simple Chinese, Mexican, or Caribbean meal that appeals to the family. Choose appropriate dinner music sung by a person of that culture. Let your children draw scenes of the country you are celebrating, and use these to decorate the dining room. If your meal revolves around China or Japan, allow everyone to eat with chopsticks, and brew tea to serve with the meal. If you are celebrating Italy, play an Italian opera while you cook and have a pasta-making party. A Caribbean feast might include reggae or steel-drum music, and the dishes could include some interesting produce like plantains and guava.

Finicky eaters

If you have a fussy eater (or two or three), here are some ideas for getting those nutritious foods in.

- Let your kids sprinkle cinnamon and sugar on cooked carrots or sweet potatoes.
- Make your own healthy version of pizza. Buy crust mix or flat bread and add tomato sauce, lean ham or turkey sausage, cheese, and your favorite cut-up vegetables. Make it a family adventure to build your pizzas together.
- Make a meal from baked potatoes and an offering of various toppings: cheese, butter, and chopped vegetables.
- Add finely chopped, cooked broccoli to a grilled cheese sandwich.
- Ask your child to try peas from pods she opens herself.
- Add brown sugar, maple syrup, or orange juice to the pan as you cook carrots.
- Make Green Bean Packages. Lay about six long, cooked green beans together. Sprinkle with brown sugar. Tie together using

GOOD TO KNOW

A study by the
Harvard School of
Public Health found
a strong correlation
between TV,
unhealthy snacking,
and obesity.

10 Commandments for Fussy Eaters and Their Moms

1. Keep it simple.

2. Refrain from feeding them lots of sugary foods and sweet drinks (even too much fruit juice can douse a good appetite).

3. Sneak in the four food groups every day.

4. Never guilt a child into the clean-plate club.

5. Find ways to make mealtimes fun.

6. Involve even the youngest finicky eater as sous-chef.

7. Never use food as a punishment or reward for other behaviors.

8. Stock proven favorites even if you get bored.

9. Keep trying to find pleasing foods.

10. Let the choosy eaters help with menu planning.

a piece of bacon that has been cut in half lengthwise. Place bundles in shallow pan; add ½ cup water and bake at 350° for 10 minutes or until warm.

- Wrap vegetables in biscuit dough. Bake and serve.
- Offer a variety of vegetables with ranch dip.
- Make Cheesy Potato Boats. Bake medium-size potatoes until soft. Slice each potato in half lengthwise, and scoop the pulp into a bowl. Save the shells. Add 4 tablespoons of butter, 4 tablespoons of nonfat sour cream, ¼ cup grated cheddar cheese, and 1 teaspoon salt. Mix well, pile back into the shells, and bake 10 minutes or until very hot. Make paper sails and stick them in the potatoes with toothpicks.
- Add cooked, pureed vegetables to your meatloaf in place of other liquid. Use tomatoes, squash, turnips, and other mild-flavored vegetables. Add shredded vegetables such as carrots or zucchini to ground beef and make into patties for burgers.

- Let your child choose the vegetables he wants to add to homemade soups.
- Fix a shish-kebab meal by arranging bite-size pieces of meat and cut-up vegetables on skewers.
- Add steamed and pureed turnips to mashed potatoes. Kids usually love mashed potatoes, and turnips are mild enough in flavor that they cannot be detected. You can also add pureed cauliflower.
- Shred carrots and stir into Jell-O.
- Add shredded zucchini or carrots to potato-pancake batter.
- Even kids who don't like spinach will like warm spinach dip. Use the recipe on a package of vegetable soup mix or from an online recipe collection.
- Add extra sautéed onions, bell peppers, and tomatoes to chili—homemade or canned. Chop the vegetables very fine.
- Add steamed and pureed carrots and tomatoes to pizza sauce.
- Add finely chopped and cooked tomatoes and bell peppers to ground beef. Season with taco seasoning. Serve on taco shells or hamburger buns.
- Place carrot strips in pickle juice for two days in the refrigerator.
- Buy pasta made from vegetables, such as spinach or carrots.
- Artichokes are so much fun to eat when each family member gets his or her own along with a little bowl of lemon butter. Snip off the leaf points; cut off the top and stem. Put whole artichokes in a large pot and cover with water. Simmer for about 25 minutes, until you can pull the leaves out easily and the artichoke is tender when poked with a knife. Drain. Pluck leaves out one at a time, and dip base in lemon butter.
- Make sweet breads that have vegetables in them, like zucchini-spice bread or carrot-cinnamon bread.
- Add grated and steamed carrots to cheesy scrambled eggs.
- Fill celery stalks with peanut butter or low-fat, flavored cream cheese. Cut carrots into sticks or thin rounds. Experiment with parsnips, zucchini, and other crunchy vegetables.
- Mix grated cucumber and green food coloring into cream cheese and use as a sandwich spread.
- Let your kids help you cut off the end of a bunch of celery. Place the stalks into red- or blue-colored water (use food coloring). Set in the refrigerator overnight, and the next day you will have colored celery to eat.
- Top pasta with steamed zucchini in tomato sauce.
- Add grated and steamed carrots to nacho-cheese dip.
- For a healthy, protein-rich snack, spread a slice of turkey

GOOD TO KNOW

Turnip greens are an excellent source of vitamin A, which helps the eyes and skin and provides defense against infection.

sandwich meat with a little mayonnaise or mustard and then wrap it around a celery or carrot stick.

- Make crazy veggie open-faced sandwiches. Spread a slice of bread with cream cheese, pimento cheese, or peanut butter. Create funny faces on top using olives, celery, carrot sticks and rounds, radish slices, or any other vegetables.
- Kids love crunchy foods, so try drizzling vegetables with a little olive oil, sprinkling with kosher salt, and roasting in a 400-degree oven for 15 to 20 minutes.
- Make a sweet-and-sour cucumber salad by marinating thin slices in white vinegar that you've seasoned with sugar and salt.
- Stir-fry carrot slices, zucchini slices, and broccoli florets in a little peanut oil, and drizzle with soy sauce before serving.
- Thaw frozen chopped spinach, squeeze dry, and stir into scrambled eggs just before they are set.

Lunches: Building a Better Bag Lunch

- Homemade or canned soup or chili can make a filling, hearty midday meal in the cold weather. Microwave a chunky soup until steaming. While it's cooking, fill a thermos with hot water. Let it stand for several minutes to warm the inside, and then pour out the water and add the soup.
- Meat sandwiches freeze well. You can pull one out of the freezer in the morning and it will be thawed and ready to eat by lunchtime. Don't spread the bread with mayonnaise or salad dressing. Instead, use softened butter, mustard, or cream cheese. Wrap tightly in freezer-safe plastic wrap and freeze for up to two months. Don't freeze any mayonnaise-based salad sandwiches, such as tuna, egg, or chicken.
- If you want lettuce and tomato on your sandwich, pack them separately in a plastic bag.
- Put together individual packets of ham or turkey slices and freeze. Then make the sandwich with the frozen filling. It will stay cold in a lunch box until it's time to eat.
- For sandwiches with meat or poultry, use several thin slices instead of one thicker slice. It makes the sandwich much easier to eat.
- Make peanut butter and jelly sandwiches the night before. Spread both sides of the bread with peanut butter to act as a sealer, and put jelly in the middle.
- Break out of the white-bread mold by using whole wheat, hard rolls, rye, pumpernickel, cinnamon-raisin bagels, or English muffins to hold sandwich fillings.

Tips for Happier Breakfasts

Breakfast is the most important meal of the day—especially for kids. Studies show that children who eat breakfast are more alert and productive at school, and develop healthier eating habits throughout their lives. Try some of these ideas to make breakfast a priority and give your kids a good start to their day.

- Have one of your kids ring a bell or set an alarm to announce when it's time for breakfast.

- Assign different jobs for each child—someone to pour the juice, someone to set out the dishes, someone to say a prayer.

- If there is a struggle in your house over what constitutes a healthy breakfast, consider having "weekday cereals" that are more nutritious and "weekend cereals" that your kids choose.

- If it's a challenge to get breakfast on the table before the bus or car pool arrives, consider setting the breakfast dishes on the table the night before.

- Over breakfast, talk about the day ahead—one thing each person is looking forward to that day and one thing everyone would like prayer for.

- Make a get-ready-before-play rule, and stick with it. Only allow playtime, TV time, or computer time after responsibilities—getting dressed, finishing breakfast, doing assigned chores—are finished.

- If you are really rushed most mornings, make sandwiches for school lunches on Sunday. Label and freeze each one in a zipper bag. Kids can choose a sandwich each morning, then add fruit, chips, or vegetable sticks. An ice pack or frozen box of juice keeps the sandwich cold until noon.
- Wraps taste best if made several hours ahead. Spread a flour tortilla with softened cream cheese or Boursin cheese, then add thin slices of turkey and either sun-dried tomatoes or pitted black olives. Cut in thirds, wrap tightly, and refrigerate.
- Think outside the sandwich. Prepare a lunch of finger foods for your children. Choose from crackers, cubes of cheese,

FROM THE HEART

One of my family's fondest memories is preparing dinner over a fire we built at a campsite. Sometimes we even fix our favorite campfire meals on the grill in the backyard. Here's our favorite open-fire menu:

Foil Dinners: Tear off a 20-inch length of heavy-duty aluminum foil. Grease one side with butter or margarine. Break up ¼ pound ground beef or turkey into small chunks, and place it on the greased foil. Layer thinly sliced potatoes and carrots on the meat. Sprinkle with half a package of dry onion soup mix, and top with three pats of butter. Fold the foil over the food and secure tightly. Then fold over each end tightly so the juices won't run out. Place the foil packet directly on hot coals for 10 minutes. Turn the packet over carefully, and cook for another 10 minutes. Unfold foil, and eat right out of the packet. Make one for each person in your family.

slices of deli meat, grapes, baby carrots, pretzels (plain or yogurt covered), almonds, raisins, dried apricots, banana chips, sugar snap peas, and other mess-free foods.

Picnics

Use this list to make sure you're ready for food and fun in the outdoors.

- food and condiments
- grilling supplies
- beverages
- water
- ice
- cooler
- paper plates
- paper cups
- eating utensils
- serving utensils
- napkins
- tablecloth or old quilt to cover a table or spread on the ground
- packaged premoistened towels to clean hands
- paper towels for cleanup
- garbage bag to take care of litter
- bug spray
- sunscreen
- first-aid kit
- toilet paper if you're in a remote location
- flashlights if you'll be out after dark
- camera

INSIDER CHEF TIPS

Cooking Crises

- If a stew or soup tastes too garlicky, simmer a sprig or small bunch of parsley in it for 10 minutes.
- If a dish tastes too salty, add a peeled, thinly sliced potato and boil until it's transparent, then remove the slices.
- If fish is too salty, add vinegar to the cooking liquid.
- For overly salty soup, stew, or tomato sauce, add pinches of brown sugar to taste.
- To eliminate strong cabbage odors in the house, put a small tin cup half full of vinegar on the stove near the cabbage. It will absorb the odor.

- Revive limp carrots and celery by placing them in the refrigerator in a bowl of ice water for two hours before serving.
- Puree overcooked vegetables, add broth or milk along with seasonings, and you'll have a delicious soup.
- To put out a grease fire, throw baking soda on it. Do not use water.
- If a soup turns out too thin, cook it longer so it thickens. Or add uncooked rice or pasta and simmer, covered, until it's completely cooked.
- Add crumbled egg shells to a cloudy stock, allow to simmer two or three minutes, then lift out the shells and strain the stock. The stock will be clear.
- If you overcook a roast and can't serve it, use the meat for hash, chili, or potpie.
- If you overcook fish and it's dry, make a rich sauce for it or mash it and make fish cakes.
- If a sauce curdles, beat it vigorously with a hand mixer, then add an ice cube and beat it in.

Kitchen Time-Savers

- When clearing the table, don't stack dishes. You'll have to spend more time cleaning off the food stuck on the bottom of each dish.
- Save butter wrappers in the freezer and use them to grease pans.
- Rinse your measuring cup in hot water before you pour in molasses or honey.
- When you make tacos, prepare an extra meal's worth of seasoned hamburger. You can freeze the ground beef in ice-cube trays and reheat it, one cube at a time, for topping baked potatoes or making taco salads.
- Put slightly diluted jelly into a squeeze bottle for cleaner spreading.
- If you don't have a pastry bag, put frosting in a self-sealing plastic bag. Cut the tip of a corner and squeeze.
- When you see bananas on sale, buy extra. Roll peeled bananas individually in plastic wrap and place in freezer. Thaw quickly by microwaving each banana for 10 seconds.
- Whenever you chop or shred veggies and cheese, prepare extra and freeze.
- Bake or poach several chicken breasts to freeze and use in future meals.
- Freeze slices of lemon or lime in plastic bags. Add the frozen slices to glasses of iced tea or water.

⚠️ CAUTION!

The USDA recommends that plastic wrap not touch food while it's cooking in a microwave oven.

- Before a dinner party, scoop ice cream or sorbet balls onto paper-lined trays. Refreeze, and they're ready to serve.
- When fruit is in season, make pie fillings. Freeze in covered pie pans lined with wax paper. All you'll need to do for fresh-baked pie is prepare crusts.

Everyday Cooking Tips

- Boil rice or potatoes in broth or bouillon rather than water for more flavor.
- Enhance reduced-fat ground beef flavor by adding bouillon, or sauté the meat with some chopped onion.
- Reduce salty flavor in ham by baking it partially, then draining the juice. Pour a small bottle of ginger ale over the ham, and return it to the oven until done.
- Keep parsley in a bowl of cold water in the fridge or wrap it in a damp paper towel.
- For enhanced flavor, cut a garlic clove in half, then rub it inside your stew or soup pot before you prepare the recipe.
- Roast chicken or other meats on top of celery stalks; they make a moisturizing and flavorful meat rack.
- Absorb grease from roasts with a piece of stale bread placed under the rack.
- Add a teaspoon of sugar to cooking peas to enhance the flavor and help retain color.
- When boiling corn on the cob, add a pinch of sugar to help bring out the corn's natural sweetness. Don't use salt.
- To retain flavor while cooking chicken, turn it with two wooden spoons rather than piercing the meat with a fork.
- Use raisin bread for French toast for a change.
- Add a pinch of cinnamon to a cup of warm honey and serve with pancakes or waffles in place of maple syrup.
- Add a pinch of baking powder to the milk-egg mixture for puffier French toast.
- Keep your meat from curling: Cut fatty edges with scissors in three or four places before cooking.
- Save juices from canned fruit to flavor baking ham.
- Make your electric stove work like a gas one by using two burners—one on high and the other on low. Switch your pan from one to another when you need to change temperatures quickly.
- Bake apples, stuffed peppers, or tomatoes in a muffin tin. They'll retain their shapes better.
- Thicken soups by adding pureed, cooked vegetables.

- Make perfect rice by sautéing it over medium heat in a little oil. Add water double to the amount of rice, stir, and reduce heat. Cover and cook for 15 minutes. Remove pan from heat and let sit, covered, for 15 minutes. Fluff before serving.
- Freeze salad plates for about an hour before use. The greens will stay cooler and crisper.
- Use kitchen scissors for small jobs such as snipping herbs into salads, cutting cold cuts and cold chicken breasts, and cutting up pita bread or even pizza. Buy a pair that's dishwasher safe.
- Use your hands to tear up lettuce, toss salad, and crumble cheese on top of a casserole.
- Prevent stuck-on food by preheating a wok or stainless-steel skillet over high heat before you add the oil.
- Make your own poultry seasoning: Combine equal amounts of marjoram, sage, savory, and thyme.
- Season quicker and cleaner: Replace the salt and pepper shakers on the stove with a bowl filled with three-quarters salt and one-quarter pepper.
- Feel free to substitute one berry for another, or limes for lemons.
- Use half the amount of dried herbs as fresh. Crush dried herbs in your hand before adding to recipes, and cook the dish for just 15 minutes after you add them. Then taste and season additionally as needed.
- Use heavy whipping cream interchangeably with light cream in recipes, except those that call for whipped cream. Light cream won't whip up to nice, fluffy peaks the way heavy cream does. Sour cream and yogurt add a zippier taste to recipes but don't boil well—they may separate.

Baking

- When baking bread, shiny pans make a light crust, and darker pans make a darker crust.
- When coating a baking pan with flour, use an empty spice jar (the kind with holes in the lid) to shake it neatly into the pan.
- For a moister cake, add two tablespoons of oil to a cake mix, then follow the directions.
- To prevent a cake from becoming too brown and drying out, place a pan of water on the top rack of the oven while baking.
- Don't overbeat cake batter. It can cause the cake to crack.
- Be sure to carefully flour the sides of a cake pan. Spots left uncovered by flour will prevent cake from gripping the sides while rising and force it to slide back down.

GOOD TO KNOW

Don't think parsley is just for garnishing. It enhances the flavor of soups, stews, sauces, salads, vegetables, omelets, and many more dishes. It is rich in vitamins A and C, and also acts as a breath freshener.

- For the same reason, do not use butter to grease a cake pan. Flour cannot cling to it evenly.
- Chocolate cakes are notorious for sticking. Be extra careful when you grease and flour the pan. Instead of flour, you can dust the pan with cocoa.
- Eggs should be at room temperature before beating them to provide the greatest volume. They should also be at room temperature when they are incorporated into butter and sugar in cake batters. Although egg whites will yield more volume if you allow them to reach room temperature first, cold eggs are easier to separate.
- If you don't have time to allow eggs to come to room temperature naturally, you can place eggs that are still in their shells in a bowl of warm tap water for a few minutes.
- Butter creams best when it's at cool room temperature, about 70 degrees. If it's been in the refrigerator, you can soften it quickly by grating the chilled butter into a mixing bowl, using the large holes on a four-sided box grater. It will be ready to cream in about five minutes. Alternately, cut the butter into small cubes and leave it for about 15 minutes, at which point it should be ready to cream. As a general rule, don't microwave butter to soften it. It nearly always winds up melted in some places and too hard in others.
- Don't fill a cake pan more than two-thirds full. Tap the pan on the counter to knock out air bubbles.
- To ensure the baked cake doesn't stick to the pan when you're ready to remove it, fit a piece of wax or parchment paper into the bottom of the cake pan when you're baking the cake. To fit paper exactly, trace the bottom of your cake pan onto the paper and trim to size.
- To make colored coconut to top a cake, put shredded coconut in a ziplock bag, add a little food coloring, and shake.
- To prevent cake crumbs from marring the frosting, apply a crumb glaze—a very thin layer of frosting that coats the cake and seals in any crumbs. Allow it to dry, then frost as usual.
- To be sure you get the right shade of icing, blend colored frostings in advance and allow them to sit. Food coloring intensifies over time.
- To get perfect results when writing on a cake, first write on the frosting with a toothpick; then trace over the marks with decorator frosting.
- If a cheesecake cracks, sift powdered sugar over the top.
- To prevent a cake from sticking to the platter, sprinkle the

bottom of the dish with sugar first. The slices will lift off easily.

- Cakes with sugar frosting will keep at room temperature for up to three days; seal any cut surfaces with plastic wrap and store in a cake keeper or invert a large bowl over the cake plate.
- Pies and cakes with buttercream or cream cheese frosting or custard filling should always be refrigerated.
- Freeze unfrosted cake layers in plastic wrap and wrapped in aluminum foil for up to four months; thaw one hour at room temperature.
- Store soft cookies and crisp cookies separately in airtight tins.
- Freeze soft cookies for up to six months in an airtight container, with plastic wrap between layers.

Successful substitutions

Certain substitutions are standard in baking recipes. For instance, margarine can be used in place of shortening or butter without noticeably affecting the texture of the baked goods. It does, however, affect the taste. Butter has an unmistakable flavor and a creamy texture that margarine just can't imitate. In some instances, substituting vegetable shortening for butter pays off. For instance, piecrust made with vegetable shortening is extra flaky. Since vegetable shortening melts at a higher temperature than butter, it's useful for sautéing and frying. Some people like to use it in their cake frostings.

- When making substitutions in baking, try to keep the ratio of liquid ingredients to dry ingredients as close as possible to the original recipe.
- Substitutions that work in the oven may not work on top of the stove, and vice versa.
- Whenever you make a substitution, keep in mind that baking times may vary, so be sure to check for doneness more frequently.

Fruit

- Choose citrus fruits by weight rather than size. The heavier they are, the juicier they are.
- Valencia oranges usually make the best juice; navel or Florida Temple oranges are great for eating.
- Don't assume a bright orange color means fruit is juicier and more flavorful. Oranges are often dyed to look better.
- Get more lemon juice by heating the fruit a bit (10 seconds in the microwave per lemon), then rolling it on the counter to soften it.

GOOD TO KNOW

To prevent discoloration, slice an apple with a stainless-steel knife. (A carbon-steel knife will darken the apple where it touches the fruit.)

- If you need just a few drops of lemon, poke the fruit with a toothpick, squeeze out what you need, then plug the hole with the toothpick. Save the lemon in a plastic bag in the refrigerator.
- A nutcracker will help you squeeze more juice from a lemon half.
- Freeze lemons by dipping them in water, then dropping them into a large, self-sealing bag. When you need fresh juice, thaw the fruit in the microwave, let it sit for a few minutes, and squeeze.
- Use a splash of lemon or lime juice to keep cut-up fruit and veggies from browning.
- Make orange peeling easier by soaking whole oranges in boiling water for a few minutes. The skin and membrane will slip right off.
- Grate and freeze citrus fruit rinds for seasoning desserts, poultry, and fish.
- A hollowed-out orange makes a great serving bowl for fresh fruit salad, sherbet, or sorbet.
- The best-tasting and freshest pineapples are large and heavy, and have dark-green leaves.
- Make a pineapple last longer by slicing it from the bottom.
- Buy big apples for immediate consumption; small ones last longer.
- Store apples in the fridge; those kept at room temperature go bad faster.
- Place a slice of apple in hardened brown sugar to resoften it.
- To keep potatoes from budding, place an apple in the bag with the potatoes.
- Freeze cranberries before chopping and grinding; the job will be much neater.

Berries: pointers for picking

- Pick ripe ones. They won't ripen further after they're picked.
- Skip the obviously misshapen ones. They're usually hard and lack flavor.
- Pick berries gently. If crushed, they'll spoil faster.
- Don't pick berries by pulling on them—pinch the stem to avoid bruising the fruit.
- Leave the green cap on strawberries to prevent moisture loss.
- Small- to medium-size berries are sweeter; very large ones tend to be hollow and flavorless.

- Look for blueberries that are indigo blue with a silvery frost. The best berries are slightly firm and uniformly sized.
- When picking berries, carry them in several small containers. Too much weight will crush the fruit.
- Pick only what you can eat or preserve within one or two days; berries spoil quickly.
- Transport berries from field to home in a cooler, never the car trunk.
- Once home, spread the berries out and remove damaged ones so they won't spoil the whole day's work.
- Wash berries only just before eating them. Store them unwashed in the fridge in ventilated containers—a colander or berry baskets. They will chill more efficiently this way. Professional chefs store berries on a cookie sheet lined with a paper towel and keep the berries from touching each other.
- Blueberries and strawberries freeze beautifully. Freeze unwashed strawberries in a single layer on a cookie sheet, and when they are completely frozen, place them in a freezer-safe plastic bag and freeze for up to a year. Blueberries may be frozen in their original containers, nested in a freezer-safe plastic bag. Use thawed berries in muffins, pancakes, as a topping for oatmeal, in smoothies and milk shakes, and in pies.

Freezing
- To find foods more easily, designate certain shelves for certain types of food, such as meats, desserts, vegetables and fruits, bread, and prepared foods. Use a label maker to label the shelves.
- Don't expect miracles: Your 19-cubic-foot freezer will not necessarily freeze 19 cubic feet of food overnight. Your freezer shouldn't be more than 75 percent full to run at peak efficiency.
- Before adding a lot of food, set the freezer at its coldest setting.
- Using a permanent marker, label every plastic freezer bag— before you fill it—with contents and date.
- Highlight "use by" dates on freezer packages. Move items you need to use soon to the front.
- Use freezer wrap liberally. Aluminum foil doesn't work as well because it turns brittle in the freezer and doesn't give a secure seal. Freezer paper works better.
- Freeze fresh produce immediately. Fruits frozen in syrup will be less mushy and more juicy when you thaw them. To make a

☆
SMART MOVE

Take 10 minutes today to rummage through your freezer and toss out odds and ends and items that have outlived their shelf life.

light syrup, boil two parts water with one part sugar. Chill this concoction, then pour about ½ cup over each 2 cups of fruit.
- Delicate fruits such as mangoes, watermelon, and papayas don't freeze well.
- Before sealing a freezer bag, squeeze out every last bit of air.
- Your freezer's temperature should be zero or less.
- Tape a list of freezer contents on the inside of the kitchen door or a cupboard for quick reference. Add and delete from the list daily.
- Store cereals, rice, flour, and noodles in the freezer if your area is prone to bugs.
- Store ground coffee in the freezer to help retain its freshness, then use directly from the freezer, as it thaws quickly in boiling water.
- Freeze raw hamburger patties between flattened cupcake liners.
- Store orange and lemon rinds in the freezer to use when a recipe calls for a little grated peel.
- Divide larger batches of food into smaller quantities so you can use them one at a time. Freeze portions of pesto, tomato paste, or cooking wine in ice cube trays, and freeze chicken breasts in pairs.

For best results, don't freeze
- hard cheese (unless it's grated or you plan to use it for melted-cheese recipes—it crumbles when thawed)
- mayonnaise, sour cream, and yogurt
- hard-boiled eggs
- cream and custard pie fillings
- meringue
- carbonated drinks or anything canned (you can freeze juice boxes)
- fish and shellfish, if they've been previously frozen
- cooked potatoes—though mashed potatoes make good thickeners for stews or soups
- garlic
- cucumbers, lettuce, and celery
- pears
- cream sauces

Grilling
- You'll have easier cleanup if you line the base of your charcoal grill with foil, which also reflects heat. Don't line gas grills—just keep the catch pan clean.

- Start a quick fire by building a pyramid with your charcoal briquettes. Then saturate them with lighter fluid (never use kerosene, gasoline, or other flammable liquids), and light them. Wash hands immediately after applying lighter fluid.
- You can also purchase easy-to-light charcoal.
- When coals are covered in a gray ash (about 25 minutes), you're ready to grill. Spread the coals across the grill bottom.
- Add flavor to food by placing fresh herbs—fennel, thyme, or rosemary—over coals minutes before cooking. The herbs will last longer if you soak them in water before use.
- To prevent flare-ups, keep oil in marinades to a minimum and cut excess fat from chops and steaks.
- Use nonstick spray on the grill before barbecuing.
- For safety's sake, when using a charcoal grill, keep a hose or bucket of sand nearby. If you have a flare-up on a gas grill, turn off the burners and step away from the grill.
- Get dinner on the table more quickly by microwaving poultry and meat before grilling.
- Add some veggies to your grilled meal: parboil new potatoes for 5 minutes, place on metal skewers, brush with oil, and grill for 8 to 10 minutes. Always cook fruits and veggies around the edges—the cooler part—of the grill.
- If your grill has no temperature control, sear meats a couple of inches above the coals; raise the grill rack higher to finish cooking.
- When cooking most meats, place the rack four to six inches from the charcoal.
- Store fire starter in a safe place far away from the grill.
- Vents may be adjusted to keep the heat level you want. When opened wide, they let in more air for a hotter fire. Partially closed, they give off less heat. Don't close them completely unless you want to extinguish the fire.
- When grilling fish, rub thick slices of potato on the grill rack first. The starch will coat the metal and help to prevent sticking.

SHOPPING FOR FOOD

Groceries
Quick tips for smart shopping

- Create a grocery shopping routine. If you buy in bulk, shop once a month at a wholesale club. Then pick a time each week to go to the grocery store.

☆

SMART MOVES

To get outside fast . . .
- Reorganize your kitchen and storage areas a bit for impromptu summer suppers outside.
- Store barbecue tools, charcoal and lighter, apron, and hot pad in an easy-access place.
- Keep hamburger/ hot dog condi-ments—ketchup, mustard, mayon-naise, relish—in a plastic tote in your refrigerator.
- Put paper plates, cups, napkins, plastic utensils, unbreakable salt and pepper shakers, and a tray in a cabinet near the back door for quick table setting outside.

- Don't shop when you're hungry or tired. It's harder to make wise, economical decisions.
- Avoid long grocery store lines by shopping when others don't. Observe the patterns at your store to determine the best time for your schedule. Be sure that the services you need are available at the time you shop; some full-service counters, such as deli and meat, aren't staffed early in the morning or late at night.
- Keep an ongoing grocery list in a central location so family members can record needs. When you open the last bottle or package of any item, add it to the grocery list.
- Keep a running shopping list. Having and sticking to a list keeps you from making a second run to the store for items you forgot and from being tempted to buy extra items you don't need.
- Running from store to store to buy advertised "specials" can actually cost you money (and time). Buy specials at the store where you plan to shop anyway and, when possible, use manufacturer's coupons—especially on double- and triple-coupon days.
- Get in and out of the store as quickly as possible. For most people, the more time spent shopping, the more money spent as well.
- If the store offers a choice, choose a smaller cart. You'll fill it faster and be more aware of putting in items you can really do without.
- Stay on task. Many items you need to buy regularly—milk, eggs, cheese, meat—are at the back of the store, and the aisles taking you there are full of eye-catching impulse items.
- For healthier shopping, spend more time around the perimeter of the store, where you'll find fresh produce, breads, fish, meats, and dairy products. With the exception of cereals, grains, pastas, herbs, and some frozen foods, the inner aisles in a grocery store contain mostly processed or junk foods.
- Don't buy health and beauty items at the grocery store. Unless they are on sale, you can usually buy them more cheaply at a discount store or drugstore.
- Keep in mind what fruits and vegetables are in season—they'll be less expensive and more likely to come from a grower or producer near your home.
- Don't assume that a larger size package is cheaper. Check out unit prices. A unit price is the cost for a small unit of measure, such as an ounce.

- Be careful when companion foods are on display. The chips may be discounted, but the salsa could be premium priced.
- Check "sell by" and "use by" dates. Make sure you plan to use the food before the expiration.
- Never buy a package that's dented, rusty, or torn.
- Be careful how you toss things into your cart. If a package gets damaged, the food is vulnerable to contamination.
- Be aware of what foods you throw out each week. If you always waste a quart of milk or some fruit, buy less.
- Select food items from the top and bottom shelves in the grocery aisle. More expensive merchandise is often placed at eye level.
- Be aware that stores stock expensive children's cereals and candy at their eye level.
- Homemade is not always cheaper. Sometimes cake, brownie, and muffin mixes can be cheaper than homemade.
- Buy a few frozen entrées to keep on hand for busy days. Even pricey frozen meals are usually cheaper than takeout.
- Compare prices of deli-sliced meats with packaged lunch meats. One is not necessarily cheaper than the other.
- Try no-frills and store brands. You may discover you get the same quality the name brands offer. Compare ingredients listed on labels to determine similarity of products. Name brands and generics are sometimes identical.
- It will take extra time, but if you know the price of everything you put into your cart, you can save yourself money. Some supermarkets give you an item free if the cash register scans it at a higher price than what is marked on the shelf. For specials, bring the newspaper ad or circular with you to the checkout and make sure the scanned price is correct.
- If the store doesn't have the advertised special you want, ask for a rain check. In some states, you have a legal right to one. When the item is back in stock, you can buy it for the sale price.
- Bag your own groceries so you can put things together the way they go in your kitchen.
- If a clerk bags your groceries, make sure all groceries get packed and every bag is placed in your cart.
- Keep a large plastic laundry basket in the trunk of your car to cut down on trips back and forth from the car when unloading.
- Put grocery receipts in an envelope and save them for a month. You may need to return an unsatisfactory product.

GOOD TO KNOW

U.S. supermarkets carry an average of 45,000 items.

GOOD TO KNOW

Shop around the store for cheese. The dairy case will have prepackaged cheeses such as cheddar, Swiss, and Monterey Jack. The deli and perhaps a cheese table may have the same products. Know what you want— types of cheese, state or origin, age—and shop all three areas for the best price. Usually, the cheese in the dairy case is the least expensive.

- Put away groceries and prepare food for the week at the same time:

> Brown as much ground meat as you'll need for the week and store it in a tightly covered plastic container.
> Chop all onions and green peppers you plan to use. Put in plastic sandwich bags and freeze.
> Hard-boil eggs. Cut up veggie sticks for snacks and lunches. Make individual-size packets of raisins, chips, cookies, etc., for lunches.

- Go to the farmers' market on Saturdays in the summer. Make it a family outing and enjoy fresh vegetables and fruit for dinner all week long.
- Buy bagged fruit and vegetables instead of loose and save about a dollar a pound. And since no two bags weigh exactly the same, use the produce scale to weigh a few bags before you choose one. You could get a few apples for free.
- Buy bread and baked goods in bulk at day-old bread stores or bakery outlets and freeze.

Meat know-how

- When buying meat, an expensive lean cut may be more economical than one that requires you to throw away excess bone, gristle, or fat.
- Instead of buying precut fillets, buy a beef or pork strip tenderloin and cut it into filets yourself. You'll save more than 30 percent.
- Buy the freshest meat possible. Hamburger should be used within a day or two of purchase, or frozen.
- A heavier turkey will give you more meat for your money. As a general rule, a 20-pound bird has more meat per pound than one that weighs 15 pounds, and you can save up to 30 cents a pound.
- Expect about 45 percent waste if you discard the skin on chicken breasts. Boneless and skinless breasts may be a better buy.
- When shopping, put packaged chicken in a plastic bag or keep it away from everything else in your cart. A wet, leaking package could contaminate other foods with salmonella.
- Either cook meat soon after you buy it or rewrap it in special freezer-quality plastic wrap before freezing. Meat displayed in the meat department is wrapped in a special kind of plastic meant for display; it breathes and helps keep the meat's red color.

- Buy a whole boneless pork loin and cut it into chops and cubes. You'll save 25 percent off the cost of presliced chops and stew meat.
- Instead of pricey center-cut pork chops, buy boneless pork shoulder and tenderize it by braising.

Don't let phrases fool you
- A product labeled "10% more free" can be tempting, but before buying, be sure to compare it to other packages of the same product to be sure it's really economical.
- "New and improved" can mean just that, or it can mean a new color, new flavor, or new formula.
- Avoid "Buy one, get something later" deals. Manufacturers know that few shoppers ever redeem rebates or mail-in offers.
- Watch out for nonfat products. Fat provides texture and bulking. If it's removed from a product, it's often replaced with sugar. Check the ingredients and calorie count—you may be better off with smaller servings of the "regular" version.
- Beware of so-called specials. Products displayed as "featured" or "new"—such as cookies, soda, paper towels—aren't necessarily bargains but may simply be promotions of regularly priced items.
- Don't be lured into buying something you really don't need just because a sign says "Limit four per customer"— consumers tend to buy more when the stores impose a limit.
- Take cash to the store with you. You'll spend much less on food than if you pay by check or credit card.

Coupons
If you're willing to invest some time and really love to get something for nothing, couponing may be for you. Depending upon how much time you want to spend, you can save anywhere from a few cents to more than half your total weekly tab. While it may hardly seem worth the trouble to cut out a coupon just to save a few cents, you'll be pleasantly surprised at how quickly those small amounts add up. These tips will help you take advantage of coupons without getting bogged down.

- Start small. Try using one or two coupons per week at first. Habits always start small.
- Establish a routine. Set aside 10 minutes every week (or 20 or 30) to clip and file coupons. If you schedule a certain time period every week, you're more likely to do it. You can work

GOOD TO KNOW

The Web site http://www .beefitswhatsfordinner. com has dozens of recipes that require 30 minutes or less.

The average U.S. household spends about $6,000 annually on food.

on your coupons while sitting in front of the TV or talking on the phone.

- Think before you clip. Don't cut out coupons for products or brands you aren't familiar with; the savings won't make up for a less satisfying product.
- Be choosy. Don't clip coupons for products you're trying to avoid, such as snacks or expensive items.
- Buyer beware. Most food coupons are for convenience foods. Even when these items can be purchased more cheaply, consider if you're introducing your family to more expensive, less healthful items that they just might acquire a taste for. You could potentially be creating bigger grocery bills in the future.
- Know when to say no. Disregard coupons for larger-size portions than you usually use. You may waste most of the food.
- Mark them up. Circle or highlight expiration dates with two different colors for easy sorting. Use one color to highlight those with a short life span (within six weeks) and another color for those that give you a year or more to use them.
- Get organized. Store coupons in labeled envelopes, an accordion file, or a coupon organizer. Or create a special coupon bulletin board. Create categories across the top of the board, such as dairy, meat, baking ingredients, cleaning products, snacks. Hang it in an out-of-the-way place like a laundry room. (It's a great way to be reminded regularly what coupons you have, but it's not very attractive.)
- Weed out. Take time at least once per month to toss outdated coupons.
- Simplify. Write your grocery list on an envelope, then put coupons for items on your list inside. Highlight the items on your list for which you have coupons.
- Increase your savings. When your store features double- and triple-coupon sales, be sure to take advantage of them.
- Share the wealth: Trade coupons with friends, neighbors, or coworkers. This way you can collect numerous coupons for items you use frequently while donating coupons that other people need. Once you get multiple coupons for the same item, you can stockpile—buy as many of that item as allowed when it's on sale.
- Save smart. Put the money you earn via coupons immediately in the bank (many stores now have branches on-site). Use the money to save for something special.

- Travel smart. Keep fast-food coupons in your glove box for easy access.
- Plan ahead. When browsing through an entertainment book of coupons, put sticky notes on pages with deals you want to take advantage of.
- Rebate deals: These are only a good deal if you are motivated to send in proofs-of-purchase or whatever is needed to get the rebate. Some products have instant rebates attached to the outside of the label that must be removed and redeemed immediately at the checkout.

Food Co-ops

A co-op is a group of people who combine their buying power to obtain quantity discounts. Groups can reach volume levels that individuals sometimes can't. Many kinds of co-ops exist: dairy, bread, spices, fruit and vegetable, organic, and more. Buying frequency and minimum orders can vary, and some co-ops require a small membership fee. Others require that you work a specified number of hours shopping, delivering, sorting, playing cashier, handling paperwork, or serving as the contact person.

Advantages
- Shopping from home. (Typically, you call in, fax, or e-mail your order.)
- Deep discounts. Savings are significant even on small quantities.
- No impulse buying. You have to make thoughtful decisions about what you want and need when you preorder.
- Fresher food. Co-ops cut out several middlemen in the grocery-buying system, so food gets to you faster. In many fruit and vegetable co-ops, you buy produce straight from the farmer. You can join health-food co-ops and purchase organic, salt-free, and sugar-free food.

Disadvantages
- Quantities. They're sometimes larger than you need. You might not need 50 pounds of rice.
- Timing. If you run out of something before pickup day, the wait may frustrate you.
- Substitutions. Sometimes what you order is deleted from the group order because too few people want the item. In this case, usually something else is substituted—and it may be something your family doesn't like.

GOOD TO KNOW

To find a food co-op, try these Web sites:
- http://www. coopdirectory.org
- http://www. localharvest.org
- http://www. purefood.org

GOOD TO KNOW

Fish that are generally low in mercury include Pacific flounder, herring, tilapia, wild Alaska and Pacific salmon, farmed catfish, and striped bass.

Restaurants

- Make dinner reservations about six hours before you want to eat—cancellations start coming in about then.
- If you order fish on Monday, remember that it was probably fresh on Saturday.
- Limit eating out on holidays. You pay more for the same meals the restaurant serves daily.
- Establish yourself as a regular customer. You'll get better service.
- Eat out for lunch rather than dinner. You may pay half as much for your favorite entrée.
- Let new restaurants get better; don't try them for at least three months.
- Want friendly service? Be friendly yourself.
- If you're trying to keep your bill down, watch what you order to drink. Soft drinks are typically overpriced.
- Don't be shy about asking for leftovers to be packaged. Tonight's dinner can become a gourmet lunch tomorrow.
- If you're eating out with kids, try to visit a restaurant early. Service tends to be quicker, and the kids won't have as much time to get restless before the meal arrives.
- Bring activities for the children in case the wait is long. Pencils, a small box of crayons, an activity book or blank paper, paper dolls, and a travel-size Etch A Sketch all fit nicely in a small bag that you can drop into your purse or diaper bag.
- Be considerate of other patrons and don't take the children to very upscale, expensive restaurants. Other adults are paying for a child-free night, and they don't want to listen to yours during a meal.
- If you have a small appetite, consider ordering an appetizer as your main course.

CHAPTER 4

MANAGING RELATIONSHIPS WITH FAMILY AND FRIENDS

If I could pass along only one secret that has made our family strong, I wouldn't explain the way we organized our closets, how we managed our schedules, or how we saved money by putting a new roof on our house by ourselves. I would tell you how Bill and I tried day in and day out to be sure the five human beings in our family showed love and respect to each other and remained committed to one another's best interests. We also made it a priority to build our relationships with others—relatives, friends, and acquaintances—in meaningful ways. Of all the roles the Family Manager performs, the one I take most seriously is fostering and maintaining significant relationships and nurturing the souls entrusted to me by God.

I like to compare the Family and Friends department to the human resources department of a company. HR fosters loyalty to the company by offering health care, wellness programs, and opportunities for employees to improve and succeed by building their skills. By providing tangible rewards—bonuses or promotions, for instance—HR inspires workers to do their best work. When there are grievances or disputes, HR steps in to resolve them.

Managers of human resource departments send employees to classes and seminars; they work with them to evaluate their performance and set new goals. In some companies, they're also the people who organize activities and events, like the company picnic or the softball team or company volunteer opportunities. These things don't necessarily add to the "bottom line" for companies, but they benefit them in the long run because they provide opportunities for people to learn how to work together, communicate better, and clarify their priorities.

In a family, HR is spelled m-o-m, and it's a critical position.

In a family, HR is spelled m-o-m, and it's a critical position. Like other managers, you are responsible for "your people." You're in charge of helping them learn to fulfill their roles and build their skills—in short, to orchestrate opportunities so each one can develop into the best person he or she can be.

I don't want to take the business analogy too far. Some people might chafe at talking about "managing" relationships, and I don't mean that at all. The key objective for managing this department is living with a conscious awareness that our most important job as wives, mothers, daughters, friends, and Family Managers is to build loving, lasting relationships. When I remember this, everything seems to fall into place.

If you suddenly won the lottery and were able to hire a full-time staff at your home, you'd discover that many responsibilities in the Family and Friends department can't be delegated. No one else can be a wife to your husband, a mother to your children, a daughter to your parents, a daughter-in-law to your in-laws, a sister to your siblings, or a companion to your friends.

The development and nurturing of personal relationships— working on your marriage, training your children, keeping your extended family together, taking soup to a sick neighbor, keeping up with old friends and making new ones—is a Family Manager's most vital mission. Nothing else is more important. But it's easy for all of us to get bogged down with the details and dilemmas of the average day and give this area less attention than it deserves.

Today more than ever, Family Managers must fight for quality time with family and friends. There are all sorts of distractions all year round that separate us from one another. Sports, for example, are no longer seasonal but year round. And look at Sundays! Sunday used to be distinct from the rest of the week. A day of rest. A day to worship together. A day to slow down, cook a meal at a leisurely pace, and enjoy it together. A day to read a book or play Scrabble in front of a fire. Yet today many families find themselves running from church to ballet practice to birthday parties to soccer fields—maybe even fighting for a parking spot at the mall. Sunday has even become the second-busiest day at grocery stores.

Not only are our schedules crammed, we seldom disconnect from the world. As much as we love our computers and portable electronic devices, if the only time we ever switch them off is between takeoff and 10,000 feet, we can be sure that we're headed for relational disaster with the people we care about most. Building strong relationships doesn't just happen. It takes work and commitment, carving out time every day to disconnect from the rest of the world so we can connect with our families.

There's good reason this department takes precedence over my other Family Manager responsibilities. Taking care of minds, bodies, and souls is inestimably more important than having a showcase home. Why do you take time to talk with your spouse about his frustrations and dreams? Why do you take your children to the doctor and dentist for regular checkups, and read to them at night? Why do you look at colleges with your children? Why do you call a friend who's going through a hard time? Why do you get your

The Most Important Things to Remember

1. The highest calling of every family member is to help each other do the will of God.

2. The family is the most important organization in the world, and Family Manager is the most important job you'll ever have.

3. Family Management is about a lot more than providing a clean house and an orderly environment. It's about nurturing your family and helping family members connect in meaningful ways with one another, with the outside world, and perhaps most important, with their own talents, skills, and spirits so they become the people God made them to be. It's about creating an atmosphere where your family can enjoy living, laughing, and learning together. It's about making your home a greenhouse where each of the human lives within it can flourish.

4. The small acts of love you show family members daily will, over time, add up to big differences that you often cannot see from where you stand today.

5. It's at home, through your teaching and example, that your children learn who they are and ultimately how to succeed in life.

6. The husband-wife relationship is the most important relationship in the family. Both the quality of the parent-child relationship and the child's security are largely dependent on the quality and depth of the marital relationship.

7. Teach your children that school is their career and equally as valuable as Mom's or Dad's career.

8. Model the behavior you want your children to embrace. Kids won't buy a double standard.

9. The relational skills kids learn at home will make it easier for them to form healthy relationships with friends, college roommates, their spouses, coworkers, and associates in the future.

10. The family is God's invention. He knows best how to make it work.

neighbor's mail and paper while she's out of town? In each of these small things, you are directly investing in a life.

While it can bring the greatest rewards, the Family and Friends department can also produce more stress and guilt than the others—for at least two reasons. First, we're dealing with human beings who have feelings, not closets that need straightening. And second, a lot of what we do in this department is constantly under scrutiny and, at the same time, is not measurable.

Let's say you decide not to mop your dirty kitchen floor so you can play Chutes and Ladders with your child. About five minutes into the game, your daughter lands on a chute that sends her back 30 spaces. Within seconds, she's wailing and pushing the game board off the table, scattering cards and game pieces everywhere. Or when you call your mother for the 13th consecutive day to check on her and she complains that she feels neglected because you never fly cross-country to visit.

Think about it. When the paint on your house is peeling off, it doesn't cry, get angry, and tell you you're a horrible home owner. When you set a goal to save $300 a month and at the end of the year you only have $2,000 saved, your online bank register won't call you a loser. Your family and friends, though, are usually quick to let their feelings show.

Despite the potential for frustration in this department, there is also the possibility for great fulfillment as we serve others. We can comfort our daughter during her temper tantrum and begin to teach her a bit about losing gracefully. We can ease the ache of Mom's loneliness by saying how much we wish we were closer too. When we sincerely give someone the gift of our time, energy, or love, we are blessed twice because of the boomerang effect. Genuine giving always gives back to the giver. All the emotion invested in taking care of others is paid back with great dividends.

If maintaining an attitude of serving others is a struggle some days, don't give up. We all feel the tension. We desire to give of ourselves to others but know that if we give ourselves to too many people or promise more than we can give, we'll end up giving and getting very little. We all have times when we have to step back and evaluate, to decide which people are the most important to us and how much we can give them.

I hope that as you make everyday decisions about friends and family members—decisions that in fact can have extraordinary consequences—you will find relevant guidance in the following pages.

Strategies and Solutions for Managing Family and Friends

BUILDING FAMILY RELATIONSHIPS

Investing in Your Marriage

Kids gain much security from knowing that Mom and Dad respect and love one another. But good marriages don't just happen. If you sense that your marriage is growing stale, review the list below and consider how you might take a step toward improving it today. (And if you're not married to your kids' dad, remember that your relationship with him is still important. See page 142 for some tips on building mutual respect.)

- Don't consider divorce as an option. Learning to really love each other takes hard work and time, and it's always too soon to quit.
- Spend time talking and listening to each other every day—even if you're tired.
- Think of your marriage as a partnership. Don't assume that certain tasks are always the husband's or wife's responsibility. Let giftedness and time availability, not tradition, guide you as you share the load.
- Ask for and learn to give forgiveness. If you do something wrong, admit it without blame or excuse and ask your partner to forgive you.
- Accept each other's shortcomings. Remember that you're both human and will disappoint one another. When this happens, talk through your differences and give each other grace.
- Learn each other's love language so you can say "I love you" in ways that are meaningful to each other.
- Find and spend time together on common interests. Working on projects or pursuing hobbies together creates a lasting bond.
- Listen to inspirational messages or audiobooks together. This is especially good when you go on short trips in the car. Talk about what you learn.
- Pray together daily.
- Exercise together regularly. Encourage each other to live a healthy lifestyle. Take walks together.
- Give each other space for different interests. Pursuing your own hobbies, friendships, and careers—in addition to spending time on similar interests—enables you to appreciate one another more and learn from one another.

⭐

SMART MOVE

Establish a day
or block of time
that's sacred
for your family.
Maybe it's Friday
nights, Saturday
mornings, or Sunday
afternoons. As much
as possible, keep
your calendar free
from outside events
and devote that time
to family activities.

- Remember that love is a verb; act on it every day. Put it on your to-do list.
- Don't stop dating. Book your babysitter ahead of time for two or three date nights each month. Plan at least two short getaways a year without the kids. Every couple needs time away by themselves.
- Set aside some time once a month to meet and discuss your schedules and family goals.
- Never go to bed angry. Keep talking.
- Invest in counseling, if necessary. When you get dangerously close to the crash-and-burn stage in your marriage, step back, take stock of the situation, and remind yourselves that a good marriage is worth fighting for, and it takes not only time but a lot of patience and prayer.

Getting Along with Your Kids' Dad and Your Ex

If you're not married to your children's father, do everything possible to keep a cordial relationship with him, for your kids' sake. Before assuming that's impossible, consider the following:

- Monitor the way you talk about their father. You don't have to praise him falsely, but be sure you're not criticizing him or unconsciously asking your kids to take your side against his.
- Learn to communicate effectively. Whether it's discussing visitation or back child-support payments, it's easy to become emotional when talking with an ex-spouse. Unfortunately, that rarely leads to a productive outcome. Learn to mirror back what he is saying ("I hear you saying that you don't know how to handle Jason when he refuses to get ready for school in the morning") or get to the bottom line ("So you're saying you can't have the kids over their spring break but you'd like them to visit over Easter weekend?").
- Find a support network. If you're a single mom, perhaps a friend or coworker is also a single mom and can offer empathy and encouragement when you feel at your wit's end. Many churches and community groups offer more formal support groups where you can share ideas and vent your frustrations. Often, they provide activities for participants' kids at the same time.
- Don't accept abuse. If your ex-spouse is verbally or physically abusive to you or your children, you must not allow it to continue. Seek help from a pastor, counselor, or battered women's shelter in your area.

Simple Ways to Be a Great Mom

If we could raise our hands in secret, we would probably all confess that there have been days when we wondered if we were cut out for motherhood. I recall some such days, like when I had to park my overflowing grocery cart and take my three-year-old to the car for a moment of discipline because he pitched a no-holds-barred fit in the cereal aisle. Or when the principal called to report that our second grader had tackled and pinned down a classmate and called him a bad name. Or when a girl showed up at our house to study with our 14-year-old and she was wearing an outfit that left a lot to be desired—like more fabric.

If you start feeling incompetent as a mom and could just kick yourself for not majoring in child psychology, please come back to this chapter and remind yourself of these truths: (1) Every mom has bad days; (2) There is no such thing as a perfect mom; (3) You do not need amazing talent, a fancy degree, or a lot of money to be a great mom. Here are things *every* mom can do to be a great mom.

Be available. Your children need to know you are there for them when they need you to be. This doesn't mean that you schedule your life according to your child's whims. It is not healthy for a child to think the universe revolves around him or her. Availability means you are open and you give yourself willingly, without regret. If you have a busy schedule, make it a priority to carve out time to give each child focused attention.

Be lavish with love and forgiveness. Assure your children that they are loved and accepted even when they fail. Never withhold physical or eye contact, even when they make mistakes or disappoint you. Make sure they know that although you disapprove of their attitudes or actions, your love is unconditional. Hug, hold, and touch your children in appropriate, loving ways every day. Look into their eyes regularly and tell them how much you love them.

Be generous with praise. Children never outgrow their need for heavy doses of praise—no matter their age. The five-to-one praise principle is a good rule of thumb to follow: Balance every negative comment you make to a child with five positive comments. Think before you speak. Ask yourself if what you want to say will build up or tear down your child. Each day, look for ways to affirm your child's unique giftedness and personality. Encourage others in the family to do the same with each other.

Be fair. We all ascribe to the fact that people are different—in theory. But when we have to live with the peculiarities of the people in our

---

☺

FUN FOR KIDS

Make up a family trivia game. Write questions on the front of index cards and the answers on the back. Stack the cards in a pile and let family members take turns drawing. If the question is answered correctly, the player keeps the card. The person with the most cards wins. Here are some ideas for questions:

- Where did Mom and Dad go on their first date?
- In what month did Mom and Dad get engaged?
- What was Ben's first word?
- On what vacation did Jonathan learn to snap his fingers?

GOOD TO KNOW

Studies show that human beings laugh more when they are four years old than at any other time in life. This is more serious than it may sound. Laugher causes our brains to create endorphins that relieve stress and activate the immune system. Laugh at yourself and with others. Teach your child to do the same. Make it a high priority as a family to laugh and have fun together.

home, the standard operating procedure seems to be "fix and repair" rather than "accept and affirm." Our children will do some things that annoy us, and sometimes they will blatantly disobey us. But before we respond, we should stop and ask, *Is this my child's problem or mine? Is there really a "perfect" way to take out the garbage, clean a room, or get homework done? Is there something inherently wrong with what my child is doing, or is she just not doing it* my *way?*

Be fun. Strange as it seems, having fun with your children has a great deal to do with how they respond to your firmness. The moments you spend laughing, playing, and enjoying life together make large deposits in your children's emotional bank account. You've expressed your love and commitment to them in tangible ways. So when the time comes for you to be firm and administer discipline, they can recognize that it's motivated by your concern for them.

I've met many parents who allow overbusy schedules and the stresses of life to crowd out any time to have fun. The results are not pretty: They begin to take life, and themselves, too seriously. They feel guilty for not playing with and relishing their family, so they rationalize their feelings by saying they choose "quality time" over quantity of time. They tuck in moments with their children between meetings, appointments, or other "important work." The problem is that they can't fool their kids into thinking they're enjoying spending time with them when their minds are somewhere else.

Other parents are with (read: physically present) their children for longer periods of time but are not really *with* them. Sitting in front of the television together or working in front of a computer screen with the child in a nearby room isn't making a substantial emotional investment. When it comes to parenting, quality time and quantity time are like the oxygen your kids breathe. Although the quality of the oxygen is important, the quantity determines whether or not they thrive.

Be authentic. Because our children don't come with handling instructions, every parent will make mistakes. As you try to customize your parenting for each child, try to remember that your children don't need an expert; they need a guide. When you blow it, just admit it, learn from it, then get up and go on. Far from undermining your position, this humility will say to the child in the most powerful way, "I am really for you. I am not trying to make you something you are not. I love you, and I am on your team."

Be willing to ask for help. If you face a more serious or ongoing issue with a child, turning to a pastor or professional counselor isn't a sign of weakness—it actually shows great courage and may be the most loving thing you can do for your child.

The Home Team
Build a family team

A good manager—of a home or company—delegates tasks to others, assumes responsibility for initiating projects, and provides needed assistance. A good Family Manager is always learning how to get her family to work better as a team. Even small children can learn to pick up their own toys, help fold laundry by matching socks, and dust the baseboards with socks on their hands.

Some moms think they are doing their family a favor by waiting on them like a personal maid. Not so. Families that share household responsibilities are usually healthier and happier than families in which one person (usually Mom) does most of the work. We do our kids a favor when we involve them in household chores. We're teaching them life skills—like running the washing machine and using a dust mop—they are going to need. We're also teaching them cooperation and collaboration skills. Plus, delegating helps balance responsibilities and workloads between marriage partners. And it builds on the idea that home belongs to everyone; therefore, everyone contributes to its care.

Use these strategies for building your own "family clean team."

Help team members buy into the cause. Your family won't buy into the idea of sharing household tasks just because Mom says so or the Smiths do it that way. If a family understands how and why a new system will improve their lives, they will be more likely to try to accomplish it. For example:

- "If the house is cleaner, you can have friends over."
- "If we all pitch in, it will get done sooner and we'll have more time for fun."
- "Mom will be in a better mood." (This has great value.)
- "Honey, if you and the kids will be in charge of picking up the day's clutter before bed, I'll have more energy for you afterward."

Be willing to negotiate. Everyone has a different tolerance level for dirt. There's a lot of truth in the old adage "Home should be clean enough to be healthy and dirty enough to be happy." In other words, I know no one who likes bugs crawling on their countertops. On the other hand, who cares if the sink gleams if Mom's always playing chief nag? It's important that you find a clean comfort level that's built on common ground. This means everyone will probably have to give a little (and maybe in some cases a lot), but that's what being a family and a team is about.

Create your family's definition of *clean.* Be specific about standards for each room, and let everyone have a say. Maybe your teenager will give a general description of how he likes the bathroom: clean. He's probably never thought about why there is or isn't mildew in the shower or what that funny little brush is in the container behind the toilet. Coming up with a definition of *clean* is a good springboard for discussion and a good way to start the process of delegating the chores it takes to maintain your shared definition of *clean.*

Aim for improvement with a positive attitude. No one will jump at the chance to be on your team if you're negative ("I'm sick and tired of living in a pigpen") or critical ("If you ever did anything around here . . ."). Barking orders is for marine platoons and packs of dogs.

Try to catch family members doing a job right and give them a pat on the back. If they're trying but not yet doing a job correctly, take a few minutes to encourage them and show them how to do the job. For example, if your daughter is supposed to clean the kitchen, praise her for putting all the dishes in the dishwasher. If she forgot that cleaning the sink and countertops is part of finishing the job, offer to show her how it should be done and express confidence in her ability to do it next time.

Be supportive and express confidence in your team's ability to do a good job. Your positive expectations and praise when the job is done often set the stage for higher performance and create a more positive relationship between you and your team members. Thank your husband and children for every task they do, even if it's something you expect of them. Always express gratitude.

Don't take no for an answer. Many moms wonder what to do when their kids won't cooperate and fulfill their responsibilities around the house. Consider these questions: Does your son or daughter watch TV? Play video or computer games? Enjoy using favorite toys or electronic devices?

- Those activities, and others like them, are *privileges*, not rights. You are actually helping your kids when you have a policy that says: Until you fulfill your responsibilities, you do not get your privileges.
- Even more important than the children's cooperation is the

lesson they learn about real life. That's the way the adult world operates—if you don't fulfill your responsibilities on your job, you won't have the privilege of getting a paycheck or maybe even having a job at all.

- Don't be afraid to trade permission for contribution. Your child deserves to learn at home, where the stakes are small, rather than in the cold, cruel world, where the stakes are enormous.

Be flexible. Unexpected events can interrupt the best routines. Bend with the interruption instead of standing against it. Your investment in spending time with your discouraged daughter will pay far higher dividends than a vacuumed house. Going on a hike or picnic this weekend might do more for family morale than a day spent wielding dust rags and cleaning musty closets.

Be proactive about how you can help your husband succeed in his work. Spouses are people, and people who feel like you're on their team are a lot more likely to want to be on your team. Take an active interest in your husband's career. Ask him about his work-related stress and successes—and then listen to his answers. Be aware of his most demanding days and help as much as you can, maybe by mowing the lawn that day or giving him an occasional night free of chores.

Broaden your team if you're a single mom. Explain the concept of working as a team to your children as soon as possible. Consider banding together with another single mom to help each other clean house. You and your kids go to her home for a couple of hours each week; she and her kids do the same for you. Children who are old enough can help with cleaning tasks or entertain younger children while jobs get accomplished. When chores are finished, do something fun to reward kids for their cooperation.

Keep in mind that team building is a process. It's not something you do once and then it's done. In that aspect it's like cleaning the bathroom, although a whole lot more fun! And on the days when you feel as if your mission is impossible, remember that God created your team and is on your team. He's ready to give you the wisdom, strength, and patience you need to get your family working together to accomplish His purposes on earth.

Team building in 10 minutes

Building a team is about having fun together as well as working together. You don't need to schedule a fancy team-building retreat, complete with a rock-climbing adventure and training seminars, to foster healthy communication and strengthen family ties. You can practice powerful team-building tactics in 10-minute segments of time throughout the week. Consider these ideas:

- Take 10 minutes every Sunday night to go over the family schedule for the coming week. Make sure all activities are listed on a centrally located family calendar. Give everyone a heads-up on important scheduling details.
- Get up 10 minutes earlier so you can eat a simple breakfast together as a family. Use these moments to talk about the upcoming day and remind your children of your love.
- Look for ways to add fun to household chores. Set the kitchen timer and have a laundry-folding contest. See who can fold the most in 10 minutes.
- Spend 10 minutes doing online research about community events this weekend. Make plans to do something fun together.
- Work on a challenging jigsaw puzzle as a family 10 minutes each night before bed until you're finished.
- Take 10 minutes to do something special for a family member. Give your child a leg massage after soccer practice. Pick up your husband's clothes at the cleaner's when he's running late.
- Carve 10 minutes out of your schedule to write your husband or child an encouraging note or e-mail on a day when things aren't going well.
- Take 10 minutes before your child's bedtime to inquire about the details of his day. Give him focused attention and listen attentively (read: turn off your cell phone, landline, PDA, and television). If you discover he isn't open to talking then, try asking him about his day over breakfast or when he first gets home from school. Eventually, you'll discover when he is most likely to tell you what's really going on inside him—and it's amazing how much you can learn in 10 minutes.
- Grab 10 minutes to make a spur-of-the-moment dinner reservation and secure a babysitter. Invite your husband on a surprise date.
- Ask family members if you can have 10 minutes of their time. Give them the opportunity to tell you honestly how you can be a better Family Manager. Your willingness to listen and learn will go a long way.

House rules

Having a set of team rules that everyone agrees to abide by relieves everyday stress. Everyone needs to know the guidelines and basic policies under which they are operating. In some families, the parents talk about the rules they want to establish and present them to the children. In other families, the Family Manager articulates the rules after getting input from all team members. The ideal is a collaborative system of setting house rules in a family meeting.

However you do it, establishing house rules, as well as a reward-and-consequence system that applies to everyone, is important. Besides saving a lot of emotional energy, there are also long-term benefits. The relational skills your kids learn at home—respecting others' feelings and their property—will make it easier for them to form healthy relationships with others later in life.

Years ago, our family established the following 10 rules for our household. Ten is not a magic number; you may decide that 8 or 12 house rules works for your family. Our rules are only meant to be a guideline when creating your own family's house rules.

Rule 1: We're all in this together. The rules apply to everyone—Mom and Dad, too. Kids won't buy a double standard. When you give them permission to call you on the carpet for a violation, they will feel ownership of the rules.

Rule 2: No yelling at anyone or "pitching fits." Yelling and screaming are appropriate in emergencies only. Make it a family policy to not speak with raised voices; teach your kids alternative ways to ask for what they want or express in a controlled way how they feel.

Rule 3: Delete the phrase "Shut up" from our vocabulary. Every human is a worthwhile, uniquely made individual, worthy of respect. Make sure everyone knows offenders will face consequences.

Rule 4: Calling names or making unkind, cutting remarks to each other is strictly out of order. Laughing together is healthy. But every family must have boundaries. It's important that when family members poke fun at one another, it's fun for everyone. It's not funny to joke about someone's big nose, deformity, seemingly stupid mistakes, fears, or weaknesses.

Make a list of the names and negative phrases you would like to eliminate from your family's vocabulary: "dummy," "stupid," "punk," "I don't like you," "You make me sick." Set a family goal to rid these terms and phrases from your conversations.

Rule 5: Take responsibility for our own actions and words. Children are not born knowing how to work through conflicts. When your kids get into a fight, sit them down and hear both sides of the story. Ask questions that make each one think about both sides of the problem. Help them learn to identify the root problem and focus on their own behavior—not what was done to them. Teach your kids that they are always responsible for their own actions.

Rule 6: Ask forgiveness when we have hurt or offended someone, even if it was an accident. Kids need to learn the importance of restoring a relationship. This may be especially challenging if they don't think they've done anything wrong. As a parent, set the example by apologizing when you hurt or disappoint a child—even if it was unintentional.

Rule 7: Keep confidential what we share with each other. Family members need to know they can trust each other. Are you considered a safe, supportive, and reliable source of counsel they can trust? Don't talk about one child's problems with another child. Never discuss with friends the confidential matters your spouse or child shares with you.

Rule 8: Respect each other's space. Everyone needs a degree of privacy. Knocking before opening someone's closed door is a good habit to start early on.

Rule 9: Respect each other's stuff. Children need to learn to respect the property of others and to share their belongings with others. To do this, they must have a sense of control over their things and respect the control someone else has over his or her things. This means if a child has a friend over and they want to play with something that belongs to a sibling who isn't home to give his permission, they must find something else to play with.

Rule 10: Agree to abide by a family chore system and get together regularly for family team meetings. Everyone who lives under the roof of a house should help with the upkeep. Identify the consistent conflicts in your home: whose turn it is to feed the dog, do the dishes, or vacuum the family room. Then schedule a family meeting and use the "Who's Responsible for What" list on pages 58–60 to divide chores among family members.

More ideas to consider for house rules:
- Put away what you take out.
- Use good manners with family members as well as guests.
- If you fix a snack in the kitchen, clean up after yourself. Rinse your dirty dishes and put them in the dishwasher.
- Everyone is responsible for his or her own laundry.
- Everyone participates in a once-a-week cleanup of common areas. In addition, each person is responsible for keeping his

or her private space (bedroom, work area) clean according to mutually agreed-upon standards.

- No leaving wet towels or dirty clothes on the bathroom floor. Clean up the tub or shower after yourself.
- Let others know in advance if you need to watch (or record) a certain TV program for work or school. Check with others before you play loud music. If you need to leave a project out overnight in a common area, get approval before you begin.
- Take detailed phone messages for one another.
- In every room, make sure your trash is in the trash can. (No matter how much we love our kids, picking up their used tissues, scraps of paper, food, and garbage is disgusting.)

Remember that your house rules may need to be revised as children grow and circumstances change. When you update the rules, make sure everyone knows about the changes.

WHAT KIDS ONLY LEARN AT HOME: ANSWERS TO SOME OF A MOM'S TOUGHEST QUESTIONS

How Can I Teach My Kids Good Values?

Taking care of our children's physical needs is important, but helping them develop strong character is at least as vital. It is our job as parents to shape the character of our children as they grow, to give them a sense of right and wrong, and to provide them with an inner compass that will guide them through life.

None of us will ever be perfect parents, nor will we raise perfect children. But one thing's for sure: If we aim at nothing, we'll probably hit it.

The following ideas are simple, everyday ways to build positive character qualities in your child.

- *Be intentional.* Set aside some time to make a list of the values you and your spouse want to pass on to your children. Here are some you might consider. Add your own to the list.

honesty	love of learning
kindness	strong work ethic
love	courage
faith	allegiance to country
patience	care for others
self-discipline	helpfulness
loyalty	compassion
leadership	respect
enthusiasm	

- *Applaud your child.* He will be less likely to look for acceptance in the wrong places.
- *Be consistent.* Remember that your child is learning even when you're not aware that you're teaching. Don't forget that one day she will follow your example and not your advice.
- *Supervise your kids' media intake.* Monitor their television-watching and Internet time. (See pages 161–163 for specific ideas.)
- *Keep the flame alive.* Make your marriage an ongoing priority. It's one of the greatest things you can do for your children.
- *Express your hopes.* Talk with your older children about your dreams for them—that they will live by strong values.
- *Build a library.* Start a collection of movies and audiobooks that entertain your kids and teach them strong values at the same time.
- *Don't shield children from consequences.* The decisions we make daily form us into what we will be tomorrow. Small decisions can have big results—for good or for bad.
- *Discuss the downside of compromise.* Make sure your kids know that if they have to do the wrong thing to stay on the team, they are on the wrong team.
- *Help kids choose their companions.* Encourage your children to invite their friends over to your house. This way you can get to know them. If you spot an unhealthy relationship—particularly one in which your child is dominated—talk about this openly.
- *Teach by your own mistakes.* Catch yourself whenever you're inconsiderate or make a mistake. Don't make excuses or try to justify your actions. Admit when you are wrong.
- *Recognize acts of kindness.* Whenever you are with your child and you observe someone being considerate to another, point it out. Always praise your child's acts of kindness.
- *Teach respect for authority.* Daily events offer many occasions for this, but children need to learn it from your example. Don't belittle their teachers or coaches. Remember, more is caught than taught.
- *Honor heroic behavior.* Point out instances in the news and everyday life in which people have been heroic.
- *Teach good manners.* Explain that good manners are a way we show respect for other people.
- *Offer unseen support.* Pray with and for your children.

How Can I Teach My Kids to Tell the Truth?

- If your child tells a lie, don't take this lightly. Lying was one of the "automatic discipline" behaviors at our house when the boys were growing up.
- When you catch your child in a lie, make sure she knows that you don't approve of what she did but you still approve of her.
- If your child catches you in a lie, acknowledge it. No excuses. If you are a truthful person, your children will be more likely to be truthful.
- Never instruct your child to lie for you. If someone you do not want to talk to calls you at home and your child answers the phone, don't ask him to say, "Mom isn't here." If you don't want to accept the call, simply have the child take the caller's number and explain that you will call back later.
- Praise your children for being courageous when they tell the truth even when they know they'll get in trouble.
- Make sure you call a spade a spade and a lie a lie. It's okay to encourage your children's ability to tell imaginative stories. Just make sure you also reinforce the difference between lying and writing or telling a story.
- Half-truths aren't really the truth. You can make a family "game" of discovering half-truths. Have each person think of an imaginary situation in which he or she might be tempted to tell only half the truth. For example, "I finished my homework—but only after I talked on the phone for an hour with my friend."
- Don't make promises to your child you are not willing or able to keep; don't make threats you are not willing to enforce. Your children need to know that telling the truth applies to parents, too.
- When playing board games or card games with your children, talk about the importance of playing fairly and telling the truth—even when playing a game.
- When you buy a house or borrow money to buy a car, let your children go with you to the bank. Explain to them the importance of signing a contract—that you are promising, or "telling the truth," that you will fulfill certain obligations.
- Do your own truth-in-advertising review. Have family members bring an advertisement clipped from a magazine or newspaper to a family group time. Look at each ad to discover how the truth is being stretched or manipulated. What's the real message of the ad? That we'll be happy, healthy, wise, loved, and pretty if we buy Product X?

- Search out books, movies, and music for your child regarding telling the truth. One sure classic is almost any version of "The Boy Who Cried Wolf." Younger children will enjoy *The Berenstain Bears and the Truth.*

How Do I Get My Kids to Obey?

It's frustrating to walk into the house and almost trip over the kids' coats, hats, gloves, and wet boots that they shed on the spot, when that very morning you had told them to take off their boots on the entryway rug and put away their winter gear before getting an after-school snack. I mean, how hard can that be? Not real hard, so it's important to think through the reason it didn't happen.

There are several possible reasons why children misbehave, ignore our authority, or do not cooperate or follow through on something we asked them to do. And each calls for an appropriate, fair response.

They didn't understand. Sometimes a child simply does not know he or she did something wrong. This can stem from either our failure to communicate or the child's inability to comprehend. If this is the case, the child needs clarification of the issue—not punishment. Especially with a young child, a fair response to disobedience is to ask, "Did you understand you were not supposed to . . . ?"

They didn't remember. Sometimes children forget because they don't take us seriously, but we need to recognize and respond fairly to honest memory lapses. This is a constant problem with younger children. Sometimes it helps to give a child a reminder and a warning concerning the consequences of regular forgetfulness: If she forgets to take her lunch to school, she may have to borrow lunch money from the school office and pay it back herself. Some kids, because of special learning styles, have difficulty remembering a series of instructions. Rather than telling them what you want them to do, you might write it down or demonstrate the action steps. Some children retain information better this way.

They are not capable. Sometimes children are physically, mentally, or emotionally incapable of following the rules. Many parents have unrealistic expectations of younger children. Milk will be spilled, not because a five-year-old is being careless, but because his hands are small and uncoordinated. Before reacting harshly to apparent misbehavior, stop and ask yourself if your expectations are appropriate to the child's capability to respond. It's not fair to ask children to behave beyond their years.

They don't trust us. A vast difference can exist between a child's perspective and a parent's perspective of a problem. For example, I'll never forget the day I was getting madder by the minute because I thought our oldest son was just being stubborn about a little splinter in his finger. When my husband and I sat him up on the bathroom counter, holding both of his legs and hands, and said, "Sit still. This won't hurt," his crying escalated to screaming and his wiggling to writhing. Then we realized that having a splinter removed with a needle was as traumatic to a young child as major surgery without anesthesia would be to either of us. He didn't know that he would feel better once the splinter was out. Our son had no basis from which to trust us, because instead of listening to his fears, we had told him he was making a mountain out of a molehill. Sometimes molehills are mountains from a child's perspective.

They simply want their own way. Much misbehavior and failure to comply comes down to a battle of wills. When a child thinks, *I'm going to do what I want to do when I want to do it*—whether the child is 6 or 16—fair and appropriate discipline is the only answer.

Discipline is much more than the ability to send a child to a corner for a time-out, skillfully wield a wooden spoon, or take away the car keys. The goal of all discipline is to change the way a child thinks so he can, in turn, change his own behavior and become a self-disciplined person.

Raising children requires a savvy understanding of the unique forms of discipline and when each is the most effective to call forth strong character and choices. You will use each of these at different times in your child's life.

- Instructive discipline: explaining the acts and attitudes that we, the parents, have decided are not acceptable
- Modeling discipline: exhibiting the behavior we want our children to practice
- Corrective discipline: rebuking bad behavior in order to call on the child's character to change
- Reward discipline: praising a child for things he or she does right
- Punitive discipline: denying privileges to demonstrate the consequences of unwise choices

How Can I Teach My Children to Manage Their Anger?

Part of being human is getting angry, sometimes for good reason. But teaching our children how to express anger in healthy ways, as well as

---

☆
SMART MOVE

Teaching respect for parental authority begins early. A two-year-old, if undisciplined, will become a disrespectful, surly six-year-old. If left untamed, that child will become a scornful teenager. Remember, when you must inflict a little pain in the short run to teach your kids respect for authority, you are paving the way for your child to be successful in the long run.

how to deal with their own faults—to ask for and receive forgiveness from themselves and others—is perhaps one of the biggest gifts we can give them. Living in a family means learning to put the feelings of others before our own. Our responsibility is to teach and show by example what to do with uncomfortable feelings such as anger. This means that Mom and Dad exhibit self-control even though they feel like slamming a door, throwing something breakable, or hitting someone. Here are some tips for teaching children how to manage this powerful emotion.

- Decide how you will and will not express anger in your family. For example: You will never go to bed angry at each other. You will settle disputes as soon as possible. You will not hit each other, no matter what. (Let your kids help in setting the guidelines.)
- Create a safe place to discuss past offenses family members are still angry about. Set aside regular times for family meetings to discern ongoing problems so resentments won't build up. Sit down and talk about these things honestly. Make sure everyone has an opportunity to add to the agenda.
- If expressing anger physically is typical in your family, remember that a home that condones violence is the breeding ground for loneliness and depression in children. Seek counsel from a pastor or family therapist if you need help.
- Be aware that viewing violence on TV and in movies increases aggressiveness, instills fear of becoming a victim, promotes indifference to victims of violence, and stimulates the appetite for more violence. Decide what you will allow your children to watch, and stick to your decision. Make sure they turn on the TV to see a specific show, not just to see what's on.
- Physical exercise is a good way to relieve angry feelings. Send yourself or your angry child on a walk around the block a few times until tempers subside.
- All of us lose our tempers at times. When this happens, ask forgiveness and move on. Don't wallow in guilt. Don't abdicate your responsibility just because you make mistakes periodically. Ask forgiveness, and give it.
- Identify the consistent conflicts in your home that cause tempers to flair: who didn't do what they said they would do, how many minutes someone gets to play a video game, how much time is spent on the computer or telephone, etc. Add specific issues to your house rules that map out simple guidelines of fairness.
- Coach your child's baseball, soccer, or other sports team. This

is a great opportunity to teach that good losers are the winners and that bad winners are the losers.

- Remember that there are always two sides to every issue. When you're called upon to referee an argument between your children, be sure to get all the facts.
- Let your children see you deal with anger and frustration in a positive way. It is unreasonable to expect your children to heed your advice and ignore your example.

How Can I Pass on My Faith to My Children?

- Live out what you tell your children you believe. The adage is true: More is caught than taught.
- Create an atmosphere in which your kids can openly ask questions and work through their beliefs. Honest wonderings, and even honest doubts, deserve straightforward discussions and answers.
- Become comfortable with your own faith. Talk about other religions with your children and compare them with your own beliefs.
- As a family, start your day at the breakfast table reminding your children of God's presence. At our house, we read a chapter from the book of Proverbs, which teaches wise living, every morning before school, then said a prayer for our day.
- Sit near the front of your place of worship so your children can see what's happening and feel more involved in the worship service.
- Sing hymns as you put your children to bed at night.
- Purchase a children's version of the Bible for your children.
- Encourage your children to get involved in a church youth group or Bible study. Peers with like values can encourage each other to live up to high standards.
- Remind older children getting ready to leave for college that their beliefs about God may be questioned and even ridiculed. Make sure they are grounded in what is true and are ready to defend their faith.
- See to it that your own spiritual life is growing so you can be a source of strength and wisdom for your children.
- Begin a prayer journal for your children. Date your prayers, your requests, and the answers you observe.

How Can I Encourage My Kids to Eat Right and Be Active?

One way to take care of your children's bodies is to establish healthy patterns. As a bonus, when you practice what you preach,

---

FROM THE HEART

Home is the spiritual forming ground for our children. It is where we initiate the moral standard bearing, the spiritual hunger, and the legacy of love we hope our children will choose to emulate. Like all worthy pursuits, teaching our children about faith and spirituality can and should be kid friendly: accessible, interesting, and developed at their own speed.

you, too, will be healthier! Set nutritional and physical fitness goals for your family. Meet together and decide on a healthy eating plan and an exercise program that fit your family's schedule and ability levels. Here are some other ideas:

- Ask your favorite fast-food restaurants for calorie and food content information. Create a multiple-choice quiz about the calorie counts of different favorite items. Your children may be surprised to learn that fries, a chocolate shake, and a large cheeseburger have 1,310 calories.
- Talk with your kids about nutrition and healthy eating. The U.S. Department of Agriculture offers some helpful materials on the food pyramid (a visual tool to help your kids quickly identify the major food groups and how many servings of each they need every day). Go to http://www.mypyramid.gov.
- Schedule a family sports night once a month or more often. Try different sports, such as basketball, bowling, racquetball, skating, or tennis.
- Hold a family crunch contest. Record how many sit-ups each family member can do at the beginning of the summer. Do sit-ups three times a week, then after a month hold another contest to see how much each person has improved.
- Go on regular bike rides. Map your route before you leave, choosing new and interesting destinations every week.
- Incorporate calisthenics into family cleanup time. Do lunges, fast-paced walking, and stretches while completing regular household duties.
- Enroll in a family recreational program at your local YMCA or parks and recreation department.
- Develop a family workout schedule. Here is a sample plan: Do 20 minutes of calisthenics or other strength-building exercises on Mondays. Do 30 minutes of aerobic activities like running, swimming, or walking on Wednesdays. Do fun recreational sports such as biking, hiking, or skating for one hour on Fridays.
- Invest in an exercise DVD and work out with your kids.
- Become a family of water drinkers. You lose the equivalent of 10 cups of water from everyday living. And you replace only about four through eating. Hidden dehydration robs you of energy and makes you feel lethargic. Drink water all day, every day.
- Take vitamins. Ask your pediatrician what's right for your kids, and at the very least, take a multivitamin yourself. Talk to your doctor about what your own body needs.

- If you live a mile or less from school, consider walking as much as possible. You'll burn calories and conserve fuel. Walks to school offer an excellent opportunity for setting goals and expectations for the day. Walks home give children special time to tell you about their day.

How Can I Encourage My Parents to Get Involved with My Kids?

Grandparents are more than those always-friendly faces at the window when your family arrives for a visit. They can also be an important part of the glue that helps hold a family together with support, love, and counsel.

Even if your parents live hours away from you, they can still be a vital presence in your children's lives. Here are some ways to build strong and loving relationships between grandparents and kids.

- Make sure you have a good photo of the grandparents placed where even the youngest child can see it regularly.
- Keep grandparents posted on what the kids are reading. They may want to read some of the books themselves so they can discuss them via phone, visit, or e-mail.
- Have grandparents record themselves reading books for your young children. Kids will learn to recognize those voices.
- Arrange a phone conversation at a regular time monthly or weekly. Put even the youngest child on the phone with grandparents. Even if she can't talk yet, she can become familiar with their voices and spread a little toddler charm to relatives far away.
- Have the kids "visit" grandparents often via e-mail. By the time your child is four or five, he will likely be learning and playing games on a computer. Once a child is able to read, there is no better instant, economical way for him to keep in touch.
- Consider having grandparents and older kids write a story: Each one writes a paragraph and mails or e-mails it to the other to work on.
- Make grandparents aware of your kids' special dates: birthdays, holidays, school programs, and extracurricular activities. That way they can call or send cards to mark those moments.
- Suggest the idea of taking up a hobby together—perhaps gardening, photography, or scrapbooking. Grandparents and kids can exchange seeds, photos, and memorabilia.

FUN FOR KIDS

Encourage grandparents to research and record your family tree. See www.rootsweb.com for ideas and instructions on how to do this.

- Arrange a win-win situation: Ask willing grandparents to babysit. They get grandkid time, and you get a much-needed break.

Before you take your kids to visit grandparents, send their preferences in an e-mail or letter. List what cereals, lunch foods, beverages, and snacks they like, as well as what their bedtimes and usual wake-up times are. What kind of pillows do they like? What do you allow them to watch on television? What would they like to do for fun?

- Suggest that a grandparent take a grandchild to visit a place he's studying in school.
- Holidays can be too busy and stressful to allow for quality time with the grandparents. Invite them to attend an event with your family that's less showy but still important to a grandchild: a school play, a children's choir concert, a midweek soccer game.
- Have the kids teach grandparents favorite games when they're together. They'll have an automatic icebreaker and tradition for visits.

Adopting grandparents

If your parents are deceased, ask an older couple with whom you share rapport and like values to become your child's surrogate grandparents. Or if the idea of grandparents is a negative concept to you because of abuse, desertion, or other forms of cruelty, ask an older couple from your place of worship or neighborhood to fill the void.

Do Good Manners Really Matter?

Good manners do more than make children pleasant to have around; they build confidence in your kids as they face new social situations. As you begin teaching, remember to avoid nagging—be gentle and consistent instead. And don't forget to affirm kids whenever they get it right!

Mealtime manners

Remind kids to:

- Sit up straight.
- Be quiet: Don't drag their chairs across the floor or bang silverware against their plates.
- Keep their napkins in their laps, and don't forget to use them.
- Keep chair legs on the floor.
- Pass condiments around, not across, the table.

- Don't start eating until everyone has been served.
- Ask the person closest to them to "please pass" whatever item they need. Thank him or her for doing so.
- Take small portions. Help themselves to seconds after everyone has been served.
- Take what they're offered. If they don't like something, politely say, "No, thank you" or take a very small portion.
- Eat slowly. Put down their spoon or fork between bites.
- Chew with their mouths closed.
- Talk only after they've swallowed their food.
- Take small bites.
- Swallow food before taking a drink.
- If food is stuck in their teeth, remove it privately after the meal.
- Keep elbows and arms off the table.
- Ask to be excused when the meal is over.

Relationship manners
- If your child is rude to you, expect a sincere apology.
- If a disrespectful child visits your home, use the occasion to discuss proper manners with your own children after the guest leaves.
- Practice good introduction manners: Teach your kids to stand and shake hands with adults when meeting them for the first time.
- Model saying, "Excuse me?" when you don't hear what someone says.
- Make sure your children arrive on time to their activities— start a lifelong habit! Show them how to call a host if lateness is unavoidable.
- Teach your child to be sensitive to the loner at a party, to invite him or her to participate or to talk.
- Instruct your children to offer kitchen help, to keep their belongings organized, and to hang up wet towels when visiting another child's home.
- Be sure your children say thank you after visiting someone.
- If the visit was special or lasted longer than a night, work with your children on a thank-you note to mail to the hosts.

How Do I Keep the TV and Internet from Monopolizing My Family's Life?
TV and kids
Television, if used properly, can be a useful learning tool. When viewed in moderation with guidance from watchful parents, TV

☆
SMART MOVE

Establish a rule that children can't play with or wear a new gift until the thank-you note has been written.

can help kids become critical thinkers. Make the most of television in your home by heeding these tips:

- Do not allow children to have TVs in their bedrooms. This promotes isolation from the rest of the family.
- Set a limit on viewing per week. Educators suggest a maximum of 10 hours weekly.
- Help children become aware of misleading special effects used on TV.
- Don't channel surf; select specific programs from the TV schedule each week.
- Encourage kids to watch shows that have positive role models and teach them cooperation, interaction, and appreciation of other cultures.
- Teach children that aggression is not the way to solve conflict.
- Keep the TV off during dinnertime and homework time.
- Encourage kids to think about and even question what they're watching rather than just taking it in.
- Whenever possible, preview the programs your kids want to watch. Approve the ones you think are suitable.
- Don't let them watch something just because "everybody else gets to." Stick to your family's values and what you've decided is good for your children.
- Whenever possible, watch programs with your children, then discuss some of the following questions:

  How would you rate this show on a scale from one to ten?
  What was the program's message?
  Could you identify with any of the characters?
  Did you feel that this program portrayed life as it really is?
  What would you have done to help any of the characters?
  Was there anything in the show you did not agree with?
  What in the show uplifted you or inspired you to be a
      better person?
  Was this program worth the time you spent watching it?

Internet safety

As responsible parents, we would never knowingly allow our children to communicate with a deviant. Yet if we allow our children unsupervised access to the Internet, we run the risk of this very thing happening. Here's how you can help protect your children.

- Restrict Internet access to a computer in the family room or

---

GOOD TO KNOW

The American Academy of Pediatrics recommends that children under two watch no television at all.

SMART MOVE

Initiate a family practice to "fast" from TV at certain times. You might even join the thousands of other families who participate in National TV-Turnoff Week, which is held each spring. See http://www.tvturnoff.org.

some other common area where you can easily monitor your kids' online activities.

- Invite your child to help you become more computer literate. Learn about the services your child uses.
- Consider subscribing to an Internet filter to block out objectionable material.
- Carefully monitor your kids' involvement with chat rooms and social networking sites like myspace.com. Pedophiles often use both as a means to find victims.
- If your child receives a suggestive, obscene, belligerent, or threatening e-mail, do not allow him or her to respond to it. Instead, forward a copy of such messages to your Internet service provider.
- Tell your children not to give out any personal information such as your address, telephone number, work number, or their school name over the Internet.
- Monitor your credit-card bill. Many pornographic Internet sites require credit-card payments in order to gain access. Consider using an online service that has special child accounts with restricted access to chat rooms and the Internet.
- If you suspect a family member has a problem with pornography, visit http://www.troubledwith.com. This site offers prevention tips and support for parents.

Do I Really Have to Talk with My Kids about Sex?

Messages about sex are everywhere, and one thing's for sure: If we don't talk to our children about sex, they will get the information on their own from the media or their peers—and it could be faulty, even harmful, information. It is parents' responsibility to give kids accurate, practical information. I'm not talking about scheduling one night to have a big-deal sex education talk with your child in hopes that he'll listen. This is not a "Whew, I got that out of the way" issue. Here are ideas for passing on a healthy view of sex to your children.

- Be positive and honest. Tell your children what you believe God's intentions are for sex. Realize that your teens probably will not listen to your opinions if you seem to be judging their friends or teachers. Know the facts and present them in love. Remind your children of your lifetime commitment to their health, security, and well-being.
- Be a role model. Practice what you preach. If you tell your children to live one way but you clearly behave in another

FUN FOR KIDS

Use your computer as a positive parenting tool by tackling computer projects with your child:

- Research types of pets you're considering, or vacation spots.
- Find directions for a new hobby, such as origami or coin collecting.
- Learn to save photos and set up files for viewing.
- Create a newsletter about your family and send it to extended family.
- Learn about the historical significance of a place to which you're traveling.
- Search for coupons from local businesses and restaurants that you can print and use.
- Read about emergency preparedness for your home, then gather supplies.
- Find kid-friendly recipes and start a file of favorites.

way, the message they will get is that you don't really believe what you're telling them is important.

- Be accessible and approachable. What they ask may shock you at times, but just be thankful they're asking and are willing to talk to you.
- Make good information available. Have appropriate books, movies, and pamphlets around the house for your children to use when they have questions. Remember, the less you push, the more likely they are to take a look.
- Find out about the sex education program at your children's school. Many schools offer informational meetings before beginning instruction. If not, ask an administrator or teacher about the curriculum. What you discover might surprise you, and it will also give you a chance to talk with your kids about your own values and opinions. Allow your children to express their opinions as well. Listening is a good way to get your children to open up.
- Remember that sex is good and hormones are real. Curiosity about sex will not go away just because you never discuss the subject. In fact, avoiding the subject can make sex seem even more exciting. Reinforce your values. Talk about what you believe. Tell your children you are proud when they make mature, healthy decisions.
- Trust them. Tell your children that you intend to trust them. Praise them when they earn that trust. When they make mistakes (and they will), talk about how they can correct these mistakes and win back your trust. Don't leave them feeling hopeless.

How Can I Help My Children through the Teen Years?

Teach them right and wrong. Don't confuse kids with the notion that there are no moral absolutes or decide to let them discover right from wrong on their own. The price they pay for this knowledge will be too high.

Don't let anything interrupt your love. If you want your teenagers to embrace your values, make sure they know you value them. Your unconditional commitment to them is the anchor that will give them stability through the stormy teen years. Your children will make mistakes and disappoint you. Make sure they never doubt your love and acceptance, even when they fail. Make sure they want to please you because you love them, not to try to ensure your love.

Speak their love language. As the older and hopefully wiser part of the parent-teen relationship, take responsibility for the communication process. Many parents are puzzled to discover that their teens don't know how much they are loved. Many times this is because parents are "speaking" a love language that their children don't understand. Take time to discover what kinds of behavior on your part get through to your teen and fill his or her emotional tank with a sense of well-being. (Recommended reading: *The Five Love Languages of Teenagers* by Gary Chapman.)

Give them freedom—gradually. Parents make a huge mistake by adopting one of two extremes: either refusing to let teens make choices on their own or giving them absolute freedom. Wise parents begin early to teach their children to make age-appropriate choices based on the following principle: Freedom brings responsibility and responsibility brings freedom. As teens show they can handle responsibility, wise parents gradually release them to make more and more choices on their own. And when they fail—which they will—certain choices need to be withdrawn temporarily to teach them that choices have consequences and that privileges can be restored when they've demonstrated responsibility.

Trust your teen, but keep your eyes and ears open. Trust is a powerful relational connector and breeds trustworthiness. Trust them until they prove untrustworthy. Then teach them how to rebuild trust. Being vigilant concerning the threats to your children is not the same as mistrust. As good as your teen may be, don't bury your head in the sand. There are powerful influences that can overpower the best kids before they realize how they've been influenced. Listen to your children's music. Ask your kids if they understand the lyrics to their favorite songs. Research shows that when our minds receive a message six times, it becomes indelibly etched there. Don't think that lyrics with messages about casual sex, rebellion, and suicide are not affecting your child's decisions. Be vigilant about your teenagers' friends. If they ask to spend time with someone whose values and habits are questionable, let them have the friend over to your house. If you see that the relationship would not be a healthy one for your child and that your child may not be strong enough to stand up to the friend, talk about this openly.

Don't shelter teens from consequences. The second most powerful "curse" parents can inflict—after requiring that children earn their love—is failing to let teens know that choices have consequences. They need to know that they can't recreate the world to

GOOD TO KNOW

The higher adolescents' perception is of their mother's expertise and trustworthiness, the more frequently they talk with their mother about the social and moral consequences of being sexually active, according to an article in the *Journal of Marriage and Family*.

GOOD TO KNOW

The more often teenagers have dinner with their parents, the less likely they are to smoke, drink, or use illegal drugs. In fact, compared with teens who have frequent family dinners, those who have dinner with their families only two nights per week or less are at double the risk of substance abuse, according to a study by Columbia University.

their liking. They must accept the world as it is. Experience is the best teacher, so let them experience failure while you're around to pick them up and help them get back on their feet.

Don't forget who's the parent. Kids don't need a best friend nearly as much as they need a parent. Don't be afraid of saying, "No!" Parents who give in to fear of their teen's anger or rejection tend to be needy people who use their children for their own sense of emotional well-being. Set limits and stick to them unless you realize they were unreasonable to begin with. It's important for parents to talk to teenagers about behavioral guidelines and expectations and the consequences of not adhering to the standards you and your spouse agree upon. Be specific about what is and isn't acceptable behavior. Make it a priority to schedule time to ask your children to describe the personal guidelines they feel they should set for themselves as they begin to go out on their own more frequently without your supervision.

Make them welcome. Your teen is an important member of the family who has changing needs, and you need to make accommodations for those needs and desires. Create a warm and welcoming atmosphere in your home so your teenagers and their friends will want to hang out there. They'll have a safe, fun place to go, and you'll know what they're doing. Keep plenty of soda and snacks on hand, and be willing to put up with some mess and some louder-than-pleasant music.

Ask forgiveness when you make a serious mistake. Teens have a heightened sense of fair play. As a parent, you will make mistakes. You will not always be the model of maturity, wisdom, and love that your children need. Hiding an offense or making excuses only heightens the problem. Better to come right out with it, confess your shortcomings, and ask forgiveness for the wrong done. You'll find that kids want honest parents rather than perfect parents. You'll also strengthen the bond between you and your teen rather than widening the gap. If your child knows that you love him or her, you discover that this love covers a multitude of parental sins.

Keep teenagers a part of family life. It's natural and healthy for teens to begin to express their independence as budding adults, but there are healthy limits that you need to set. Teenagers have a natural tendency to think the world revolves around them, their needs, and their friends. This I'm-the-center-of-the-universe thinking must be interrupted for the emotional health of the child, for his or her future relationships, and for sanity in the family. Here are some suggestions.

- Put them to work. As busy as their world might be, teens need to know that you expect them to be contributing members of the family team. Studies show that kids who don't have chores to do around the house don't feel valued.
- Interrupt their demand to spend time continually with their friends with regular family trips or outings. Make sure it's fun for them.

Never let them push you away. As cocky, arrogant, and hostile as teens can sometimes be, they are haunted by a soul-deep question of insecurity: "Do you love me?" Rather than seek to earn love, at times teens will "test" for it by trying to push you away. Make sure you answer their do-you-love-me questions with "Yes!" by staying engaged. As frustrating as it may be at times and as tempting as it may be to drop to their level of emotional immaturity, don't forget your responsibility to keep communicating—hopefully at a calm level.

Create learning opportunities for them to grow physically, emotionally, socially, and spiritually. Your example is your children's most important teacher in life.

- Take them to work with you and let them see how you handle life.
- Send your child to a good summer camp. It helps tremendously for kids to learn how to make wise decisions from older peers they admire—as well as from their parents, of course. At camp kids can learn flexibility, independence, and responsibility. They can also enhance their athletic and social skills, develop self-discipline, and grow in character. If your church doesn't promote a good summer youth camp, visit http://www.cciusa.org for a list of camps by region.
- Help your teenagers start a business or get a job. Brainstorm about their talents and resources, then think of a need they could meet. Help them write a good résumé. Teach them the importance of looking people in the eye and shaking hands firmly when being interviewed.

Support their dreams. Let your teenagers know you're on their team. Show an interest in their friends, schoolwork, and activities. Discuss your teenagers' strengths and abilities, and help them dream grand dreams about what they can achieve. Show your teens you care by treating their schoolwork and desks as you would your own business. Make sure they have plenty of supplies, good lighting, and a pleasant atmosphere in their "offices." Work with teens to establish some guidelines about whether music can be played, snacks can be eaten, etc., while they are studying.

Help teens make wise decisions. Although most teens think they are smarter than their parents, they don't have the experience and wisdom to make all their own decisions or to face life's problems alone. They still need discipline and love. And most of all, they need to be encouraged to begin to think and behave responsibly on an adult level.

As children enter the teenage years, hopefully they have internalized a code of ethics you have been teaching them and drawn their moral boundaries. Whether you feel their standards are firmly anchored or still a little fuzzy, it's a good idea to talk about this important issue. Make it a priority to schedule some time to ask your children to describe the personal guidelines they feel they should set for themselves as they begin to go out on their own more frequently without your supervision. If they don't know how to verbalize their answers, you can help them out by presenting some scenarios in which they could likely find themselves faced with hard decisions. For example, ask how they would respond in the following situations.

- You learn that a friend is using or selling drugs.
- You find out that many students at your school think it's no big deal to cheat on tests.
- You are date raped.
- You are asked to do something "just for fun" that you know is against the law.
- You are at a party that's getting out of hand. Kids are drinking, and you begin to question the safety of the people at the party, including yourself.
- You are offered the opportunity to make money doing something that goes against your conscience.
- You have the opportunity to get a false ID.
- You learn a simple way to sneak in and out of a friend's house.
- A friend starts talking about suicide.

When your growing child faces a tough choice, the fact that he's thought through the situation beforehand doesn't guarantee a better response, but it will make it easier for him to make a wise decision. And remember, you know your child better than anyone else— sometimes even better than he knows himself. Every human has blind spots—the black holes of life we get sucked into because of our personalities, natural tendencies, or upbringing. Maybe you've

TEEN/PARENT CONTRACT

It's important for parents to talk to teenagers about behavioral guidelines and expectations, and the consequences of not adhering to the standards you and your spouse agree upon. Be specific about what is and isn't acceptable behavior. A good way to do this is with a contract between you and your son or daughter. You and your child should sign and date the contract so that if an infringement occurs, he or she won't be able to use "I didn't know I wasn't supposed to do that" as an excuse.

Here are some sample points you might include in your contract.

▶ My opinion matters a lot, but this is not a democracy, so my parents have the final say.

▶ I will express my freedom responsibly. I will ask permission when I'm not sure what my parents would want me to do.

▶ Every member of my family is valuable, so I will treat each person and any guest in my home with respect and thoughtfulness.

▶ I will also not abuse family members physically or verbally—including rudeness, swearing, or name-calling.

▶ I will treat my body and anyone else's with deep respect. No drugs, cigarettes, or alcohol are allowed. No pornography or sexual contact between unmarried persons is allowed.

▶ Unless I have previously discussed an exception, I will be home by _____ on weeknights and by _____ on Friday and Saturday nights and let Mom or Dad know where I am at all times.

▶ I agree to be truthful in all things.

▶ I understand that having belongings is a privilege not a right, so I will take care of my possessions and respect others' property as well. I will ask before borrowing, knock before entering, and treat someone else's possessions as I would my own.

▶ I will exercise responsibility with my time. Responsibilities come before privileges, so I will get homework and chores done before television, computer time, or goofing-off time.

GOOD TO KNOW

New parents typically lose between 400 and 750 hours of sleep during baby's first year. See http://www.abc.net.au/science/sleep/facts.htm.

never thought about it in this way, but you've probably noticed some of your child's black-hole tendencies from a very young age.

Talk openly with your teen about behavioral guidelines and expectations, and the consequences of not adhering to the standards you and your spouse agree upon. Be specific about what is and isn't acceptable behavior. A good way to do this is with a contract between you and your son or daughter. You and your child should sign and date the contract so that if an infringement occurs, he or she won't be able to use "I didn't know I wasn't supposed to do that" as an excuse.

See the sample contract on page 169.

DEALING WITH THE EVERYDAY— FROM FAMILY MILESTONES TO THE MUNDANE

Preparing for Baby

The day a baby arrives is a joyous one. Grandparents, extended family, and friends will likely want to visit and "help." Though well-intentioned, all these people can actually create more work. Siblings are excited about their new brother or sister but may feel ignored in all the hoopla. Here are tips for sharing the joy without getting a headache—and for smoothing the adjustment period for siblings.

Before the birth

- Purchase a three-ring binder and pocket dividers to organize the mounds of information surrounding the birth: records, doctor's information, emergency numbers, and tips and articles to read when you find a few spare minutes.
- Be gracious but clear before the birth about which family or friends you want in the delivery room, the waiting room, and at home when you return with the baby.
- Create a list of tasks people can do when they ask if they can help. This way you can take them up on their offers in practical ways once the baby is born. For those eager to help, in addition to bringing in meals, let them do laundry, run errands, and chauffeur older kids to their various commitments. They could also babysit one night a week so you and your husband can go out.

Helping siblings cope before the birth

- Have a family meeting to announce this blessing. Consider the ages of your children—a kindergartner might be able to handle news of a new baby sooner than a teenager would.

If anyone reacts negatively, don't get defensive—be honest about your own apprehensions.

- Present the change in a positive light, even if you have mixed feelings yourself. Don't say, "I don't know how we can fit another person into our already-crowded house and schedule." Do say, "It's going to be exciting to all work together to fit the baby into our family."
- Talk about the change often. Bring it up in daily conversation. Start a countdown on the calendar. Be aware that acting out is often kids' way of expressing their insecurities—talk with them. Let them know how much you love them and what great big brothers or sisters they will be.

After the birth

- In the first few weeks after the baby arrives, be sure to give yourself and your family plenty of space to adapt to a new schedule—and a new personality in the house.
- Avoid drop-ins when you or your baby is sleeping by hanging a friendly "Do not disturb—family napping" sign on the front door.
- Without guilt, take the personal time you need to bond with your child.

Helping siblings cope after the birth

- In the first few days at home, explain to young children that you need to rest. In age-appropriate ways, tell them that having a baby makes big changes in your body but that you'll soon be back to your old self.
- Show some extra affection to the baby's siblings. Try to spend a few minutes alone with each child each day. Ask about each one's day, or read a favorite book together. Let them talk about their concerns.
- Give siblings time to adjust. No matter how much you've prepared them, the reality takes time to sink in.

Babysitting Co-ops

By forming a co-op with other busy parents, you'll be able to handle those middle-of-the-day appointments as well as evenings out more easily. And since no money changes hands, it's always affordable!

Why they work

- Children stay with friends who are parents themselves. You can rest easy, knowing that your child is with experienced, loving adults.

☆
SMART MOVE

After maternity leave, consider returning to work at the end of the week. Starting on Wednesday or Thursday will give you enough time to see how you will have to adjust your schedule without causing too much stress. You may also wish to consider working partial weeks for the first month to help you and your baby ease back into your work schedule.

Work with your child-care or day-care provider to make your transition back to work as smooth as possible. Consider doing a "test run" where you arrange child care for a half day only. Time how long it takes for you to get yourself and your baby ready and out the door, then add in plenty of buffer.

- Your kids see these outings as a treat: Instead of being "left behind" by Mom and Dad, they get to play with other kids—and other kids' toys.
- Because you exchange babysitting, you need never feel guilty about asking someone to sit. Everyone benefits, so everyone gladly contributes.

How to start a babysitting co-op

- Make a list of local, like-minded families who might be interested.
- Have a meeting to organize prospective participants to discuss membership requirements, whether you'll elect officers, the size of the co-op, how often you will meet, dues for supplies, general guidelines for managing emergencies, what to do in case of a child's sudden illness, how to handle discipline issues, how to deal with late pickups, and how members will be added or eliminated.
- Set up your exchange system. Use tickets or points. For example, "charge" one ticket or point (or more) for babysitting one child per hour. If you use points, you'll need a secretary to record points accrued and spent for each co-op member.
- Arrange for members to rotate the management of secretarial tasks: typing and distributing co-op rules, meeting information, and medical consent forms.
- Set up a personal record-keeping system for each child. This includes every child's food allergies or special medical needs, pediatrician's name and phone number, what hospital you prefer, your insurance information, emergency contacts, and a notarized permission slip for medical attention.

Playgroups

Starting a playgroup (in which moms with similar-aged kids take turns either hosting the entire group of moms and kids or planning activities and supervising just the kids as they play) is a great way to give each other a break. To start a playgroup with moms in your area, schedule a meeting to discuss the following:

- How many children will be in the group. Four kids in the group is optimal for the under-four set, especially if only one parent will be on duty.
- What the schedule will be. Two hours is plenty for toddlers and preschoolers to play in a group. If the moms have chosen

---

to take turns supervising all the kids, you might decide to allow 15 minutes to get settled, 30 minutes of a preplanned craft or activity, 15 minutes for a snack, 45 minutes for outdoor or free play, and 15 minutes of rest while listening to a book or music.

- When the group will meet, and how often. Mornings tend to work best because young children are less tired before lunch and more willing to cooperate with other kids and try new things.
- Where the group will meet. The host's home is typical, but you can also decide to meet at a local playground or community center.
- How you will handle fights, separation anxiety, and other issues.
- Special dietary or activity restrictions or allergies. You might want to create a master list of mom-approved snack foods and activities.
- Safety precautions and how you will handle emergencies.
- Contact information. Make sure you get each mom's address, home phone number, cell phone number, e-mail address, and an additional emergency phone number in case she cannot be reached.
- It's a good idea to put everything in writing and give each mom a copy of the guidelines before the children get together the first time. If you're taking a turn at entertaining all the tots, plan ahead so the supplies and snacks you'll need for hosting are easily accessible.

Child Care

The child-to-caregiver ratio

The National Association for the Education of Young Children recommends the following:

Birth to 2 years: A maximum of 8 children per two caregivers.
2 to 2.5 years: A maximum of 12 children per two caregivers.
2.5 to 3 years: A maximum of 14 children per two caregivers.
3 to 5 years: A maximum of 10 children per two caregivers.

Is your child in good hands?

For many moms, child care is an issue that's sometimes hard to feel good about. If arranging child care is a necessity for your household, talk to other moms in your area and check with local churches for recommendations of quality child-care options. And before visiting a day-care center or home-based day-care provider, familiarize yourself with the state licensure regulations for these places. (Go to the "Family, Home, and Community" section at http://www.usa.gov to find your state's database.) As you interview possible options, keep in mind that a great caregiver will:

- honor your values
- be someone with whom you could be friends
- gladly answer questions about herself
- greet your kids
- show character you'd like your kids to learn
- offer a safe, simple routine
- explain rules in a firm, kid-friendly way
- give special attention when a child is ill or upset
- show and teach respect for people who are different
- encourage a child's good behavior with praise
- obviously like kids and encourage their individuality
- talk to and hold babies
- manage special needs without complaint
- refer to children by the names they prefer (e.g., Randy instead of Randall)
- talk to your children, asking about their day and answering their questions
- teach health habits like washing hands after bathroom visits
- pay more attention to your child than to you
- encourage independence and skill building, such as washing hands and face, and picking up toys
- know when to offer help and when to let the child do for himself
- be alert to your child's needs
- not tolerate children's bullying each other or calling each other names

Signs of a poor caregiver
- raises her voice and use severe punishment: spanking, isolating children, withholding food
- ignores your children
- spends hours in front of the TV or on the phone
- uses negative language, saying "don't" frequently and threatening discipline unnecessarily
- overlooks bullying and bad behavior

Babysitters: Important Information They Must Know

In addition to your contact information and other emergency numbers, your babysitter should know the following:

- guidelines for child's eating and drinking, including foods that are off limits
- nap- or bedtimes, and how to enforce them
- activities your child likes
- things your child is not allowed to do when you're away
- TV limits and acceptable programs
- disciplinary measures
- instructions for using car seats or other equipment
- policies about not opening doors to strangers and how to answer the phone
- guidelines for phone use, TV use, computer use, drinking or smoking, and having visitors
- instructions for pets
- what to do in case of an emergency
- locations of fire and burglar alarms, first-aid supplies, fuse box, flashlights, all entrances and exits
- your address with clear directions to your home, posted in case of an emergency

Medical consent form

Provide a consent form in case your child requires medical attention. The form should include:

- your child's name
- his or her date of birth
- your insurance carrier and policy number
- doctors' names and phone numbers
- vital medical history, such as medications, allergies, and chronic conditions
- this statement: "Any licensed physician, dentist, or hospital may give necessary emergency medical service to my child [your child's name] at the request of the person bearing this consent form."
- both guardians' signatures

Education

Giving your young child a leg up on learning

Acquiring the skills needed to excel in school starts well before your child ever sets foot in a classroom. By involving your toddler or preschooler in simple, creative tasks and fun games designed to

GOOD TO KNOW

If you want to check the background of potential sitters, consider sites such as www.crimecheck.com, www.integctr.com, and www.nannybackgrounds .com.

FamilyManager™

GENERAL INFORMATION FOR BABYSITTERS

Cell Phone _____ Beeper # _____

Destination _____ Destination # _____

Security System Instructions _____

Monitoring #_____Code _____ Password _____

Location of . . .

    Flashlights _____

    Fire Extinguishers _____

    Fuse or Breaker Box _____

    Water Shut-off _____

    U.S. Poison Control Center: 1/800-222-1222 _____

Fire Escape Plan _____

_____

Food/Beverages/Snacks _____

_____

Meal Instructions _____

_____

Medications _____

    Dosage/Times/Instructions _____

_____

House Rules

    Bedtime _____

    Homework _____

    TV/Computer _____

    Friends _____

Animals _____

_____

FamilyManager™

Child's Name_____ Date of Birth _____/_____/_____

Social Security Number _____

Address _____

_____

Child's Regular Physician _____ Phone _____

Address _____

_____

Health Insurance Company _____ Phone _____

Name of Primary Insured _____

Social Security of Primary Insured _____

Policy Number _____ Certificate Number _____

Health Benefit Plan _____ Customer Service Phone _____

I, _____, the parent having legal custody or legal
guardian of the above named child, authorize any of the following adults,

Name _____ Relationship _____

Address _____

Name _____ Relationship _____

Address _____

to consent to any X-ray examination, anesthetic, medical or surgical diagnosis or treatment, and hospital care, to be
rendered to the minor under the general or special supervision and on the advice of any physician or surgeon
licensed to practice, and to consent to any X-ray examination, anesthetic, dental or surgical diagnosis or treatment,
and hospital care, to be rendered to the minor by any dentist licensed to practice.

_____   _____
SIGNATURE OF PARENT OR LEGAL GUARDIAN   DATE

Notarized by: Acknowledged before me on this date: _____

_____
SIGNATURE OF NOTARY

State of: _____   My commission expires: _____

*Check with your physician for any special requirements for your state.

GOOD TO KNOW

The best predictor of children's success as adults is that they began helping with chores by age three or four. The study found that early participation in household chores was deemed more important in adult success than any other factor, including IQ, according to Dr. Marty Rossman at the University of Minnesota.

enhance learning, you'll be giving them one of the greatest gifts: a love of learning.

Reading

- Read to your kids daily. This helps them develop listening and observation skills, and it stimulates the imagination.
- Establish a reading corner with a comfy chair, good reading light, and a basket of books.
- In your collection, include books with story lines they can personally relate to: the addition of a sibling, going on a trip, visiting a doctor or dentist.
- Before reading a new book to young children, tell them the title and ask what they think the story might be about. When you're almost finished reading the book, ask your children to make up an ending to the story.
- Link reading books with television programs. If your child watches a show about birds, check out a book at the library on the same subject and read it together.
- Teach children letters of the alphabet by having them look for all the A's or B's on a magazine page. As the child finds the letter, she can color it with a highlighter pen.
- Make an alphabet book. In a spiral notebook, write each letter of the alphabet on different pages. Look through magazines and help your child find pictures that begin with each letter. Cut out the pictures and paste them in the notebook.
- Make up stories that stimulate your children's imaginations. When you're in the car or around the dinner table, have one family member start a story and each person after add more to the adventure. For example:

> Dad: There once was a dog named Banjo, who lived . . .
> Mom: in a small town in Colorado. He was a medium-size dog . . .
> Child 1: with black and white spots. Everyone loved Banjo because . . .
> Child 2: he had rescued many people who had fallen into snowdrifts that winter. But one afternoon . . .

Life skills

- Teach young children to follow directions. When showing children how to perform a new task or skill, model each part of the job. Then let them participate with you until they can do the task alone. And remember to give instructions one at a time, followed by doing that part of the task.

- When taking children to the bank, bakery, dry cleaner, post office, or service station, tell them about the kinds of work the people do and why their services are needed.
- Talk about sounds with your child: workers repairing the street, a train whistling, dogs barking, a cash register ringing, or birds chirping. Try to mimic the sounds together.
- Young children need to build with blocks, play with clay, put together puzzles, and do simple exercises such as bending, crawling, hopping, stretching, and walking. This helps them develop their large and small motor skills and prepares them to learn tasks that require physical dexterity at school.
- Teach art education on the go. Look for shapes and lines while you're in the car. Highway stripes are straight; rooftops have angles; roads are curved; traffic signals have circles; manholes are also circles.
- Assign your child to be the daily weather reporter. His job is to learn the forecast each day from the newspaper, a local radio or television station, or the Internet and report to the family so you can plan the day's activities. Check the thermometer to see if he was correct about the temperature high for the day. Keep track of the predictions and results on a dry-erase board.

Starting school: diminishing school daze for first timers
Starting school is a major life change for kids. You can make the transition as smooth as possible by visiting the school beforehand, as well as introducing new routines and activities prior to the start of school:

- When you visit the school with your child, show him or her what activities will happen there; go over the names of his or her classmates and teacher; find out where the classroom will be and where the restrooms are located. If possible, get a class list with phone numbers so you can arrange a few playdates with classmates before school starts.
- A week or so before the first day, implement schedule changes in household routines. Get up, get dressed, and eat breakfast as you will when school begins.
- Walk together to the bus stop or school a few times. Review safety rules and any after-school pickup arrangements. Remind your child never to go home with anyone else or get in a car with a stranger. (Don't write your child's name in

large letters on his backpack or schoolbag; a stranger may fool a child into thinking he's a friend by calling the child's name.)

- Make a special day of buying school supplies and a first-day outfit.
- Buy "fast" clothes—shoes with Velcro fasteners, tagless T-shirts, and shirts with ample openings to slip easily over the head. Buttons, snaps, zippers, and shoelaces slow kids down.
- Make sure your child is comfortable with using a public bathroom. Remind your child always to wash his or her hands when finished.
- Have your child practice using a lunch box or carrying a cafeteria tray of food.
- Plan to spend a few extra minutes before dropping off your child on the first day. Be sensitive; even a confident child can get stressed in a new situation.
- Celebrate the moment! Take pictures at home of your child in his or her first-day outfit.

Back to school

Countdown to back to school

Two weeks before

- Plan a special dinner to celebrate the end of summer and start anticipating the new school year. Talk about how school is your children's "career" and is as important as yours. After dinner, pass out paper and pencils, and help your children list individual goals for the school year. Save the lists in a file folder to review at the end of each month. This will remind you to praise your kids for sticking to their goals in certain areas and make needed adjustments to get on track in other areas.
- Schedule a day to purchase school supplies. Pick up extra supplies to keep on hand for homework projects, such as construction paper, colored pencils and markers, folders for reports, and poster board. Set up a designated space where kids can do their homework, and store supplies nearby.
- Shop for school clothes.
- Set up a home base of operation—your Control Central from which you keep track of your family's schedule and other important details—in a central location, like a countertop or a desk in your kitchen. Keep your family calendar, phone messages, and grocery list here, as well as office supplies, phone book, takeout menus, and a trash can.

- Purchase stackable in-boxes—one for each child—and let kids personalize their own. Place them near Control Central, and give instructions for kids to unload school papers and forms from their backpacks and into their in-boxes immediately after school. It's Mom's or Dad's responsibility to look at papers at night and follow through on any necessary actions.

One week before
- Talk with your children about safety. Chart the path your children will take to travel to and from school. Develop a family code word. If an unfamiliar person has to pick up your child at school, the person can use the code to show it's safe to get into the car. This word can also mean "Help" if your child must call you in a frightening situation.
- Purchase an alarm clock for each child. Put it on the opposite side of the room from the bed so each child must get out of bed to turn it off.
- Start putting younger children to bed 10 to 15 minutes earlier each night to reset their biological clocks. Ask older children to begin adjusting their bedtimes and morning routines too.
- Discuss and confirm your morning schedule. Decide how much time each person needs in the morning.
- Assign kids tasks that encourage teamwork and responsibility for smoothly running school days. Make a rotating schedule that allows kids to try various tasks.
- Another child can act as the "town crier" in charge of giving everyone a 10-minute warning each morning—10 minutes before it's time to walk out the door.
- Charge your camera for first-day-of-school photos.

First day of school
- Work the plan you've created over the past two weeks.
- Have a special send-off prayer with your children.
- Take pictures!

Ways to encourage learning away from school
- Encourage children to read for pleasure and always have a book "in progress." Show interest in what they're reading by asking questions about the story and the characters. Offer rewards for reading.
- Promote exploration. If your child asks why an animal behaves a certain way or why stars twinkle, make it a point to research it together on the Internet or at the library.
- Plant a small flower, herb, or vegetable garden together. Use

☆
SMART MOVE

Have a contingency pickup plan in place if your child gets sick at school at a time when you're tied up.

plant catalogs to guide your choices. Read the directions to find out planting and care requirements.

- Appoint your child to be the scorekeeper during a miniature golf game. Ask her to figure the average strokes for each player.
- Provide your children with the opportunity to do creative projects they show interest in, such as drawing, sewing, building models, caring for animals, learning simple geology, or working on mechanical projects.
- Help your child submit pictures, poems, riddles, or stories to children's magazines.
- Keep a good dictionary and thesaurus handy. When your children read a word they don't know or hear an unfamiliar word on TV, teach them to look it up.
- Put old magazines to good use. Give two or more children a list of 25 things to hunt for, such as a boy, a girl, a car, flowers, a flag, or a horse. Have them tear the items out of the magazine. Allow 20 minutes to find all the items. The one who finds the most wins.

Homework hints

Show interest in your children's schoolwork and display papers they're proud of on a bulletin board. Look at their textbooks and ask them what they enjoy learning about the most. Ask which subjects are difficult for them and where they need help. Let them know you struggled with some subjects too.

- Teach kids to make a list of what they need to accomplish each week and then prioritize what they need to do first.
- Help kids guess how long it will take them to finish homework, then let them time themselves. They will begin to learn about time management.
- Help them understand the importance of doing advance work, such as making sure their sports uniforms are clean and getting all equipment together in plenty of time before the game.
- Teach your children to multitask while watching TV. They can clean out their notebooks or backpacks or organize art or school supplies during their favorite shows.
- Model the behavior you want your kids to embrace. If they see you procrastinating about a project you need to tackle, don't expect them to behave differently. Talk about how you can learn together to be better managers of time.
- As they get older, encourage kids to keep their own calendar notebook where they can record important facts and dates.

- Help them break a big task—writing a book report or preparing for the science fair—into smaller segments.
- Create homework incentive programs. Children earn points toward an award by doing homework on the day it is assigned, completing it on time, and having a good attitude.
- Discuss with your children how to do special projects or papers before they start them. Help your children think through the following: What does the teacher want? What items do you need to complete the project? What is available? What other resources need to be checked? Help them make a list of needed steps.
- See what resources are available before starting projects and reports. Your public library often houses special collections on various subjects. It may also carry clippings or memorabilia on local history. Grandparents may have antiques, old books, newspapers, or photographs that could be used for an interesting report. If a child has to write a paper on the judicial system, for instance, arrange for him to interview a lawyer. If you have a hobby, your child might be able to use it as a source for a project.
- Study with your kids. One mom I know enrolled in an algebra refresher course at the local college so she could help her freshman son with his studies.
- Stress the importance of neatness. Teachers are influenced by the way work looks. If your children have poor handwriting, encourage them to take the time necessary to write legibly. Reward them for practicing penmanship at home. When possible, let your children do their work on a computer.
- Talk about the grades your child brings home and what was required to earn them on different assignments.

Test-taking skills

Help your children learn to study effectively for tests. Encourage them to:

- review notes soon after class
- color-code essential information with a highlighter pen in textbooks (if they own them) and highlight class notes to make it easier to review the important points
- ask the teacher what a test will cover if they're unsure about it
- save old tests to use as study guides
- study with several other students to review material before a test

GOOD TO KNOW

Only a quarter of the nation's fourth and eighth graders are performing at or above proficient levels in math, according to the U.S. Department of Education.

SMART MOVE

To help children sleep, experts recommend keeping televisions and computers out of their bedrooms.

- study according to their biological clocks (When is each child most alert—in the early morning or evening?)
- for optimal retention, commit information to memory when they're rested
- learn how to use memory strategies, such as acronyms, key words, linking ideas, and rhyming
- proofread papers before turning them in, and use a dictionary to check for spelling errors if they're not using a computer

Car Pool Guidelines

Part of a Family Manager's job is to make sure kids get to the right place at the right time with the right equipment. If it looks like your chauffeuring duties will be too much for one person to handle this fall, it may be time to start a car pool. These guidelines will get you going.

Gather a group
- Find other parents who might also benefit from a car pool.
- Let your child react to each of the names of car-pool candidates—see if he or she is comfortable with them.

Set ground rules
- Learn about the school's security procedures for kids being dropped off and picked up.
- Make sure drivers have adequate insurance to cover kids in their care.
- Discuss a backup plan for drivers in case of illness.
- Decide whether you want to commit to daily or weekly driving duties.

Get information
- Have parents write down their names, children's names, essential information, addresses, and contact numbers. Make copies and distribute. Keep this information in the car in case of an emergency.

Spell out safety rules
- Urge drivers to carry cell phones but not to talk on them while driving.
- Agree that seat belts should be available and used by all children. Make a policy of not starting the car until everyone

is belted in, and be sure kids under age 12 are not sitting in the front seat (or other locations with an air bag).

- Discuss and make policies on:

  eating and drinking in the car
  keeping doors locked and windows rolled up while car
    is moving
  what to do if no one is home when a child is to be
    dropped off
  disciplining unruly kids

Kids at Home Alone

Knowing that your child is coming home to an empty house after school isn't easy for you or your child. The following tips will help you pave the way for safety and accountability, and let your child know that you care—even when you can't be there.

- Leave sticky notes with words of encouragement and affection in a prominent location. Write out notes on Sunday night and tuck them away, so all you have to do is pull one out on your way out the door in the morning.
- Post a list of snack ideas on the fridge. To keep appliance use to a minimum, suggest only no-cook snacks.
- Discuss and establish home-alone rules. Post agreed-upon rules in an easy-to-see place, so "I forgot I wasn't supposed to do that" won't be an issue. Your rules should cover the following questions:

  Are friends allowed to visit? Must your child ask permis-
    sion first?
  What chores should be tackled each day?
  When should homework be done?
  How much TV and computer time is allowed, and what
    programs are permissible?
  Are your kids allowed to go anywhere after school? Where
    and how will they let you know where they are?

- Talk about how your child should handle the following:

  answering the phone and taking messages
  losing the house key
  staying after school
  missing the bus or car pool
  illness or accidental injury

FUN FOR KIDS

Every week, post brainteasers, riddles, and word puzzles in a central location. The first one to tell Mom the right answer wins. Announce the winner at dinner on Saturday night.

SMART MOVE

If you receive an e-mail that you think is deceptive, forward it to spam@uce.gov.

☆

SMART MOVE

Pick four or five easy dinner menus that you can prepare in less than 30 minutes, and keep the ingredients on hand for those days when after-school activities run late and you don't have time to fix the fajitas you'd planned on.

weather emergencies or fire
a stranger on the phone or at the front door

- Be wise about your volunteer commitments. Let's say you want to get more involved in your church and you've been asked to serve on the missions committee, which meets twice a month on Monday nights. This would mean spending more time away from your family. You also learn that the youth pastor is looking for adult volunteers to accompany students to the homeless shelter where they serve dinner on Thursday nights. When weighing the benefits of both options, you realize that since your son is involved in the youth group, you'd get to spend time with him and share the satisfaction of serving others together—an additional benefit. Once you realize which activity would allow you more time with your child, your decision is made.

- Talk to your boss ahead of time about important school events. Advance notice will increase your chances of getting someone to cover for you at work. Here's a list of school functions to consider:

  drop-off and pickup on the first day of school
  parent open house and meetings with teachers
  assemblies, performances, or holiday programs in which
      your child has a role
  one or two field trips
  science or art fair in which your child is a participant
  athletic games in which your child participates
  graduation or other important end-of-the-year celebrations

- If you can't attend an important event, ask a relative or close friend to stand in for you. If possible, have someone videotape the event so you and your child can enjoy watching it together later.

- Maximize time with your family at the end of the day. Change into comfy clothes and disconnect from the world so you can connect with your family. Turn off all electronic devices for a while, including your telephone, cell phone, pager, PDA, television, and computer.

Activity Overload

In a recent study reported by KidsHealth.org, 41 percent of children polled between the ages of 9 and 13 reported feeling stressed most of the time or always because they had too much to do, and 77 percent wished that they had more free time.

- Children need unstructured time to recharge their batteries. Free time helps them learn to entertain themselves, fosters creativity, and helps them discover the things they enjoy doing and how God designed them. They need time to work on crafts or experiment with a musical instrument, socialize with friends, read books, play games, and daydream.
- Don't overload your child's schedule with practices and activities. You may need to delete some things from the schedule if your child shows signs of overload, such as:

> leaving homework unfinished or completing it late at night because there's not enough time in the day
> rushing through meals to go places
> complaining about having to go to practice, games, or lessons
> not getting enough sleep
> overall moodiness due to a busy schedule

- Also consider your own stress level about getting your child from activity to activity. It may be time to make some changes.

Sick Days

Sick days with children are inevitable, but there are ways to make them easier on you and your child.

- Be prepared. Have numbers handy for your doctor and pharmacy. When you call your doctor, be prepared with this information:

> the child's temperature
> symptoms—headaches, pulling at ears, sore throat, vomiting, diarrhea, stomachache, rash, unusual sleep patterns
> medication you've given so far

- Keep your medicine cabinet well stocked with necessary over-the-counter medications and medical supplies.
- Call ahead before you take a sick child to an appointment at the doctor's office since doctors tend to run late with appointments. Ask the receptionist for a realistic arrival time so you won't have to spend unnecessary time in the waiting room.
- Create a "medical bag" filled with books, games, stickers, and other fun objects for your child to enjoy only when visiting the doctor.

SMART MOVE

When taking a sick child to the doctor, try to schedule the first appointment of the day or the first appointment after lunch. It's less likely that you'll have to wait.

- If you have other children, arrange to leave the well kids with another mom or caretaker while you take your ill child to the doctor. That way, you can focus your full attention on your sick youngster as you wait. Then return the favor when your friend's children have doctor's appointments.
- Create a special box that you keep out of sight and get out only on sick days. Fill it with things like activity and coloring books, crayons, stickers, a new puzzle, or a model to work on.
- Designate a spot in your pantry for "sick foods," such as chicken noodle soup, clear soda pop, flavored gelatin, electrolyte drinks, and soda crackers. (Flavored gelatin is more fun for kids when it's prepared in a 9x11-inch cake pan and cut into fun shapes with cookie cutters. Dry toast is more appealing when it's cut into shapes.)
- Create a fresh atmosphere for a child with a lengthy illness. Put on clean pillowcases, and let fresh air into the room daily. Send your child a small gift each day "through the mail"—new markers, a pack of gum, a package of flower seeds, a small book. Watching for the mail carrier will be something fun to do each day.
- Brighten your sick child's room with colored crepe paper and a cheery poster taped to the ceiling.
- Call your child's teacher and ask if you can pick up schoolwork. Encourage getting as much done as possible while at home.

Bedtime Routines

Without proper sleep, kids' bodies are not able to fight infection as effectively. Sleep deprivation can also affect a child's outlook on life. When you and I are tired, we realize that the day is more difficult because we're sleepy—but children don't understand this.

- Set a bedtime for school nights and stick to it. Thirty minutes before bedtime, encourage children to finish any projects or activities and begin their bedtime routines—wash face, brush teeth, and put on their pajamas—so they'll have a sense of daily rhythm. Although they may stay up later on the weekends, don't alter the schedule greatly if you want the school-day routine to be easy to maintain.
- Include activities in the routine that will help your child slow down and relax (like taking a shower or reading a book). Spend a few minutes recapping the day together, and pray with your child.

- Anticipate bedtime distractions. Make sure kids go to the bathroom before going to bed. Put a glass of water by the bed of a child who frequently needs a drink. Provide a night-light or flashlight for children who tend to be frightened of the dark.
- Enforce a lights-out time by installing a timer on kids' lights. Let them read or listen to books on tape until the light goes out.

BUILDING OTHER RELATIONSHIPS

Making Time for Friends

As much as you love your family, you need friends to talk, laugh, commiserate, and pray with. Probably most of us are regularly making new friends—in the neighborhood, at the office or gym, at school or community meetings, or at church. We have a great deal to do with how far each relationship develops.

The reality of friendships is that they ebb and flow in our lives. And perhaps one way to know if a friend is really a friend is if she understands this.

If you're already overwhelmed by the demands of your family, home, church, job, and other outside activities, you may think investing in your friendships is simply impossible. Before giving up, consider trying one or more of the following ideas:

- Whenever you plan activities for your kids, consider hooking up with a friend and her children. If you're going to a one-time event like a school picnic or a Fourth of July parade, why not invite another mom and her kids to come along? Or if your daughter has been begging you to sign her up for gymnastics, why not see if a friend's daughter might want to sign up for the same class? Your kids will enjoy playing together—and you and your friend will have some one-on-one time.
- Plan a monthly lunch date. Even if you just meet your friend and her kids at the local fast-food play area, you can count on some uninterrupted time to talk while your kids play.
- Keep all-occasion greeting cards on hand. You may know a friend is hurting but be unable to find the time to stop by or call. Simply receiving a brief note from you acknowledging her struggle will brighten her day—and deepen your friendship.
- Find your own extracurricular activities. Whether it's scrapbooking, bunco night, or a weekly Bible study, you deserve to make some time regularly for an activity you enjoy. Just anticipating the next meeting is likely to lift your spirits.

☆

SMART MOVE

Create the routine of getting together regularly with a few friends you enjoy but don't get to see often. Maybe you decide to go antiquing together on the first Saturday of April and October each year. Or you might begin a tradition like attending the same women's retreat every year or eating lunch together on the first Tuesday of every month.

Although my parents never formally taught me any principles of friendship, I watched their lives, learned, and identified three stages of building friendships:

1. Take the initiative.
   - Be friendly; be the first to say hello.
   - Say the other person's name often.
   - Show genuine interest in the other person's life.

2. Establish rapport.
   - Think to yourself, *I accept you as you are.*
   - Listen attentively—for feelings as well as thoughts.
   - Express approval and affirm when appropriate.
   - Give sincere compliments when due.
   - Look for ways to give, not take.
   - Watch for occasions to spend time together.

3. Build the relationship.
   - Let them know your opinions.
   - Seek their advice.
   - Make time for them.
   - Remember important dates.
   - Share personal resources.
   - Honestly share your joys and pain.
   - Avoid being possessive or controlling.
   - Pray with and for them.

Network Your Neighborhood for Fun and Safety

Getting to know your neighbors is important: You can work together to make your neighborhood a safer place for outdoor play, designate "safe" houses where children may go if they are being harassed, and warn each other of suspicious goings-on in your area. You can watch one another's homes and pick up one another's paper and mail during vacations.

Here are ways to promote friendship, networking, and safety in your neighborhood:

- Create and distribute a master contact list. Interested families can provide names, addresses, phone numbers, ages of children, and family hobbies. Also, get everyone's input on favorite stores and services in your area. The list is also a good opportunity for teens to indicate interest in babysitting.
- Develop a neighborhood Web site to post important and just-for-fun information, exchange recipes, list coming events, etc.

You can do this for free via Yahoo (http://www.yahoo.com) and Neighborhood Link (http://www.neighborhoodlink.com).

- Start a monthly potluck dinner held at different folks' houses. You could also form a gourmet club or bunco group.
- Coordinate a neighborhood-wide garage sale or start a crime-watch program.
- Join in a common cause. Gather a group to lobby officials for a needed stop sign or to add speed bumps to your street.
- Be alert for ways to celebrate each other's occasions—big and small: Tie helium balloons on a mailbox on a child's birthday; tie a big pink or blue bow on a lamppost when a new baby arrives; welcome a college student back home with his favorite pound cake.
- Pitch in and help elderly neighbors with yard work and light maintenance.
- Practice generosity by loaning yard tools. (Painting handles a bright color before loaning them out will help neighbors remember the tools belong to you.)
- Host a "New Kid on the Block" party for new neighbors.
- Begin an annual tradition—an Easter egg hunt, a Memorial Day picnic, a Fourth of July barbecue, or a chili cook-off.

CHAPTER 5

MANAGING YOUR FINANCES

Financial management, like any other kind of management (even cleaning bathrooms!), is really a process rather than a goal to be achieved once and then forgotten. Your priorities about how you manage your family's money will fluctuate as your family grows. After all, feeding a family of five costs more than feeding a family of three. Automobile insurance for a teenager is more expensive than owning a tricycle. College costs more than preschool.

Some of the financial concerns you must deal with as the Family Manager are:

- establishing and periodically reviewing your family's financial priorities
- setting up and following a budget
- stretching limited dollars
- preparing tax forms and keeping records
- selecting appropriate investments
- selecting appropriate charities
- calculating the amount of insurance your family needs
- setting up a retirement plan
- filing health-insurance claims
- shopping smart for a car
- stretching your child-care budget
- shopping smart for groceries, clothing, furniture, gifts, and appliances
- establishing credit
- teaching your kids the value of a dollar
- dealing with sensitive issues such as wills and after-death decisions
- getting ready to send kids to college

Financial management is really a process rather than a goal to be achieved once and then forgotten.

. . . .

This list covers the basics. But given your family situation, there will always be something else. Maybe it will be creating a crisis plan to weather a financial storm. Needless to say, that will be easier to do if you already know how to shop smart, have a monthly budget (so you know where cuts will hurt the least), and are living by the priorities your family has agreed to.

All of this may sound overwhelming if you, like me, don't consider yourself a numbers person. But don't be discouraged. I am pleased to announce a hard-won and deeply comforting truth: You don't need a degree in accounting to effectively manage the finance department. I should know. The word *budget* was foreign to my vocabulary until I married. Up to that point, my parents provided everything I needed. When I was a teenager, I had my own checking account, but I never bothered to balance it. I had no clue how much money was in it, and it didn't matter. If I ran short, our banker would call my mother and she'd deposit the additional funds right away. Yes, it was a sheltered life.

Making financial decisions will be easier if you are living by the priorities your family has agreed to.

Financial reality set in early in our marriage. All of a sudden, money wasn't always there. I wasted much of what we had on food we didn't eat, clothes I didn't need, and dust-catching knickknacks to decorate our cinder-block apartment. Bill attempted to show me the error of my ways, but I got defensive. To me, money was for spending—not saving.

But that changed pretty quickly when we had our first child, a big hospital bill to pay, and another person to feed, clothe, and send to college someday.

All of a sudden learning to manage our finances came front and center. At first it wasn't easy, but eventually I learned that bank statements aren't written in a foreign language and tracking monthly cash flow is nothing more than simple addition and subtraction. And I can still remember the boost to my confidence level when this non-numbers person caught an error on our home mortgage escrow account.

You, too, can become a better manager of your family's money. In this section you'll find practical advice on developing a financial strategy and concrete financial goals for your family, as well as tips on organizing your financial information and teaching your kids about money.

The Most Important Things to Remember

1. Everything you have is a gift from God.

2. What you cultivate *in* your children is more important than what you leave *to* them.

3. It's not what you make but what you give that makes life rich.

4. Difficult financial times can make you bitter or better—it's your choice.

5. Fewer monthly financial commitments give you more freedom and flexibility to spend money in the ways you prefer.

6. The joy of a purchase made on credit usually doesn't outlast the payments.

7. If you haven't decided what you value in life, when money is tight, you can easily feel insecure, discontented, and unable to enjoy the blessings you do have.

8. If you strive after wealth at the expense of family life, personal health, and a healthy marriage, you will find that you really don't control your wealth—it controls you.

9. Don't use wealth as a security blanket or a scorecard, but rather as a tool.

10. Managing money is not about the money. It's about how you view money.

Strategies and Solutions for Managing the Finances Department

CREATING YOUR FAMILY'S FINANCIAL STRATEGY

More couples divorce over financial issues than any other problem. Talking through and deciding on a financial strategy for your family will save a lot of angst. The keys to a solid financial plan for your family include:

- determining your view of money
- deciding on your priorities
- creating a budget and spending plan

If the idea of thinking through all these issues and creating some solid plans feels overwhelming right now, just remember you can take each of the following steps a little at a time. Any time you invest in creating a solid financial plan will pay off big later!

Your Family's Financial Philosophy

All of us have a philosophy about money and, whether we're aware of it or not, we live out our philosophies all day, every day. It's important to understand what your philosophy of money is, because this will influence your priorities and spending habits.

To some extent, each of us was influenced by the way our parents handled finances and what they valued. So when two people unite in marriage, they bring with them separate philosophies of money and a lot of standards they think are perfectly normal.

- What are your views regarding money?
- What are your husband's?
- Have your two views brought conflict? How?

Take some time to sit down by yourself (if you're a single parent) or with your husband and clarify your philosophy toward money. Consider what the following mean to you when you think of how you use your money.

Be responsible.
Be productive.
Be honest.
Be generous.
Be yourself.
Be realistic.

Your Family's Financial Priorities

Once you have your philosophy pretty well nailed down, you need to set priorities. Otherwise it will be easy to lose perspective about what's really important to you. Without priorities, you're more likely to make impulsive decisions and spend money you shouldn't spend—which will make you feel worse than you did before you tried to make yourself feel better by purchasing something!

Or maybe you feel frozen, unable to spend any money right now. Unless you've decided what you value in life, you can easily start to feel insecure, discontented, and unable to enjoy the blessings of life you do have.

Carve out some time soon to think about financial priorities for your family. Do it by yourself or with your spouse. Include older children if it's appropriate—whatever seems best for your family situation. Use these questions and fill-in-the-blanks to guide you in developing your priorities.

1. What do you each value most about your life today?

2. If you had the money, what would you say are your top three desires?

3. What three things do you want that money can't buy?

4. How much is enough? I'll feel okay about money when we have _____ (amount) in the bank. I'll be content when we have _____.

5. List the causes you'd like to give money to. How much would you like to give?

6. Where would you like to be financially in 12 months? in 5 years? in 20 years?

7. How do you feel about going into debt? About getting out of debt?

8. Given the choice between a job you'd love for less money and the job you have now and dislike at your current income, which would you choose? If you want a job you love, what can you do to either cut expenses or increase income in other ways?

9. Ask yourself this question: "If I had more money, I would spend it on _____." (Sometimes looking at what we want to spend money on and where we actually spend money can help us do some shifting without increasing the amount of money we spend.)

10. Fill in the blank: "If we suddenly found ourselves in a financial crisis, I could do without _____."

11. If you were suddenly blessed with wealth, do you know how you would react? How might your priorities change?

Your Family's Financial Plan

Once you've decided on your philosophy and your priorities, you need a strategy to make those things happen. Because each of our situations is different, I can't tell you exactly how to create a financial plan for your family. I can tell you, though, the issues we all need to deal with as we formulate a personalized strategy for our families' financial well-being.

- You need a budget.
- You need a savings plan.
- You need to decide how much to give to religious and/or charitable organizations.
- You need an easy, organized way to keep important records.
- If in debt, you need a strategy for reducing that debt.

- You need to know what your insurance covers—and what it doesn't.
- You need to have a plan for making major purchases.
- You need to file tax returns.
- You need to plan a way to meet children's education costs.
- You need to know when you'd like to retire and what you plan to live on when you do.

Budgets and spending plans

You need a spending plan that details exactly where all your money needs to go. You don't go to the grocery store without a shopping list, and you don't want to face a stack of bills and expenses without a plan to pay for them. Here's how to develop that plan.

1. Determine your monthly income.
   Figure out your family's average monthly earnings after taxes.

2. Calculate your monthly expenses.
   - child care
   - credit-card and other loan payments
   - entertainment
   - food
   - health care and insurance
   - housing
   - utilities
   - school tuition and supplies
   - transportation costs and car loans
   - drugstore items and cosmetics
   - gifts
   - tithing and other charitable contributions
   - membership fees (fitness centers, clubs, home-owners association)
   - any other miscellaneous expenses

   Now total all these categories and determine your monthly expenses.

3. Determine whether you're operating with a surplus or a deficit, then decide what to do about it.
   - Subtract your total monthly expenses from your total monthly income.
   - If your monthly expenses are less than your monthly income, you are holding your own. You might consider beginning to build a savings fund for emergencies, but only if you have no outstanding high-interest debt.

GOOD TO KNOW

Banks want to keep their customers satisfied and are often willing to waive charges, reduce fees or interest rates on credit, or make other compensations to keep your business at their institution.

SMART MOVE

When a car is paid off, continue to make "phantom" car payments monthly to a savings account. That way you will be able to save for a future car down payment (or have money for major repairs for the paid-off car). Also, it keeps that money in your spending plan so that when you do have another car payment, it's easier on the budget.

- If your monthly expenses equal your monthly income, then you're cutting it too close. You need a spending plan that helps you spend less of your monthly income.
- If your expenses are more than your income, you face a difficult choice. Either increase your income or reduce your expenses.

4. Create a mandatory savings plan.

After all your credit-card debt is paid off, start a savings plan. Or use this plan as a goal toward eradicating credit-card debt. Review these points below and determine the minimum amount you need to save:

- Write down your financial goals—both short-term (being able to pay bills in full, paying down credit-card debt) and long-term (buying a house, saving for retirement)—and consider what kind of spending plan will help you reach those goals.
- Put at least three to six months' salary in a savings account for emergencies.
- Set aside at least 5 percent of each paycheck in an individual retirement account (IRA), a pension fund, or a 401(k) plan.
- To pay for major purchases, figure out how much you can save each month. Pay for the item once the money is available; don't buy it on credit.

Now subtract the amount you need to save to meet these goals from your monthly income after taxes. You may be left with a small number. Don't be discouraged. If it seems absolutely unreasonable, revisit savings goals. But also keep an eye on where your money goes.

5. Track how your money is spent.
- Keep a spending diary (on paper or electronically) for one month. This will give you the most accurate picture of your spending patterns. It's always a revealing process.
- Split your expenses into two categories: fixed (mortgage, car payments, insurance premiums, etc.) and variable (clothing, credit cards, entertainment, etc.).
- Consider how you might reduce the variable expenses.

6. Put your plan into action.
- Create a worksheet or spreadsheet to track your spending plan.
- Each month, fill in actual expenses and savings next to the projected numbers.
- Compare the two columns to see how well you've stuck to your plan.
- Revise the spending plan as your income and expenses change.

GOOD TO KNOW

If you pay only the minimum balance on a $4,500 credit-card bill, it will take about 44 years to pay it off.

Ideas on Cutting Your Expenses

Step 3 on page 199–200 notes that if you discover your expenses exceed your income, you have one of two choices: You need to cut your expenses or increase your income. Let's look at some ways you might trim costs first; then look at the ideas on how you might be able to provide additional income for your family.

Smart money moves

- Break down large financial goals into smaller pieces. For instance, if you want to save $2,500 over the next year, that works out to $6.85 a day. Think of ways you might cut back on spending by $6.85 a day. Could you downsize your morning latte? Make sack lunches for the kids? Read the newspaper online? Consolidate errands and use less gasoline? Consider opening a special savings account for your goal so you'll be less tempted to access the money for everyday expenses.
- Use one low-interest credit card that gives you air miles or points for other purchases.
- Keep receipts. Have an easy-access file at your Control Central to keep all credit-card and cash receipts in case you need to return something.
- Consider how many hours you need to work to pay for something you want to buy. For example, if you earn $20 an hour and an item costs $160, ask yourself if what you want is worth eight hours of work.

Fast and easy cash savers

- Open a savings account at a bank branch inside your grocery store. When you use coupons, rather than having coupon amounts deducted from your bill, ask for the refund in cash. You can then immediately deposit the money at the in-store bank.
- Limit trips to the ATM. Withdraw the cash you'll need for the upcoming week or two. Store it in an envelope in a secure place. Track spending by noting how much and when you or family members take cash out of the envelope.
- Comparison-shop online before buying a car, household appliance, or just about anything else. You can save big bucks.
- Avoid shopping for gifts at the last minute, which can be costly. Next time you're at the mall, spend a few extra minutes picking out some generic gifts such as books, candles, or movie gift certificates to keep on hand.

SMART MOVE

Compare deals on credit cards at http://www.bankrate.com.

GOOD TO KNOW

As much as 2 percent of your fuel can be wasted if your tires are not fully inflated.

GOOD TO KNOW

Americans spent $17.5 billion in overdraft checking fees in 2007. The average fee paid for each overdraft was $34, according to the Center for Responsible Lending.

Before-You-Buy Questions

Whenever you're thinking of acquiring something new, no matter what it is, ask yourself these 10 questions before surrendering more space:

- Do I/we really need it?
- Can I/we make do with what I/we have?
- How often will I/we use it?
- How much space will it take up?
- How much care does it require?
- Is it durable?
- Does its design and quality meet my standards?
- Is there information available to help me make my decision?
- Is the price right? Could I/we find it at a secondhand store?
- How much difference will its addition to our home really make?

- Start a routine of collecting change from your purse or pockets at the end of each day. On average, Americans carry $1.28 in change, so if you save $1.28 a day for 365 days, you'll have $467.20! Get your family in on the fun and save for something special.
- Become a savvy coupon clipper. See pages 129–135 for ideas on saving money at the grocery store. See also pages 279–280 for a list of some of the best sources of coupons on the Internet.
- If you purchase makeup at a department store, ask the salesperson for samples of other products that you would like to try, such as a moisturizer or cleanser. Usually they are willing to do this, and these sample sizes of products can stretch the time before you need to purchase these items.
- The end of a quarter is a good time to find deals—especially on high-ticket items. Often stores need to boost quarterly revenue reports so they'll mark down inventory to move it out quickly.

Shopping smart for clothes and accessories

Few things are more frustrating than planning to wear something new and realizing when you put it on that it doesn't look as good on

you as it did on the hanger in the store. Avoid stress, and save yourself time and money by becoming a savvy shopper.

- *Before purchasing something new, consider the cost of maintenance involved.* Perhaps you found a beautiful linen suit on
  sale. Take into account that linen wrinkles badly, so you'll
  have to press it after each wearing and dry-clean it when it
  gets dirty.
- *Consider alteration costs.* Look at clothes as an investment
  and alterations as a part of it. If you aren't willing to pay for a
  tailor or hem a skirt yourself, don't buy the item.
- *Shop in comfort.* When you shop for clothing for yourself,
  wear easy-to-slip-off garments, panty hose if you usually wear
  them, and your usual amount of makeup, and fix your hair
  as usual. If you're shopping for a skirt or dress, take a pair of
  heels with you. This way you'll have a more accurate idea of
  how it looks on you and if it will need to be hemmed.
- *Leave tags on clothes.* Before paying for items, make sure
  you can return any items you decide not to keep—particularly
  those that have been marked down for final clearance. When
  you get home, see how they look and feel in the comfort of
  your own bedroom, in front of your own mirror. What else
  do they go with in your closet? Do you have appropriate
  accessories? Only when you're sure you're keeping an item
  should you remove tags.
- *Learn discounting patterns.* Many clothing stores mark down
  items on a reliable schedule—maybe four or six weeks after
  a new line is introduced. Observe your favorite store's pattern
  (you can track it online if you don't have time to go to the
  actual store) or ask a helpful salesperson for the schedule.
- *Return items politely.* Remind the store clerk that you are
  a steady customer, smile, and respectfully ask to see the
  manager if necessary.
- *Understand the refund policy.* Getting a store's refund policy
  in writing before you purchase something will simplify any
  return headaches.
- *Understand the adjustment policy.* Some stores will offer a
  credit if an item you purchased goes on sale within seven days.
- *Remember that displays can be deceiving.* Think twice
  before running to the register if something catches your
  eye. For example, if a silk plant arrangement looks lush and
  overflowing, you'll need to purchase more than a handful
  of flowers to achieve the same look. Find out everything the

GOOD TO KNOW

The average U.S.
woman spends
about 400 hours
each year shopping.

floral designer used, and tally the cost before deciding to make it yourself.

- *Mannequins wear small sizes, and they've never been pregnant!* Avoid dressing-room depression by choosing clothes that fit your body type and lifestyle.
- *Don't hunt for damaged items, but don't ignore them either.* You could receive a generous discount because a silk jacket is missing a button or a leather tote bag has a scratch. It's perfectly fine to ask for a price reduction.
- *Don't assume the designer brand you discover at an outlet store is a must-buy.* Check to see if patterns match and if there's extra fabric at the seams. Sometimes manufacturers cut corners on items made especially for their outlet stores.
- *Check your receipt before leaving the store.* Cash registers are not infallible.

Be a smart Internet shopper
- *Comparison-shop.* The Internet is ideal for comparison-shopping for things like airline tickets, hotel rooms, and cars.
- *Get the details.* Make sure you understand shipping and handling fees, expected delivery dates, warranties, and return policies before finalizing your purchase.
- *Know your merchant.* Be careful about making purchases from companies whose names or reputations you are not familiar with. If you're in question about a business, visit http://www.consumer.gov. You will find buyer's guides, lists of tips, and links to helpful resources.
- *Monitor personal information.* Know what a merchant is planning to do with the information collected about you. The Web site should have a privacy policy posted.
- *Say yes to e-mail sale notices.* Agree to receive e-mail notices from Web sites you like. These often include special sales and free-shipping notices. At the same time, be willing to delete notices unopened if they tempt you to shop even when you don't need to.
- *Keep records.* Know what you ordered and what you were promised. Be sure to print out and file a copy of the receipt.
- *Inspect carefully.* Check out products upon delivery.
- *Keep everything.* Store all paperwork and packaging should you need to return the merchandise.

Be a smart holiday shopper
On average, Americans spent between $700 and $1,100 on holiday gifts in 2007. People who charge these purchases often end

up spending 20 to 25 percent more than those who pay with check or cash.

- *Start early.* Start as early in the year as you can stand it and keep an eye out for gifts on sale. Designate a shelf or area of a closet to store your early purchases.
- *Keep a list.* Having a list makes the process easier. Add ideas for each person on the list throughout the year, especially when you hear them mention something they'd like to have.
- *Set a spending limit.* Know how much you can spend for holiday gifts, and stick to the spending plan.
- *Buy in quantity.* If you can buy the same gift for a teacher and a coach, do it.

Bartering

Bartering is a smart business practice you and a friend can use to share expertise or items and to save each other time and money. For example:

- *Exchange services.* If you are strong in the Special Events or Food departments but you're less confident when it comes to the Financial department, ask a friend who's an expert money manager if you can pick her brain. Return the favor by suggesting menu ideas and decorating themes for her big dinner party.

- *Host a swap party.* Decide on a theme such as toys, baby equipment, or children's clothing. Invite friends to bring a few of these items along to swap, and everyone goes home with "new" things without spending a cent.

- *Barter around the holidays.* During the holiday season, use bartering to maximize your strengths and minimize your weaknesses. If you're not a great cook but you excel in wrapping beautiful packages, tell a friend you'll wrap her gifts if she'll bake holiday treats for you.

- *Trade home-maintenance or decorating tasks.* Suggest to a friend that you will help her paint her child's bedroom if she helps you wallpaper a bathroom.

Ideas on Increasing Your Income

When the budget gets tight, many couples immediately consider sending a nonworking spouse (usually the wife) into the workforce. Before you take that step, be sure to do the math. You may discover that the added income doesn't really add much to the bottom line.

☆

SMART MOVE

Before you head to the store to buy anything, check for discounts on the Internet. There are online coupons for almost everything you need.

How much money do you really make?

One of the reasons a mother sometimes takes a job, in addition to the job of being a mother, is to earn extra money for her family. If that is the only reason for taking a job, take a good, long look at the numbers and make sure it's still a financially sound idea. Sometimes, after all the expenses are tallied, it's cheaper to stay at home. This is especially true if the job is something you don't enjoy. Another alternative is to find work you can do from home and decrease or eliminate some of these expenses.

Complete the following worksheet and see where you stand on the cost of working:

Gross weekly salary: _____

Less total taxes: _____

Other payroll deductions: _____

Take-home pay: _____

Less transportation and parking: _____

Work clothes: _____

Food (lunches, snacks): _____

Pocket money:
Convenience spending
  (takeout foods, eating out): _____

Child care: _____

Total income remaining: _____

Working from home

If you've decided you need to contribute to your family's income, don't assume that means you must take a nine-to-five job in an office. Working from home, either independently or telecommuting, is becoming more popular and doable for many dual-career women. Here are six questions to help you decide if it's a viable alternative for you.

1. Are you self-directed, and do you work well independently? In past evaluations, how has your employer rated you on time management and productivity? If you have received good scores, you can present that as evidence to prove to your employer (or yourself) that you can work at home.

2. Realistically, can your job be done away from a corporate office environment? Does it require uninterrupted concen-

tration? Do you need a lot of space and special equipment? Can your job be done using a computer, fax, modem, e-mail, pager, and/or voice mail? Will the company provide those? If not, can you cover the costs?

3. Would a compressed workweek—three 12-hour days or four 10-hour days—work as well or better than your current system?

4. How will your boss supervise you? How often will you need to attend meetings at the office? Can he or she evaluate your work if you work at home?

5. What benefits can you sell to your employer? Fewer days off work (a sick child no longer means missed hours)? Increased flexibility to meet client and corporate needs (special projects can be done after regular work hours)? Reduced need for office and parking? Increased employee satisfaction? The company will save money if you reduce your hours? The key to negotiating the job schedule you want is to make your employer see that he or she will gain from the arrangement as well.

6. If you lose some or all of your benefits, can you afford to cover them yourself?

If telecommuting or working from home looks viable for you after you've answered these questions, research child-care options. Find short-term child care for your children for when you are away from home. Also, have a child-care plan during the summer. Make sure your employer knows that you will not care for your children on company time.

Then write a formal proposal that states your request to work from home. Include the date you want to start. Summarize why you believe your job is appropriate for telecommuting, and describe your proposed daily routine. Suggest a specified length of time for a trial period. Remember that your boss may need approval from another management level, especially if your company has never had an employee work from home. A well-written proposal will get him on your side.

Home-office sanity savers

One of the biggest pluses of telecommuting or a home-based business is the flexibility. But being able to balance your paying job with your Family Manager job requires an extra dose of discipline and organization, as well as setting some basic house rules with your family.

Here are some guidelines on how to achieve that balance.

- If you have young kids at home, hire someone to watch them while you work. This will allow you to work for several focused hours at a clip rather than having to wait for naps or evenings. Consider trading child care with other mothers from preschool or the neighborhood.
- If you choose not to hire a sitter, you must be extremely disciplined with your time. Work your schedule around your children's naps or school hours and create a backup plan for days when your child won't nap, has vacation, or is home sick from school.
- To protect your high-focus time, screen all phone calls with an answering machine or voice mail while your child is in preschool, school, or day care.
- Develop phone rules. One mom painted a Ping-Pong paddle red on one side and green on the other. When she's on a casual personal call, she holds up the green side, and when the children need to be silent and wait (barring an emergency), she holds up the red side. Reward your children for following the rules.
- Establish work-space boundaries. Being able to work behind a closed door is ideal for eliminating distractions. If that's impossible, have some indicators that mark out your work zone; for example, those orange cones you can buy at sports equipment stores. You need something that alerts passersby that "Mommy is working—do not disturb."
- Think of projects in their component parts. If you don't have time to finish an entire project, use your available time to finish parts of it.
- Set up a "home office" for your child with art supplies, paper, pencils, tape, and an old briefcase. One of my toddler's favorite games became "working," and he became so engrossed in his own project that I got extra chunks of time to work.
- Schedule specific personal time for chores, errands, exercise, time with friends, and so on. The flexibility of blending home and other work makes it tempting to whittle away your productivity with housework, errands, or just chatting on the phone with friends.

If You're Really Strapped for Money

Call the creditors and explain the problem. Taking the initiative and working out a payment plan is better than avoiding or not returning their phone calls.

Some payment is always better than no payment, and creditors appreciate your efforts. Visit a local debt consolidation service for free advice on contacting creditors and structuring payment plans.

Financial downsizing

If you or your spouse loses a job, the shock wave runs through the entire family. You have bills to pay and need to find another source of income. If you're now eligible for unemployment, collect it. While it may not replace your previous salary, it is some money for the checking account. Then get an action plan in place to minimize spending until the next job comes along.

- A critical first step is to talk with your children about the change. They may welcome ideas for earning money for extras themselves; involve them in dealing with this change.
- Tighten the budget now, not when money runs out. Take a long look at your spending plan and see what adjustments are possible. Be tough.
- List some free or inexpensive activities your family can enjoy. Free videos from the local library, community events, and stargazing are all good family entertainment.
- Don't dip into savings. Every family needs a safety net, so leave your savings intact. Make an effort to set aside one dollar each day and put your loose coins into a piggy bank. Similarly, resist the urge to charge on your credit cards.
- Schedule an old-fashioned date with your spouse. Just listen to each other and omit all criticism. Working together as a team is important, especially now. Keep a positive focus on each other and on finding work. Create action plans for preparing a revised résumé, networking, and interviewing toward a new position.
- Begin searching for a new job immediately. Think of your new job as finding the right new job. Don't think of this as vacation time. But do take time to be thankful for a good interview or a networking session by rewarding yourself with a Friday afternoon off or a long morning walk—something you couldn't do while working at your old job.
- Consider counseling if family stress becomes too great. Talking to a minister or pastor, therapist, or social worker about the situation often lessens family tension and anxieties. Payment, if any, is usually on a sliding scale, and insurance often reimburses a portion of the cost. If one of you still has a job, investigate the company's employee-assistance program.

SMART MOVE

The U.S. Department of Housing and Urban Development advises families to spend no more than 30 percent of their gross income on housing.

GOOD TO KNOW

In 2007, annual health insurance premiums averaged $4,479 for individuals and $12,106 for families, according to the Kaiser Family Foundation.

- Be flexible in your plans, and tell everyone you're looking for a job. You never know who will have the next great job that's perfect for you in an unexpected industry.
- Some expenses are essential to the welfare of your family and better left untouched. Here are the payments you *must* maintain.
  - *Medical and dental insurance.* Your entire family should be covered by the working spouse's insurance plan. If no one is employed, look into COBRA benefits through the old employer or contact your personal insurance agent for more affordable options.
  - *Rent or mortgage.* You have to have a place to live.
  - *Life insurance.* Consider increasing the value of the working spouse's life policy.
  - *Medications.* Dropping a needed medication may save you a few dollars today, but the long-term consequences could be devastating.
  - *Food.* Stick with nutritious meals—grains, fruits, vegetables, and meats. Eliminate convenience and junk foods, and processed foods and drinks.

ORGANIZING YOUR MONEY MATTERS

Bill Paying

Paying your bills online will save you hours each month. Most banks offer online bill-paying services. It's easy to learn and greatly simplifies the chore of paying bills by setting up files for every payee and balancing your accounts. You can even arrange for the system to make automatic payments, so you'll never miss a rent or mortgage payment.

You can also set up online payments using a software system like Quicken or create online accounts with individual companies. Many offer the option of receiving your bill via e-mail, which cuts down on paper clutter.

Prioritizing Bills

If you're unable to pay all of your bills one month, it's important to know which unpaid bills generate what consequences. This will keep your credit rating as strong as possible.

Here's what happens when payments are skipped:

- Mortgage payments are a top priority. The foreclosure process only starts if several payments are missed, but late fees and marks on your credit record show up immediately.

- Bank cards also report missed or late payments immediately. Attempt to pay at least the minimum amount due each month.
- Insurance payments for cars and houses are usually paid in advance and include a 30-day grace period, so some lag time may be permissible. (If you live in a state where you must carry proof of auto insurance in your car, be sure the date of coverage is current or you may be fined if you get pulled over.) Health insurance must be kept current or you risk losing the coverage.
- Car payments may allow a late or partial payment if your prior payment history is strong. Repossession usually happens only after several months of nonpayment.
- Utilities are usually forgiving, allowing the occasional late or skipped payments.

Of course, should you find yourself continually falling short every month, you have a serious problem that needs to be addressed. Revisit your spending plan, and look for outside help. Some churches offer financial counseling services or referrals to outside agencies that help families in financial crisis.

Taxes
Taxes remain a perpetual headache for most families, annually wreaking havoc in the days and weeks leading to the April 15 deadline. But there are ways to simplify the process and organize the paperwork, and eliminate that last-minute rush.

A note on refunds
If you're one of the families that celebrate getting a refund every year, rethink your partying. A refund means the government has had the interest-free use of some of your hard-earned money during the year. Instead, balance your withholdings so they equal your deductions at year-end.

Getting organized
Keeping organized tax records throughout the year makes tax preparation much easier. Make separate file folders or large envelopes for each category of deductions. Then toss in receipts, bank statements, and other documents during the year. If there is any question about saving some document or throwing it away, always save it. Try organizing according to these categories:

Charitable contributions. Keep all canceled checks or credit-card receipts for any donations. For donations more than $250, you

★

SMART MOVE

Help your children
learn that fun
isn't necessarily
expensive. Nurture
low-cost hobbies
and activities, such
as gardening, playing
card games, walking
and hiking, creating
inexpensive crafts,
and going on picnics.
Get up early, watch
the sunrise, and
cook breakfast
over a campfire, or
grill at a park. Go
on a bike-hike as a
family—ride to a
favorite eating spot,
then ride back. Call
your local parks
and recreation
department and ask
about inexpensive
programs and
activities that your
family might enjoy.

need a receipt from the organization acknowledging your dona-tion. When you donate noncash items like clothes, your old car, or unused furniture to a charity, submit an itemized list with an appro-priate value and have someone from the organization authorize the receipt. Remember to keep track of any transportation and mileage costs you incur traveling to perform any volunteer work. This is deductible.

Business and job-related expenses. Depending on your type of business, several items are deductible. These could include uni-form costs, magazine and newspaper subscription costs, and course fees. When you're looking for a new job, all related costs are deductible as well, such as travel costs to interviews. Also, moving expenses to start a new job are deductible. Home-office expenses are somewhat more complicated, as only a percentage of some costs are deductible. Consult a tax guide or CPA for clarifi-cation before filing.

Dependent care. All the expenses you incur to care for your depen-dents, such as child care, alimony, medical care, and any special costs incurred to care for disabled dependents comprise dependent care. Many of these expenses are deductible, based on whether or not you work and the age of your dependents.

Income sources. Each year you'll receive statements from all employers who have paid you for work in the prior year. Also, keep all dividend and interest statements together, as those are also tax-able income sources. Real-estate sale and rental information goes in this folder also.

Investment expenses. All costs of purchasing accounting software, all fees to prepare your taxes, and the cost of the safe-deposit box are deductible. Keep careful track of the sales of all investments, so your profits and losses from these transactions are accurately calculated.

Medical expenses. Each dependent is allowed a specific deductible for all medical expenses during the course of the year. Expenses above this amount are then itemized on the tax forms. For every family member, keep a separate folder of all medical bills, includ-ing drugstore charges.

Mortgage expenses. At year-end, your lending institution will mail you a summary of the interest you've paid on your home. All of this interest, along with any interest from any home-equity loans, is deductible.

MONEY MANAGEMENT FOR KIDS

The best way to teach good money values to your kids is to look for everyday opportunities to apply them to your kids' lives.

Guidelines for Teaching Kids about Money

Be responsible. Make sure your kids know that you will not automatically replace items that are broken, destroyed, or stolen because of their irresponsibility.

Be productive. As soon as children can help around the house, they need regular chores. Even two-year-olds can fold dish towels and pick up toys.

Be honest. Kids need to learn it's wrong to take what doesn't belong to them—including nonmaterial things, such as time from an employer, credit for something someone else accomplished, or services they use but haven't paid for.

Be generous. Young children can be taught to share their resources and time with others. As kids get older, encourage them to become involved with religious organizations, local charities, and not-for-profits. Become a family of givers.

Be yourself. Kids need to understand that they are not what they own, wear, or drive. Each of us is valuable as a unique human being.

Be realistic. Kids need to know that none of us always get what we deserve, but most of the time we will have more than we need. We need to nurture contentment with what we have.

Everyday Economic Lessons for Kids

You can use all kinds of daily situations as a springboard for discussing financial matters. Here are a few.

- The next time you use an ATM or cash a check, take a few seconds to explain that the machine isn't printing money. The money is coming out of your account—a connection your child won't make without your help.
- In the grocery store, show your children how to decipher the unit-price tags on grocery shelves, and they can help you shop for the best deal in the cereal or soft-drink aisle.
- At home, make money a game—literally. Getting the whole family together for Monopoly, Life, or Pay Day provides fun lessons in taking out mortgages, paying bills or tuition, or buying stock.

SMART MOVE

Never do anything or buy anything on a regular basis for your children that they are capable of doing or buying for themselves. Your job is to help them become independent, self-sufficient adults.

FROM THE HEART

The privilege of having money brings great responsibility. One of the most important lessons we can teach our kids is the proper perspective toward money and material possessions—and they won't learn that at school. Our homes must be the classrooms.

- When you pay bills, get your children involved so they see how much things cost. Emphasize that your family finances are private and the details should not be shared with others.
- As your children enter their teen years, consider giving them a clothing allowance so they can begin to learn to budget. Give them guidelines on items they will be responsible for buying and what types of clothing are appropriate.
- If you buy something in a store and the clerk mistakenly gives you back too much change, let your child see you return the extra money you received.
- Do you have anything in your home that you should be paying for but aren't? Extra cable channels that you get by mistake? A neighbor's magazine subscription that comes to your address? Turn the situation into a teaching opportunity by correcting it and telling your child it's wrong to accept something without paying for it.
- Let kids be responsible for late fees. Have them return DVDs to their cases immediately after watching and place them in a designated location near the door. When they forget, they pay the late fee.
- Check out local consignment shops before buying seldom-worn clothing such as ski clothes and formal wear. Ask kids to compare prices and note savings.
- Have a child take a calculator to the grocery store and add up the price of everything you put into your cart.
- Create a rule that if kids leave their belongings where they can be stolen or broken, they help pay to replace them.

Allowances

Giving children an allowance is a great tool for helping them learn money-management skills, as well as for teaching them the value of being part of the family team. Kids need to learn at an early age that every member of the team contributes to the family's well-being.

Adopt the philosophy at your home that in addition to each family member's career (school is a child's career, just as important as Mom's and Dad's careers), everyone is responsible for certain household duties. Consider a base allowance amount for doing their share of housework. Here are other ideas to think about.

- Begin giving children an allowance at age six, depending on their ability to count and their understanding of money. Consider giving a half-dollar or dollar for every year of your child's age.

- Establish spending rules up front about what their allowance can and cannot buy and when they will need to spend their own money to purchase something.
- Encourage them to save part of their allowance. If they want to buy a more expensive item, help them set goals for saving. Consider matching their savings dollar for dollar.
- Encourage your kids to give away part of their allowance to a charity or to church. Inspire them to give by showing them what the money provides.
- If kids don't fulfill their responsibilities, suspend their allowance. When they're grown, if they haven't learned the importance of fulfilling their responsibilities, they won't have the privilege of getting a paycheck.
- Pay only for jobs that are completed. Half-done jobs do not earn half an allowance.
- Provide opportunities for kids to earn extra money by taking on extra jobs, such as cleaning out the garage or basement. Post "Help Wanted" ads on your bulletin board or refrigerator that list kids' opportunities to earn extra cash.
- Help your kids brainstorm ways they could earn extra money outside the family. They might consider such jobs as babysitting, pet-sitting, distributing flyers for small businesses, mowing lawns, or starting an errand or odd-job service. If they'd like to start their own small business, be sure to check with your local government office to see if a business license or permit is needed. Then create an advertising flyer or a business card to distribute to homes or post on public bulletin boards.

FUN FOR KIDS

Make a big deal out of your child's first paycheck. Make a copy and frame it.

CHAPTER 6

MANAGING SPECIAL EVENTS

Here's reality: Your kids won't remember how many loads of laundry you washed or if the kitchen floor was mopped daily. But they'll remember the annual Christmas party your family threw for neighbors and friends, the vacation when they lost Dad's fishing pole at the bottom of the lake while learning to fish, your tradition of hiding clues throughout the house that led to a special Valentine's Day gift, and the spur-of-the-moment celebrations you created to commemorate good report cards. They'll remember the family reunion at the dude ranch that ended up being a dud ranch, even though you all had tons of fun.

In most homes, Mom usually organizes and coordinates special events and family celebrations. These occasions may be small or large, once-in-a-lifetime or annual events. What they all have in common is that they fall outside the normal routine of your daily tasks and activities. Parties, birthdays, graduations, vacations, showers, weddings, anniversaries, Christmas, and other holidays all fall in the Special Events department of a Family Manager's job. Each event calls for a certain amount of planning, researching, compiling information, delegating, meeting intermittent deadlines, and following through until the event is over.

Depending on the makeup of your family and what holidays and occasions you consider special and worthy of celebrating, you may oversee a few or many special events each year. They needn't all be scheduled in advance; some of them can be quite spontaneous. But they all require some planning and execution, which may happen in a few hours or over a period of weeks or months.

You'll do yourself and your family a favor by deciding to welcome fun— in whatever way it comes.

Even though precious family memories are formed during special events and celebrations, this department sends many moms over the edge. More than the researching, planning, or even the events themselves, expectations—our own and other people's (as we perceive them)—can make us shut down or spin out of control. You'll do yourself and your family a favor by deciding to welcome fun—in whatever way it comes—by ably managing your carefully prepared plans or laughing at how your plans flopped. Setting an agenda in stone for the sake of your mother, your in-laws, or your best friend is a predictable path to frustration and disappointment. But a relaxed, "roll with it" attitude will pave the way for everyone (including you!) to enjoy any occasion more. Cut yourself some slack. Do you really need to make homemade potato salad for the Fourth of July when the deli offers a perfectly good substitute? Remember, the object is to promote positive memories, not to drive yourself crazy. There are no set standards for how your family should celebrate holidays and special occasions. Your family's priorities are the ones you should strive to live by.

Although many moms buy into the philosophy that celebrations are important, they find that weeks and months slip by without purposefully making any special memories—any positive ones, at least. Maybe you can relate, and just the thought of planning one more activity makes you want to scream. If that's the case, please consider this idea. Fix yourself a cup of tea, find a quiet place to sit, and just remember. Remember the happiest special occasions you've had as a couple or a family. Remember the disasters that seem funny now—even if they didn't then. Remember the times you pulled off a memorable special event—and also the things you'd do differently for events that didn't work out the way you wanted them to.

Then as you read the solutions in this section, mark the ideas you'd like to implement. Many will help you plan and simplify—while at the same time add pizzazz to your family's special occasions and celebrations. And keep in mind that the process is just as important as the party, the trip, or the holiday itself. You're teaching your kids the value of planning for something special, honoring someone or car-

> **The process is just as important as the party, the trip, or the holiday itself.**

rying on a family tradition, working on the details together, feeling the satisfaction of making progress, and watching all your hard work come together into a wonderful event. All these elements are part of the memory-making experience. You're carrying on traditions, creating shared memories, and creating opportunities for your family to enjoy life's special moments together. That's big.

The Most Important Things to Remember

1. Like any project, planning a graduation party or holiday celebration requires planning, research and development, delegation, follow-through, and deadlines.

2. Don't wait until you have enough money to plan the perfect party. If something is worth celebrating, it's worth celebrating no matter how simple the event.

3. Every child's mind is a curator of memories.

4. Traditions and common experiences cement a family. There's something about being able to say, "This is the way our family always does it."

5. Share the work, as well as the joy. The idea is not only to save yourself a trip to the therapist but to promote family bonding and team spirit—and to make memories that last.

6. Don't expect your children to be perfect just before or during your special event. Hang on to your emotions and deal with misbehavior calmly and in private.

7. People are more important than any occasion. Dropping everything to console a sad child is a lot more important than making sure your table decorations are perfect.

8. Sometimes it's better to carry on a tradition that's been scaled down rather than go to either of the other extremes—dropping the occasion completely or doing it so big that your stress meter reaches the danger zone.

9. Accept the fact that calamity and confusion are often uninvited guests at celebrations. Food will burn, toilets will overflow, and your power may go out. But you can still make positive memories if you are able to laugh about mishaps and plans that go awry.

10. You don't have to wait for a new year, a new month, or better circumstances. There is no better time than now to start creating positive memories for your children.

Strategies and Solutions for Managing Special Events

ENTERTAINING

10 Steps to an Unforgettable Event

Applying the same strategies a company uses—planning, research and development, delegation, and deadlines—works for birthdays, vacations, holidays, family reunions, and all the other events you oversee as your family's manager.

Here are some steps for making special events a priority, and making them doable, no matter the occasion.

1. *Brainstorm with family members about events they'd like to celebrate.* Decide what's important to your family: Certainly birthdays, graduations, and holidays are part of every family's calendar, but you don't have to place the same importance on them everyone else does. Each family is free to decide what days—no matter how "silly" or unexpected—they deem worthy of some streamers and balloons. Use the list of holidays on page 222, and make a list of the dates you want to commemorate.

2. *Get out your calendar.* Mark it, month by month, with the special occasions and events you know will occur—birthdays, holidays, weddings, etc. Then list the events you want to occur: a birthday party for your daughter, a family ski trip, a Super Bowl party, a Fourth of July neighborhood barbecue. Once they're on the calendar, they serve to remind you to keep an eye out for menus, party items on sale, and so on.

3. *Consider special events penned—not penciled—onto your calendar.* Once you've marked these events, don't let anyone talk you out of them. "Just say no" to invitations and demands that infringe on times you've designated as special for your family.

4. *Use a planning checklist for each occasion.* As you determine the tasks that need to be accomplished, items you need to buy, and people you need to invite, put them on your list. Then decide what you can delegate, what you might want to delete, and what you might want to do yourself. This will help you think more clearly and feel less

overwhelmed. By keeping all the information in one place, you'll stay on top of the details.

5. *Delegate and delete.* This is where you remind your family, "We're in this together." Working as a team promotes bonding, develops family spirit, and celebrates creative expression. So once you've roughed out a to-do list for a special event, call a family meeting. Ask for input and volunteers.

Remember, you manage your family. You do not have to do things the way anyone else does—including your mother. So be bold: Are there some items on your list you don't need to do yourself (or at all)? Can you buy a bakery cake instead of spending a whole weekend trying to make a cake the size and color of Elmo or Spider-Man? If you're hosting a holiday dinner for your extended family, can you ask others to bring some of the food? Or ask someone to come early and help set up or to stay late and help clean up? Be generous in sharing the workload and in letting yourself off the hook.

6. *Conduct research and development.* To make an event all it can be, you may need to make some phone calls and do some research on the Internet. Start collecting the information you need, such as rates for the hotel you'll stay at on vacation, dates a certain park area is available for your son's baseball-themed birthday party, or the supplies needed for the baby shower you're throwing for your best friend.

If others in your family are responsible for these tasks, give them deadlines and follow up to make sure everything gets done.

7. *Practice the five-minute maxim.* Watch for snippets of time here and there to accomplish something toward the occasion. For example, if you don't have a block of time to address all the party invitations, fill out a few when you have five free minutes. You'll eventually make it through the entire list.

8. *Execute and enjoy.* Now you get to enjoy the fruits of your labor: All the planning, purchasing, researching, packing, calling, inviting, and deciding prove their worth. Don't forget that special events are primarily to enjoy, not to labor over. As the Family Manager, you set the tone. So let loose and have a great time!

9. *Appreciate your team and honor your own labor.* After an event is over, be sure to thank family members for their

---

☆

SMART MOVE

I like to use a ½- to one-inch three-ring binder for each event. This way, I keep all the information I need in one place and can easily take it with me on preparatory errands and to the event itself. Keep a list of who attended, the activities, the decorations, and so on. Make notes of what did and didn't work. You'll save time and trouble next time!

After the event, I clean out the binder, saving only the information I need for future reference, and store this information in a labeled file in the Special Events Archives section of my file drawer. There have been times when I've had three small binders in use simultaneously—one for a family vacation, one for a wedding shower, and another for the information surrounding a child leaving for college.

Holiday Dates

Use this list to remember upcoming holidays or to choose ones that sound interesting. Once you and your family agree on which days to highlight, research what each is all about to get ideas about how to honor the day.

New Year's Day . . . January 1

Feast of the Magi (Epiphany) . . . January 6

Martin Luther King Jr. Day . . . Third Monday in January

Inauguration Day . . . January 20

Chinese New Year . . . January or February

National Freedom Day . . . February 1

Groundhog Day . . . February 2

Lincoln's Birthday . . . February 12

Valentine's Day . . . February 14

Washington's Birthday . . . February 22

Ash Wednesday . . . February or March

Presidents' Day . . . Third Monday in February

St. Patrick's Day . . . March 17

First Day of Spring . . . March 20 or 21

Passover . . . March or April

Palm Sunday . . . Sunday before Easter

Good Friday . . . Friday before Easter

Easter . . . March or April

Easter Monday . . . Monday after Easter

April Fools' Day . . . April 1

Pan American Day . . . April 14

Earth Day . . . April 22

Arbor Day . . . Last Friday in April

Administrative Professionals' Week . . . Fourth Week in April

May Day . . . May 1

National Day of Prayer . . . First Thursday in May

National Teacher Day . . . Tuesday of the first full week of May

Cinco de Mayo . . . May 5

Mother's Day . . . Second Sunday in May

Armed Forces Day . . . Third Saturday in May

Victoria Day . . . First Monday preceding May 25

Memorial Day (observed) . . . Last Monday in May

Flag Day . . . June 14

Father's Day . . . Third Sunday in June

First Day of Summer . . . June 20 or 21

Canada Day . . . July 1

Independence Day . . . July 4

Bastille Day . . . July 14

Labor Day . . . First Monday in September

Grandparents' Day . . . First Sunday after Labor Day

First Day of Autumn . . . September 22 or 23

Citizenship Day . . . September 17

Sukkoth (Jewish harvest festival) . . . September or October

Rosh Hashanah (Jewish New Year) . . . September or October

Yom Kippur (Day of Atonement) . . . September or October

Columbus Day . . . Second Monday in October

National Boss Day . . . October 16

Thanksgiving in Canada . . . Second Monday in October

Mother-in-Law's Day . . . Fourth Sunday in October

United Nations Day . . . October 24

Halloween . . . October 31

All Saints' Day . . . November 1

All Souls' Day . . . November 2

Election Day . . . First Tuesday after the first Monday in November

Veterans Day . . . November 11

Thanksgiving . . . Fourth Thursday in November

Hanukkah . . . November or December

First Day of Advent . . . Fourth Sunday before Christmas Day

Christmas . . . December 25

Boxing Day . . . December 26

Kwanzaa . . . December 26–January 1

New Year's Eve . . . December 31

contributions and allow yourself the satisfaction of knowing you've added another great memory to your family's account.

10. *Recap.* Talk together and make some notes about what worked and what didn't, and list ideas for next time. Print a lot of photos and take some family time to remember the day. Consider letting a creative family member compile a scrapbook or special photo album of the event.

When to Do What
Three to four weeks before the party
- Decide on a theme—if you want one.
- Make your guest list. If you have a bigger list than your home can comfortably handle for a seated dinner, consider an informal buffet dinner or a Sunday-afternoon open house. Or choose a day when you can be outside. For a large, special-occasion party, don't rely on the weather. Unless you're positive it won't rain, rent a party tent or have the party at another location.
- Send invitations. (Don't forget maps!)
- Plan menu; figure food amounts; make shopping list.
- Plan cooking schedule—when to bake and freeze—or meet with the caterer.
- Shop ahead for nonperishables and supplies.
- Tape an envelope for receipts to the front of your refrigerator. This will help you track expenses.
- Take inventory and start gathering equipment. Reserve rentals, if needed.
- Consider hiring a teenager to help during the party and with cleanup afterward.
- Start polishing silver or brass serving pieces during spare minutes.

Two weeks before the party
- Finalize decorating plans.
- Prepare foods you can freeze.
- Decide what you'll wear for the party. Mend clothes or take them to the dry cleaner if needed, or shop for something new. Be sure to check accessories.
- If you're planning an adult party, make arrangements or plan entertainment for your children.
- Plan music; assemble CDs; prepare any musical equipment.

FROM THE HEART

Entertaining should be about enjoying a special meal or occasion with people you enjoy, not about trying to impress people with your decorating or culinary competence.

One week before the party
- Organize your kitchen for the party.
- Keep an eye on guest acceptances and regrets; work on seating plan. Write names on place cards.
- Store countertop appliances and other items you won't need.
- Clean your oven to avoid "smoking" your food rather than baking it.
- Begin setting up stations for specifics, such as preparing drinks, assembling food platters, and stacking dishes between courses.
- Clean out your refrigerator to create more space.
- Buy bags of ice, or make ice cubes every day and store them in plastic bags.
- Get party linens ready. Press tablecloths and napkins. Store carefully so they won't wrinkle.
- Wash or wipe off plates, glasses, and serving dishes, if needed.
- Confirm arrival time for any professionals you've hired or friends you've asked to help.
- Purchase your beverages.

Two to three days before the party
- Finalize the number of guests.
- Cook food to be reheated or served cold.
- Give bathrooms a thorough cleaning.
- Rearrange furniture.
- Start decorating.
- Clear space for coats.
- Shop for everything except last-minute perishables.
- Make a list of jobs for helpers and hired staff.
- Prepare wood in the fireplace.

One day before the party
- Wash lettuce and produce; store in plastic bags.
- Set table and label serving pieces with what they will hold. (This will help you remember the vegetable salad that's marinating at the back of the refrigerator.)
- Chill beverages.
- Set up music.
- Do last-minute housecleaning.
- Buy ice, if needed, and fresh flowers. Arrange flowers in containers.
- Prepare foods that can or need to be stored before serving.

The Best Buffet

- Use varied tableware, food, and accessories for an interesting look.
- Put plates at the beginning of buffet, followed by the side dishes, main course, then salad and vegetables.
- Place relishes, breads, napkins, and silverware at the end of the table.
- Serve drinks from a separate table.
- Leave room between food items so guests have somewhere to put glasses or other items.
- Leave space for maneuvering behind a buffet table.
- Tape down all electrical wires for safety.

☆
SMART MOVE

Light citronella "bug bucket" candles one hour before a backyard party to ward off mosquitoes.

The day of the party

- Buy any last-minute perishables.
- Fix remaining foods as early as possible.
- Do a quick-clean run-through on your house.
- Freshen bathroom towels.
- Go outside and walk through your front door as if you were the first guest. Are there any last-minute things you need to do?
- Light a fire in the fireplace.
- Get dressed one hour before guests arrive, but put on an apron.
- Check bathrooms: Stock with toilet paper, towels, and soap. Turn on a night-light or leave a light on if the switch is hard to find.

The final 60 minutes

- Finish hot food in the oven.
- Put out canapés and snacks.
- Turn on the music.
- Light the candles.
- Set out food and beverages.
- Enjoy greeting your guests at the door.

After the party

- Depending on your style, do only the cleanup necessary to prevent food from spoiling or being eaten by pets during the night.

- Start a special-occasions notebook, in which you make notes about what did and didn't work. You can refer to this resource next time you entertain.

Tips for Entertaining: Details, Simplicity, and Ambience

- If you're planning a large party or reception, reserve your location, caterer, and entertainment at least three months in advance.
- Lower the room temperature before guests arrive.
- For a more dramatic presentation, serve canapés on a small mirror instead of a platter.
- Don't put foods on your menu that require a lot of last-minute kitchen preparation.
- For a buffet, choose foods that will look good after sitting out for more than an hour. Avoid foods such as green salads with dressing, congealed salads, and crackers with spreads that will wilt and become soggy.
- Set out platters the day before your party to plan how traffic flow will work.
- Set up a drink table in a different room from the food.
- Serve chunky punches and iced drinks from a pitcher that has a lip to prevent fruit pieces and ice from pouring out with liquid.
- In addition to the main food table in the dining room, place hors d'oeuvres and finger foods in strategic areas in your living room and family room.
- Choose music carefully. Keep the volume low so conversations can take place. Classical works well for a formal dinner or buffet; introduce guests to your favorite composers, or ask a local music store to help you find selections by Mozart, Beethoven, or Vivaldi.
- Country-and-western music adds flair to a casual dinner or cookout.
- Light jazz (George Benson, Peter White) or instrumental music (Jim Brickman, George Winston) are good general choices. And seasonal varieties are appropriate and enjoyable for most any occasion.
- Consider using live music. Call your local high school to inquire about band students who play in string quartets or combos for parties.
- Student groups are usually inexpensive, but be sure to check on their fee and repertoire of songs before you book them.

- If you have wet weather, place mats inside and outside the door. Provide a plastic container for holding umbrellas.
- Make a smaller table work for large parties by cutting a piece of plywood to the shape and size you need. Lay a blanket over your own table, then place the cutout on top, followed by a tablecloth.
- If you're having a large party, let your kids be servers, door openers, or coat checkers. Use paint pens to decorate T-shirts to look like tuxedos for them to wear. Buy inexpensive plastic top hats at a costume or toy store.
- Before the party, line several paper grocery sacks with plastic garbage bags and hide them in your laundry room or pantry. They'll be ready to use for quick cleanup between courses.
- Have an empty flower vase or two standing by. If a guest brings fresh flowers as a hostess gift, you won't have to run around searching for something appropriate to put them in.
- Make arrangements for your pets. Some guests may have allergic reactions to animals.
- Be sure to have plenty of extra bathroom tissue. Parties tend to tax plumbing to the maximum, so it's considerate to keep a plunger in a discreet but accessible location.
- If children are coming, make sure at least some of the foods are kid friendly.
- Be aware of guests' special dietary needs. Have on hand plenty of chilled sparkling water, fruit juice, and soft drinks. Plan to have at least one meatless dish that is hearty enough to serve as a main course for vegetarians.
- Start a sink of hot water, a squirt of dish-washing liquid, and one tablespoon of bleach after the main course. Soak dinner dishes while you're eating dessert. The bleach will kill germs.
- If your party will be large and noisy, be a good neighbor. The easiest way to avoid potential conflicts is to invite the neighbors. In any case, at least inform those neighbors who are likely to be affected by your party, and ask them to let you know if they are having problems with noise or other aspects of the party.
- Invitations should include whether the party has specific hours or is open ended, if dinner is served and at what time, whether it's a potluck, the type of dress expected, any special activities, and any parking directions.
- If you are expecting more cars than your property or adjacent streets can hold, find alternatives: nearby public parking or neighbors who will allow people to park on their property.

GOOD TO KNOW

When seating a crowd, the rule of thumb is to estimate 24 inches per person at the table.

SMART MOVE

Have upbeat music playing when guests arrive at your home for an event. Lively music stimulates conversation and creates momentum for the gathering.

☆

SMART MOVE

To make flower
blooms last longer,
change the water
daily and diagonally
cut one to two
inches off the ends.

Let your guests know in the invitation where to park. If space is really tight, suggest that they carpool or use public transportation.

A Few Decorating Details

- Use a number of smaller flower arrangements and a low centerpiece on your serving table. This will enable guests to chat with those on the other side of the table as they stand in line. And low centerpieces don't fall over.
- Place lots of votive candles around your dining room and the rest of the party rooms. They won't tip over like tapers might, so they're relatively safe to burn without your constant supervision.
- When choosing fresh flowers for your party, remember that irises wilt fast. Choose heartier flowers such as daisies, lilies, or alstroemeria.
- Consider decorating your mailbox to help guests find your house: Use balloons, flowers, or streamers.
- Create a glamorous atmosphere on a party table by tying up a small piece of dry ice in cheesecloth and putting it into a bowl of punch. (There will be a lot of smoke, but the punch won't be affected.)
- Use nonpoisonous fresh flowers to turn an ordinary cake into a fabulous dessert. Fill small plastic water picks (available at florists) halfway with water and insert flowers. Push them into the top of a frosted cake.
- For an autumn luncheon, carve out miniature pumpkins and fill them with chicken, tuna, or pasta salad.
- Use tiny American flags to decorate foods if your party is on a patriotic holiday.

Rental Know-How

- Obtain price lists from local rental companies for their party items.
- Before choosing a company, ask:
  Does the cost include same-day or next-day return?
  Are the quantities and styles you need available on your party date?
  Are delivery and setup charges included in the price?
  Is there an extra fee for returning dirty dishes, linens, or cutlery?
  What is the charge for broken items?

- Place your order early to ensure a wide choice of colors and styles.
- Have the items delivered as early before your party as possible.
- When items are delivered, check off each item and make sure it works before the driver leaves.
- Schedule the pickup time after the party.

Catering Queries

Interview potential caterers with these questions:
- Do you order rental equipment?
- Do you serve food such as hors d'oeuvres, or do you set it out on tables?
- When will rental equipment arrive? Who will deliver it? When will it be picked up, and by whom?
- Do you offer different dessert options?
- Do you order flowers?
- Do you offer coffee service?
- Do you decorate tables?
- How early do you arrive?
- What cleanup do you do? How much time do you think this will take?
- What kind of insurance do you have?
- What table linens do you provide? Do you have a variety of fabrics and colors from which we can choose?
- Do you provide dishes and silverware? What kinds do you have?
- How many staff people do you bring along?
- Do you charge extra for reserving rentals or other services?
- What is your fee? Do you add a gratuity?
- What menu options are available? Do you take requests? What are your most popular dishes?
- How many electrical outlets do you need?
- Do you suggest a seated meal or a buffet?

Quantities

- Hors d'oeuvres: Expect guests to consume about four per hour. Plan to serve four or five kinds.
- Ice: A 10-pound bag will fill about forty 12-ounce glasses.
- Meat: 18 pounds of bone-in meat or poultry, or 6 pounds of boneless meat or poultry, will feed 24 guests.
- Salad: A head of iceberg lettuce feeds 10; romaine, 8; Boston, 4.
- Dressing: three cups of dressing will serve 24 guests.

CAUTION!

Most candle fires are caused by combustibles being too close to the candle or by the candle falling over or being knocked over by wind, doors, children, or pets, according to the Consumer Product Safety Commission.

- Bread: A large loaf provides 18 to 20 slices. A single baguette feeds 10.
- Butter: Two tablespoons will spread seven slices of bread.
- Cake: A sheet cake weighing five pounds will serve 50 people.
- Ice cream: One gallon will serve 24 people when you're serving cake or cookies as well.
- Coffee: For 24 servings of coffee, you'll need 18 cups of water and 3 cups of ground coffee.

Nine Entertaining Disasters—and What to Do about Them

Disasters can be big or small, depending on how they're handled. Some of them can be avoided altogether.

1. Your electrical system blows a fuse, causing a blackout during your party. A few days before the party, have a trial run to test your home's electrical capacity. Turn on all lights, ceiling fans, music source, and any extra appliances you'll be using. If you blow a fuse or flip a breaker, decide what can be turned off without disrupting the party. You may need to use appliances at differing times or use candles as an alternate light source.

2. More guests show up than anticipated. Make the most of the situation without making your guests feel awkward. Cut food into smaller servings and fill glasses less full. Stretch iced tea by adding orange juice or lemonade. Always keep ingredients on hand to fix extra spur-of-the-moment hors d'oeuvres or a side dish. Enlist an older child or teenager to run the dishwasher midparty so you don't run out of glasses and plates. Or use your stashed paper plates if you have to. If you can't squeeze extra place settings on your table, use inexpensive bamboo lap trays for creating an additional conversational dining group. Note: Your guests will feel more comfortable and welcome if a host or hostess sits at each location.

3. Fewer guests show up than anticipated. Avoid this problem by sending out invitations early—at least three weeks in advance. People are more likely to respond to an invitation that says RSVP than Regrets Only. Also, be sure to mail an invitation back to yourself. If you don't receive it, you'll know to check with the post office to see if a bag of mail was misdirected. If bad weather or unforeseen circumstances arise and guests cannot come, be sure to make those who do come feel welcome. Keep the party on a positive note by not drawing attention to the missing guests.

4. A guest spills something and stains your carpet. Clean up the spill with as little fuss as possible. Let the guest help if this eases the embarrassment. If the carpet is treated with stain repellent, most spills will blot up. Douse the spot with club soda and clean it later.

5. A casserole bubbles over and smokes up your kitchen 30 minutes before the party. Cover the smoldering drips with baking soda immediately. Open windows and doors, and use a portable electric fan to disperse smoke.

6. Your guests are strangers and conversation is slow. Get things moving by asking each guest to tell where he or she was when a significant event occurred. For example: Where were you on New Year's Eve at the turn of the century? For humor, have each person at the table, one at a time, make three statements about him- or herself, two of which are true. Other guests try to guess which one is false. Or introduce one of the guests to the group and say how you know him or her. Ask the rest to introduce themselves and tell how they know you.

7. Someone chokes. The Red Cross recommends to first deliver five back blows between the person's shoulder blades with the heel of your hand; next, perform five abdominal thrusts, known as the Heimlich maneuver. Stand behind the person, put your arms around the waist, make a fist with one hand and grasp the fist with your other hand. Lean the person slightly forward and press hard into the abdomen, underneath the breastbone, with a quick, upward thrust. Repeat five times. While you are doing this, have someone call 911.

8. You (or a guest) are burned or cut. Keep a first-aid kit handy at all times for such unforeseen emergencies as these. Butterfly bandages work wonders on cuts caused by a slip with a paring knife. Apply ice-cold water (never butter) to burns. Apply firm pressure to a deep cut, and keep that part of the body elevated until the bleeding stops. If it's obviously a more serious injury and requires a trip to the ER, have another family member accompany the guest. Stay as calm as possible since your mood is contagious and guests will look to you for a sign as to how to react to a medical emergency.

9. A dessert turns out truly horrible. Always keep a quart of premium ice cream and a bottle of dessert sauce on hand. Paired with some packaged cookies or chocolate, this is a sweet, festive way to end any meal.

☆
SMART MOVE

Master a quick-fix appetizer and a dessert recipe, and keep those ingredients on hand all the time.

Party Ideas

- **Pasta Potluck:** Invite five couples to bring their favorite sauces; you supply the pasta. (Allow two ounces of dry pasta per person, and serve a variety.) Serve crispy breadsticks, an antipasto tray, green salad, and garlic bread. Create atmosphere by setting up card tables with red-checked tablecloths and green napkins. Raffia tied around old wine bottles makes festive candleholders. String tiny white lights in houseplants, and play soft background music.
- **Family Bowl-Game Party:** Decorate with pennants, banners, balloons, and streamers. Create a dining-table centerpiece with cheerleader pom-poms and a basket of mums. Provide popcorn and peanuts for snacking. At halftime, serve steaming bowls of chili, jambalaya, or chowder, and French bread.
- **Dessert Drop-In:** Offer guests seven or eight confections. Include an assortment of tastes and textures—crunchy, creamy, rich, and dense. Provide cheese, fruit, and nuts for those who don't eat sugar.
- **Beat the Winter Blues Beach Party:** Turn up the furnace just a tad higher. Serve summer foods you might take to the beach—cold fried chicken, potato salad, deviled eggs, and fruit punch—or use tropical recipes. Splurge on plenty of flowers, and play music that reminds you of summer.
- **Afternoon Tea Party:** Offer guests three or four kinds of tiny crustless sandwiches, such as cucumber and watercress–cream cheese, along with scones, jam, miniature pastries, and an assortment of hot teas.
- **International Cheese Tasting:** Plan to have a variety of different tastes and textures of cheeses from around the world: a French Brie, an English Stilton, a crumbly, tangy farmhouse cheddar, and Swiss Jarlsberg. Crackers and thin slices of a fresh baguette, along with pears, green grapes, and apples make the perfect accompaniments.
- **Pizza Party:** Buy a big batch of pizza dough from your local pizzeria, or buy frozen balls of dough at the supermarket. Gather the sauce and all the toppings: fontina cheese, sausage, basil leaves, black olives, goat cheese, cooked crumbled hamburger, sun-dried tomatoes, and whatever else you like. Let everyone assemble the pizzas, and while they bake, have everyone sit down for the salad course. Have plenty of cold drinks on hand.
- **Teenagers' Party:** Make a three- to five-foot submarine sandwich. Line up foot-long sandwich buns on a long piece

of aluminum foil. Let the kids layer favorite sub-sandwich toppings and cut the sandwich into serving pieces.

Special Event Seven-Day Countdown

Sometimes you won't have weeks or months to plan a special occasion. Perhaps you want to throw an impromptu celebration for your husband's promotion or your daughter's championship softball team.

Here's a plan for pulling off a special occasion in only a week. On the day of the event, you'll be amazed at what you were able to accomplish in a short period of time. Use these ideas for a Thanksgiving feast, an Easter gathering, a Fourth of July cookout, or anytime you wish you had a magic wand!

Seven days before the big event

- Plan your menu. Include as many make-ahead dishes as possible, and include favorites. Don't knock yourself out fixing winter-squash-and-kumquat pie when plain apple pie is what everyone wants. Fruit salad doesn't have to be in a fancy mold to be festive. And it's just plain smart to buy prepared foods that the bakery or deli can make better than you can.
- Make your own checklist or use a three-ring binder, as described on page 221. Divide tasks among able family members. Write family members' initials by their tasks and post the list in a central location.
- Make a guest list, then phone or e-mail guests to invite them. Be sure to ask for RSVPs. If you're inviting extended family or close friends, consider assigning each of them a dish to bring to the meal.
- Check to see if you have enough dishes: dinner plates, dessert plates, coffee cups and saucers, silverware, glasses. Do the same with napkins. It's perfectly fine to use paper dishware for festive occasions to make cleanup simple. If the occasion calls for fine china, consider hiring someone to help clean up so you can enjoy your guests.
- Check to see how you're doing on bakeware, serving dishes, platters, bread baskets, and such. Now is the time to buy or borrow what you need.
- Cut yourself some slack. Consider hiring a responsible teenager to run errands, grocery shop, clean the house, or play with the kids while you bake or work on decorations.

♡

FROM THE HEART

Entertaining can be a great way to build friendships, and it can be done by anyone, on any budget. One of my fondest memories of our early married years is of a Gourmet Club my husband and I organized with seven other couples, who, by the way, are still good friends 25 years later. (I hope it is obvious that since I was a member of the club, you didn't have to be a gourmet cook to belong.) We met once every seven weeks and took turns hosting a dinner party for the other couples. We only had to "do it up big" once a year, which was doable—and enjoyable.

Six days before

- Carefully check recipes and your list of who's bringing what, then make your grocery list.
- Relieve your refrigerator of unnecessary items to make room for special-event foods. Ditto for your freezer.

Five days before

- Shop for groceries, as well as batteries for your camera, and film, if you use it.
- When putting away groceries, organize foods in your pantry and refrigerator according to each recipe.
- Buy kids' craft items to keep young cousins and friends creatively occupied on the day of the event.
- Delegate someone to be in charge of helping kids with crafts while you're in the kitchen.
- Start making side dishes or portions of recipes that you can freeze ahead.
- Plan your centerpiece.

Four days before

- Check napkins and tablecloths. Launder and iron if needed. Spray with fabric protector for easier cleanup of spots and spills.
- If you're feeding a crowd, count chairs and tables and round up extras from the patio, friends, or a rental company.
- Write a timetable of what needs to be done when on the event day. Start with what time you want to eat, and work backward. What should you prepare first? How long will it take to get the grill going and barbecue the chicken? How big is your turkey, and how long should it cook? What's the last thing you want to take out of the oven? Schedule some time to relax.
- Make sure you have enough burners and pots for cooking and warming right before dinner. Think about what dishes could be warmed in the microwave. Remember that a slow cooker can also serve as a warmer. Fix one or two dishes you can freeze.

Three days before

- Scout serving pieces you'll use, and check glassware and china. Clean or polish as needed.
- Make more space for food preparation by clearing off kitchen countertops and storing anything you won't need.
- Fix one or two dishes you can freeze.

Two days before

- Plan seating arrangements. Make place cards if you're hosting a big crowd.
- Set the table and arrange your centerpiece.
- Fill salt and pepper shakers.
- Start storing ice in bags in your freezer.
- Fix one or two dishes that you can freeze or that you can serve cold.

The day before

- If you need some uninterrupted kitchen time, ask a friend to watch your kids for a couple of hours. Repay the favor when she's having a party.
- Take out frozen dishes to defrost.
- Prepare any dishes you couldn't freeze.
- Buy bread and flowers.
- Give your house a quick once-over.
- Chill beverages.
- Make room in a closet for guests' coats.
- Set the table.

The big day

- Carry out your event-day timetable.
- Enjoy yourself!

Short-Notice Party Shortcuts

- Keep colorful paper goods, candles, and decorations on hand at all times.
- Surface-clean only the rooms guests will see. Close the doors to others.
- Master a quick-fix appetizer and dessert recipe, and keep the ingredients on hand. For example: (1) Keep an eight-ounce package of cream cheese in your refrigerator and a box of gourmet crackers in your pantry. Place the brick of cream cheese on a pretty plate. Then pour a small jar of strawberry jam, jalapeño jelly, or fruit chutney over the top of the cream cheese. Surround with crackers. (2) Keep a bag of chips and the makings for a dip (sour cream and dehydrated soup mix) in your pantry. (3) Keep a frozen pound cake, frozen berries, and paper doilies on hand. Serve a slice of cake with berries on top of a doily. Beautiful and delicious!
- Store drinks to serve guests in a place that is off limits to

the kids. Let the kids have their own special place for their beverages.

- Keep a frozen family-sized entrée (such as a vegetable lasagna) and a tube of refrigerated dinner rolls handy. If company drops in and you want them to stay for dinner, you're ready.
- If you keep on hand a canister of air freshener, a bar of nice soap, and some decorative paper finger towels, your bathroom will always be ready for company.

Party Protocol When You Are the Guest

- Respond promptly to invitations whether you can go or not. If an emergency disturbs your plans, contact the host with your apologies as soon as possible.
- Arrive on time—not early, not late. It is often more trouble to the hosts if you are 10 minutes early rather than 10 minutes late. Call from your car if you will be more than 15 minutes late.
- Never take an uninvited child or guest to a party without asking your host first.
- When you're stopping by several parties in one evening, be polite: Let the host know you can stay just a few minutes.
- Consider taking a small gift, such as a small book, a potted plant, or a loaf of interesting bread, to the host or hostess. If it's a big dinner party, don't take fresh flowers. Your host will need to search for an appropriate vase. If you want to give flowers, have them delivered the day before.
- When going through a buffet line, never eat anything directly off of the serving table. And don't nibble while you are walking back to your table. If no seating is provided, you can eat while standing up or circulating through the crowd.
- If you want to sample the food off someone's plate (with their permission, of course), pass your plate to have a small portion put on it for you to try. Don't reach over and eat off their plate.

BIRTHDAY PARTY PLANNING

Children's parties are becoming more and more elaborate. Many families hire magicians or clowns, set up backyard petting zoos, or schedule outings at skateboard parks or pizza places with indoor playgrounds. But keep in mind that most young children are happy with the basics. Below are tips for making your child's day special without going nuts in the process.

- Plan ahead. Begin planning a month in advance, especially if you're hiring entertainment or renting equipment. Ask around for referrals from neighbors and friends.
- Determine how much you can afford to spend and how many children your child can invite. (The general rule is that the number of guests should equal the child's age, but that doesn't always work. Some children don't enjoy the chaos of a large crowd. In that case, two to three friends may be the perfect party. On the other hand, if you do schedule a party at a site that handles the logistics and provides a party hostess, you may be able to accommodate more kids.)
- For two- or three-year-olds, you'll need to invite a parent, too. This will help the kids feel more comfortable and provide extra hands for games and refreshments.
- For four- and five-year-olds, you'll need lots of energy-busting activities.
- Since six-year-olds are fairly independent and capable of helping during the party, you can handle more of them. Again, it's generally best to come up with a number of short, vigorous activities to use as necessary.
- Plan to have a party assistant—your husband, a friend, an older child—to help with younger children's celebrations. Or hire a responsible teenager to help with preparations, picture taking, and cleanup.
- Let your child's age determine the length of the party. The younger the child, the shorter the party. For teenagers, the length of a party might depend on parental tolerance for late hours and loud music. Negotiate the length of the party beforehand with your teen.
- Come up with several themes for the birthday girl or boy to choose from, or ask your child for ideas. You can build a party around almost anything your child has an interest in.
- Don't feel obligated to buy party products covered with licensed characters. If your child wants a Bob the Builder party, buy Bob the Builder napkins and then buy coordinating solid-color plates and cups. You'll achieve the themed look while saving some money.
- If you choose to give party favors, consider what sort of favor you'd like your own child to come home with. Don't overload children with too much candy or too many junky toys. Consider buying each child a coloring book or an inexpensive paperback book.

GOOD TO KNOW

The melody of "Happy Birthday to You" first appeared in 1893 with the lyrics "Good Morning to You."

GOOD TO KNOW

The top five ice cream flavors, based on U.S. consumption, are vanilla, chocolate, butter pecan, strawberry, and chocolate chip mint, according to the International Dairy Foods Association.

- Select a kid-friendly location. Home is always a wonderful choice, if you have room to accommodate the guests.
- Decide what foods to serve. Be mindful of choking hazards for kids three and under (hot dogs, popcorn, and grapes are generally considered too risky).
- On the party day, make each guest feel special. Place a smiling greeter at the front door to welcome children as they arrive.
- Encourage your child to write thank-you notes to his or her guests, even if they were thanked at the party. It's a great habit to begin that can develop into a lifelong courtesy.

PLANNING A FUN FAMILY GATHERING

In this age of supermobility, it's easy to lose touch with extended family. When that happens, we lose more than regular contact—we miss out on traditions, memory making, and enjoying the bonds of kin.

To keep this from happening, try to make family get-togethers a regular occurrence. The adventure of planning a reunion, whether a yearly occasion or a one-time event, can really be fun. The following tips will help simplify the project so you can enjoy it too.

- Decide what type of reunion you'd like to have: a backyard barbecue for 20 to 50 family members; a weekend reunion held at a camp, resort, or hotel for 50 to 200 family members; or a weeklong camping excursion in which 20 to 80 family members gather. Calculate the cost per individual/family for each idea. (Before you go any further—particularly if you're hoping for a large gathering, survey your family to see how many are interested.)
- If desired, choose a theme or event to celebrate: someone's significant birthday or anniversary, or a pivotal family event.
- Make it easier and more fun: Ask another family member to share the responsibilities.
- Set a date. You should begin planning a year before the reunion. Though you probably won't find a date that fits everyone's schedules, talk with a few key family members who will definitely attend, and set the most accommodating date you can. Or consider sending out a letter that asks about each family's availability.
- While you're discussing dates, ask around about activities everyone might enjoy, who might like to help plan, and so on.

- Consider what locations might work well: state or city parks, recreational clubs, or scenic spots such as lakes. Call or write for information on each possible meeting place. Make sure the location you choose offers opportunities for everyone—a place to play softball, walk, or swim—as well as wheelchair accessibility if needed.
- Create a notebook or file folder that will hold all pertinent details: what must be bought, who's bringing what, a list of those who have RSVP'd, housing arrangements, and a schedule detailing what you will do each day of the reunion and when.
- Make realistic reservations: If the event requires a large per-family fee, plan on fewer to attend than you hope. If your day will be relatively inexpensive, overestimate attendees. Play it safe—base your reservation on the moneys you've already collected, not those you hope to collect.
- Notify family members well in advance with a detailed letter that lists the date, location, and other information. Include:

  > How much money each attendee will need to pay, and when, for expenses. Be clear if any of the fees are nonrefundable.
  >
  > A questionnaire that asks all about the family, and a request for a recent family photo. You'll copy and compile this info into a booklet that will help family members get reacquainted before they meet again. (If you choose to get T-shirts printed for the reunion, ask for shirt sizes.)
  >
  > A list of any special supplies, such as hats for the crazy-hat contest, instruments for a family band, or necessary props for a talent show.

- Assign who will bring what—beverages, meat dishes, salads, desserts, paper plates, and silverware.
- Assign cleanup teams. Also consider appointing a reunion photographer, children's playtime organizer, song leader, adult activity director, video-camera operator, family historian, etc.
- Two weeks before the reunion, send a letter confirming details and adding any last-minute information. You might suggest that family members work together to create fun, matching name tags to wear at the reunion.
- If you don't ask families to bring their own, make name tags or have them ready for families to make themselves when they arrive.

☆

SMART MOVE

A few weeks before the reunion, start talking as a family about who you will see and what you'll do. This will help young children know what to anticipate. If possible, get out photos of out-of-town family. Seeing pictures will help your family remember names and faces of people you haven't seen in a while.

GOOD TO KNOW

The best day to avoid the post office during the Christmas season is Monday—it's typically the busiest day of the week.

JOYFUL IDEAS FOR OVERCOMING CHRISTMAS CHAOS

Seasonal Stress Relief

Each year do you promise yourself that you'll relax and enjoy the holiday season, only to find that by mid-December you're in such a frenzy you can't wait for it to be over? It doesn't have to be that way. These tips will help you keep your vow.

- View unexpected delays as opportunities to slow down and regroup.
- Give up trying to do 20 things when you have time for only 10.
- Plan at least one evening alone in December with your husband. Go out to dinner or send the kids to a friend or relative.
- One day this month, don't schedule anything.
- Don't feel guilty because you can't do everything. Just say, "No, we need this time together as a family," or "No, I can't make a side dish for the office party, but I can buy one at the deli."
- Don't fill your calendar with appointments that can wait until after the holiday season.
- Hang mistletoe and encourage your family to use it frequently.
- Check for loose or burned-out bulbs before you put the lights on the tree.
- Give up making your own elaborate bows or baking difficult recipes you don't like anyway—in fact, anything that makes you nuts.
- Feel free to not attend some functions. You really don't have to accept every invitation or attend every Christmas program at church.
- As much as possible, see that young children follow their normal routines.
- If your office is at home, be realistic about how much you'll be able to accomplish during the holidays when the children are out of school.
- If you have a blended family, avoid misunderstandings during the holidays by settling schedules and other controversial matters well beforehand.
- Don't let a grumpy person spoil your holiday spirit.
- Avoid being frustrated by snooping kids. Wrap gifts before you hide them, then put a color-coded dot on each one so only you know whose it is.

- Don't wait until 1:30 Christmas morning to put together "some assembly required" toys.
- Eliminate confusion about gifts on Christmas Day. Write each family member's name at the top of a separate page, and as each package is opened, note the giver and the gift. Each person will have his or her own list of people to thank.
- If you feel stressed over some holiday jobs but don't mind others, trade with a friend—she bakes your breads; you wrap her gifts.
- Keep your exercise routine as much as possible. Exercise relieves stress. Park far enough away to give yourself a brisk walk to and from the office or the mall. Take the stairs whenever possible.
- December is not the time to start a diet, but be sure you eat some fruits and vegetables every day.
- Give yourself a tea break late in the afternoon or whenever your energy flags. Taking time for yourself allows you to finish chores with renewed vigor.
- Keep inspiring holiday books around your home or office for some quick positive thoughts.
- Be flexible when things don't go as you expected. Remember that the only thing predictable about life is that it's unpredictable.

How to Experience Holiday Joy
Focus on giving

- Have a family brainstorming session and write down ways you can give others joy this season—decorate the room of a nursing-home resident, give blood, buy a book and donate it to a local library, send e-mails of appreciation and encouragement to men and women in the military.
- Ask children, "What are you giving for Christmas?" instead of "What are you getting for Christmas?"
- Take your children with you when you make a donation to a charity. Talk to them about what the money will be used for.
- Volunteer as a family at a food bank or homeless shelter.
- Pack up some goodies and take them to the firefighters and police officers who are on duty on Christmas Eve.
- Take your children to the grocery store and let them help you pick out foods for an extra sack of groceries to donate to a citywide food pantry.

Disconnect from the world and reconnect with your family

- Purposefully disconnect with the outside world—turn off cell

GOOD TO KNOW

For every live Christmas tree harvested, the National Christmas Tree Association reports that up to three seedlings are planted in its place the following spring.

SMART MOVE

If one family member lives far away and can't afford to fly home for Christmas, suggest that other family members chip in and buy him or her a ticket in lieu of a present.

phones, PDAs, landlines, TVs—for a designated time each night, and spend time doing something fun together.

- Set aside one weekend in December as a "family-bound" weekend. Spend time visiting holiday exhibits, working a giant puzzle, wrapping packages, and baking treats. At night, sip hot chocolate and watch favorite holiday movies.
- Get out holiday photographs and videos of your children from years past. Praise them about how much they've grown and learned each year.
- Start a special project early in the month and work on it together a little each night. You might work a giant puzzle, build a dog house for a new puppy, create a table to display a model train, or sew a holiday outfit for a favorite doll.

Put Christ back at the center of Christmas

During Advent, the period leading up to Christmas, take time each night to talk with your children about the meaning of Christmas. Visit a Christian bookstore to find various kinds of Advent calendars, candles, wreaths, and books to enhance your family's tradition.

- If you have young children, buy a Nativity set that allows them to handle and move around the pieces.
- If you have a Nativity scene, consider wrapping the figure of baby Jesus and either hanging it on your Christmas tree or putting it under the tree. Either way, you can begin a family tradition of making that the first present opened each Christmas morning. It's a great way to remember the greatest gift of the season.
- Consider setting up a small tabletop tree in your kitchen reserved for ornaments related to Christ. After dinner each night, let your kids take a turn hanging another one of the ornaments.
- Read part of the Christmas story (Luke 1:5–2:52) together as a family after breakfast or dinner each day.
- Open holiday cards as a family at the dinner table. Take turns reading the messages. Say a prayer for the friends who sent the cards.
- Attend a worship service together as a family.

CREATIVE GIFT GIVING

Quick Gift Baskets

Whether it's Christmas, a birthday, graduation, or just time for a thank-you, gift baskets are fun to give and receive. Line a pretty box or basket with bandannas or various colors of tissue paper, then fill with theme-related items. Your basket can be as simple or as extravagant, as large or as small, as your budget and creativity allow. Here are some ideas to get you started.

Athlete's basket: balls (golf, tennis, or racquetballs), socks, deodorant, sweatbands, energy bars, and a sports magazine.

Beauty basket: fingernail polish, hair ornaments, bubble bath, lotion, a manicure set, and a makeup bag.

Camper's basket: beef jerky or granola, mosquito repellent, a small first-aid kit, a pocketknife, a flashlight, and an astronomy book.

Car-care basket: a large sponge, glass cleaner, a chamois cloth, car wax, a travel coffee mug, a new key chain, an ice scraper, and a whisk broom.

College survival basket: a roll of quarters, a mug and instant cocoa mix, candy bars, chewing gum, highlighter pens, pencils, and other study supplies.

Craft-lover's basket: items for the types of crafts the recipient enjoys, such as painting, woodworking, or embroidery.

Dog-lover's basket: dog biscuits, a rubber toy, a new collar, a package of chew sticks, and a bandanna.

Fisherman's basket: hooks, lures, a jar of bait, flies, fishing line, needle-nose pliers, and a fishing magazine.

Kitchen-lover's basket: spices, a fun-shaped timer and/or other kitchen gadgets, new measuring cups and spoons, gourmet spices, and a cookbook. (Instead of a basket, use a colorful colander, an unusual-shaped cake pan, or a pretty bowl or platter. Line it with tea towels or cloth napkins.)

Newlyweds' basket: handy household items such as tools, picture hangers, twine, refrigerator magnets, and a small book on home repair.

Outdoor enthusiast's basket: waterproof sunscreen, compass, flashlight, bungee cords, snacks, waterproof matches, and a water bottle.

Sewing basket: a package of needles, iron-on patches, small scissors, thread, a thimble, a tape measure, fusible webbing, straight pins, and a sewing/crafts magazine.

Shoe-care basket: shoelaces, buffing brush or cloth, leather cleaner, water repellent, polish, and shoe trees.

GOOD TO KNOW

The gift card market is expected to reach $52 billion by 2012.

☺

FUN FOR KIDS

Start a collection—
of Christmas
ornaments,
hardcover copies
of classic novels,
charms for a charm
bracelet, or other
meaningful items—
for each of your
children. Add to it
at Christmas and
on birthdays.

Last-Minute Gifts

It happens to the best Family Manager—you suddenly realize you have no gift ready and your office assistant's birthday is tomorrow or your son is expected at a birthday party on Saturday.

Prevent needless stress by keeping a few all-occasion gifts for kids and adults on hand. The post-season Christmas sales are a great time to stock up on interesting items at deep discounts. A few such ideas are:

For kids

a small plastic box of activities and art supplies
fast-food or ice-cream shop gift certificate
game or educational software
costume jewelry

For teens and adults

journal and pen
coffee mug—travel or large size
photo album or book
movie-rental or coffee-shop gift certificate
body lotion or spray

Buying Your Children Gifts That Matter

1. *Look beyond their wish lists.* You may not be doing your kids a favor by purchasing gifts on their list if they've seen only the items on TV commercials. Ask yourself, *What are my children's needs?* At their current state of development—physical, emotional, intellectual—what else should be on their lists? Incorporate some of these items along with your children's desires.

2. *Look for toys that stimulate rather than entertain.* Beware of toys that tranquilize kids with mindless entertainment. Instead, choose gifts that encourage creativity and stimulate the intellect or senses.

3. *Look for ways to provide experiences.* Consider giving lessons for special interests, such as arts and crafts, computers, music, or sports. Or give tickets to concerts or travel money to visit family or friends.

4. *Look for ways to emphasize the uniqueness of the child.* Celebrate your child's individuality by giving presents that correspond to his or her special gifts or talents.

PLANNING THE BEST VACATION EVER

Research makes the difference between a trip that leaves you broke, exhausted, and resentful and one that lets you enjoy extras and come back refreshed and optimistic about future family vacations.

Choosing Your Vacation Destination

- The New Year is a great time to look at your calendar and mark out the dates you want to reserve for your family's vacation. If you or your spouse will need to schedule time off from work, it may not be too early to make those arrangements.
- Your family's spending plan should include money set aside regularly for your vacation. Consider how much money you'll have available for your trip. If you think you'll need more to cover lodging or special activities, begin brainstorming the ways you might secure extra funds in time. Could you hold a garage sale in the spring? Could your spouse agree to a few overtime hours?
- Schedule a family meeting to talk about the trip budget and each member's expectations. Estimate the costs of different ideas, then prioritize the list.
- If your vacation fund is small this year, don't despair. This might be the year to take a number of day trips close to home. And take advantage of local, free entertainment: tours, museums, and concerts. The important thing is to schedule a block of time for your family to spend together, enjoying activities that provide a break from the everyday routine.
- Make sure your destination has something for everyone. Don't expect kids to like the same things Mom and Dad do. Plan around the kids.
- As you brainstorm vacation ideas, consider trying something different: going on a bicycle tour, taking a family cruise, working at a guest ranch.

Long-Term Planning

- Search the Internet or write to the visitors bureau or chamber of commerce in the state and city of your destination, as well as the ones you will pass through. Ask for sightseeing brochures, a map, and info about lodging, local activities, and restaurants.
- Choose your mode of transportation. If you're driving, plan to make long drives pleasant by stocking a cooler with drinks

GOOD TO KNOW

The typical household spends $1,500 on a vacation trip and travels 1,200 miles from home, says the Travel Industry Association.

and snacks, packing a picnic, and bringing along music and audiobooks.

- If you belong to an auto club, request copies of maps and guidebooks.
- Search for affordable lodging. Ask friends or travel agents for tips, and compare brochures. For each hotel, compare the number of beds, baths, rooms, laundry and kitchen facilities, activities for children, babysitting services, and sports amenities.
- Research which local restaurants have kids' menus.
- Be sure to ask about all discounts before you book a room.
- Read the fine print. Brochures and photos don't guarantee anything.
- Beware of travel packages that require a tour of resort property.
- Consider vacations at a national park.
- Start a reading program for the trip. If kids meet their reading quotas, they can earn a cash prize on the last day. (Reading fiction or nonfiction about the place you are visiting will build their excitement when they see the place for themselves.)
- Let your kids start earning spending money.

Short-Term Planning

- Guarantee your room for late arrival, no matter when you plan to arrive.
- Know the existing balance and credit limit on each of your credit cards.
- Decide how much cash and traveler's checks you will need to take with you.
- Put your name and business address on all your luggage, and always keep it within sight in public places.
- Plan to start driving early. On longer trips, reserve motel rooms ahead.
- Before the trip, plan your meals and make a shopping list for when you arrive. Bring small items like spices from home. If you're driving, freeze a casserole ahead and transport it in a cooler.
- Cut out the portion of a map with the highways you'll be traveling, then highlight the route with a yellow marker. Glue your map to a piece of cardboard and laminate it with clear contact paper. Kids will enjoy tracking your progress. Get the car tuned up and check the air pressure in your tires.
- Make arrangements for any pets that will not be traveling with you. Contact your local kennel, or contact a friend or neighbor to pet-sit.

FamilyManager™

- ❏ Wallet/Cash
- ❏ Credit cards and/or traveler's checks
- ❏ Eyeglasses/contacts
- ❏ Sunglasses
- ❏ Watch
- ❏ Medical insurance cards
- ❏ Prescription and other medications
- ❏ Itineraries, tickets, and reservation-confirmation numbers
- ❏ Maps and directions
- ❏ Tote bag or backpack for day use
- ❏ Camera, film batteries, charger for digital camera
- ❏ Toys, playing cards, small games
- ❏ Flashlight and batteries
- ❏ Umbrellas, rain ponchos, or jackets
- ❏ Large plastic bags for laundry and wet items
- ❏ Small plastic bags
- ❏ Disposable wipes
- ❏ Travel alarm
- ❏ Sewing kit
- ❏ First-aid kit
- ❏ Snacks/gum
- ❏ Water/juice, no-spill cups
- ❏ Paper towels, tissues
- ❏ Cell phone programmed with emergency numbers, charger
- ❏ Maps/road atlas
- ❏ Toothbrushes, toothpaste, dental floss, and mouthwash

- ❏ Deodorant
- ❏ Combs, brushes, hair accessories, blow dryer (check hotel online to see if it provides such things)
- ❏ Shampoo, conditioner
- ❏ Sunscreen and lip balm
- ❏ Lotion
- ❏ Insect repellent
- ❏ Sunburn and rash salves
- ❏ Shaving items
- ❏ Makeup
- ❏ Nail clippers scissors and emery board
- ❏ Tweezers
- ❏ Cotton balls and swabs
- ❏ Feminine hygiene products
- ❏ Sneakers or walking shoes
- ❏ Outfits for each day
- ❏ Underwear
- ❏ Sleepwear
- ❏ Swimwear
- ❏ Hiking gear
- ❏ Accessories
- ❏ Outerwear
- ❏ Pillows
- ❏ Address book and stamps
- ❏ Extra duffel or tote bag for souvenirs
- ❏ Stain-removal stick

For baby:

- ❏ Car seat
- ❏ Diaper bag
- ❏ Disposable diapers
- ❏ Changing pad
- ❏ Baby powder and lotion
- ❏ Zippered plastic bags
- ❏ Wet wipes
- ❏ Nursing pads/burp pads
- ❏ Bibs
- ❏ Baby food and spoon
- ❏ Bottles, nipples, and caps
- ❏ Formula and/or juice
- ❏ Pacifiers

- ❏ Changes of clothing
- ❏ Jacket or sweater
- ❏ Collapsible stroller with canopy or umbrella
- ❏ Front or back child-carrying pack or sling-style child carrier
- ❏ Portable crib/playpen
- ❏ Blankets
- ❏ Waterproof sheets
- ❏ Bathing supplies
- ❏ Large plastic bags for wet clothes
- ❏ Lotion for diaper rash
- ❏ Teething medicine
- ❏ Nasal aspirator

☺

FUN FOR KIDS

Take along
Colorforms for
young children on
trips. They work
great on windows.

- Arrange to have your mail and newspaper delivery stopped, or ask a neighbor to collect your mail and newspapers while you're away.
- Take along a book you can read aloud to the family before you go to bed at night. Choose one you can start and finish on the trip.
- Get office clothes dry-cleaned while you're away.
- When you get home, plan to do your laundry at a Laundromat, where you can do it all at once, and sort the mail while you're waiting. And always build in a one-day buffer between returning home and going back to school and work.

Planning a Kid-Friendly Vacation

To make sure the kids have a great time, keep them in mind as you plan. Here are some tips.

- Do less than you think you can during the trip so that no one comes home exhausted.
- Schedule alone-time for family members who need it.
- Forget about the office. Focus on your family.
- Have your kids start a trip scrapbook, collecting things each day to put in it, such as postcards, a leaf, etc. Record humorous incidents and special memories.
- Make trip videos as you go, and watch them at night in your hotel. An older child could be in charge of making the video. Or rent videos from a local store rather than from the hotel.

Saving Your Sanity on a Road Trip

Days on the road can stretch too long for kids and adults. By planning ahead, you can save yourself from the bickering in the backseat—and the front.

1. Don't wait until the last minute to prepare. Share the many errands required before a trip: servicing the car, filling up with gas, installing the proper safety seats, and packing the night before you leave. Go to bed early if possible.

2. Pack smart. Place pajamas, toothbrushes, hairbrushes—everything you need for going to sleep—on top of your suitcase or in a separate bag so it will be ready for your first night at your destination.

3. Let your child pack a travel box with small toys, art supplies, and other treasures. Add a couple of new toys for surprise

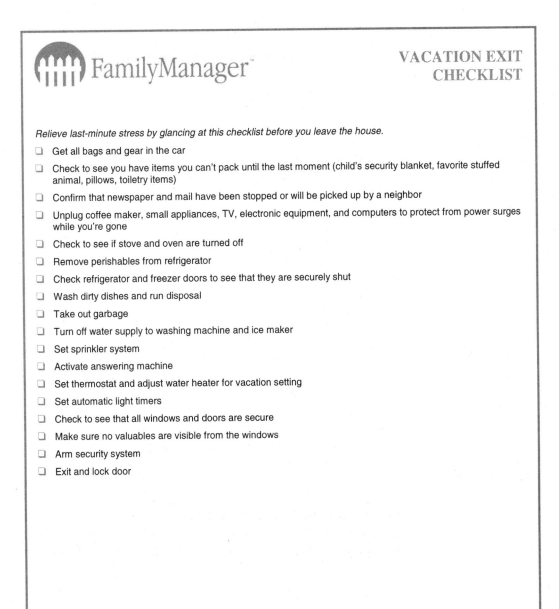

FamilyManager

VACATION EXIT CHECKLIST

Relieve last-minute stress by glancing at this checklist before you leave the house.

❏ Get all bags and gear in the car

❏ Check to see you have items you can't pack until the last moment (child's security blanket, favorite stuffed animal, pillows, toiletry items)

❏ Confirm that newspaper and mail have been stopped or will be picked up by a neighbor

❏ Unplug coffee maker, small appliances, TV, electronic equipment, and computers to protect from power surges while you're gone

❏ Check to see if stove and oven are turned off

❏ Remove perishables from refrigerator

❏ Check refrigerator and freezer doors to see that they are securely shut

❏ Wash dirty dishes and run disposal

❏ Take out garbage

❏ Turn off water supply to washing machine and ice maker

❏ Set sprinkler system

❏ Activate answering machine

❏ Set thermostat and adjust water heater for vacation setting

❏ Set automatic light timers

❏ Check to see that all windows and doors are secure

❏ Make sure no valuables are visible from the windows

❏ Arm security system

❏ Exit and lock door

SMART MOVE

Have a tote bag or small plastic crate in the car specifically for kids to put their socks and shoes in when they take them off.

En Route Money-Saving Methods

- Drink water with meals.
- Use your cell phone (depending on your plan) or the pay phone in the hotel lobby rather than the one in your room.
- Buy snacks somewhere other than the in-room refrigerator.
- Skip room service.
- Don't wait until you're running on fumes to buy gas, so you can look for competitive prices. Check oil and tires occasionally.

treats. A 13x9x2-inch metal cake pan with a lid doubles as a storage box and lap desk in the car.

4. When traveling with a baby, pack enough formula, diapers, and other supplies to more than cover the estimated time spent in transit. Be prepared for delays.

5. Pack your sense of humor and a positive attitude. These will help you survive bad weather, rude people, poor service, and a host of other inconveniences.

6. Plan the end of your trip too. Leave a meal in the freezer at home awaiting your arrival.

7. Wear loose, comfortable clothing and shoes. Make sure kids' clothes are easy to get in and out of during restroom visits.

8. Relieve last-minute stress by glancing at the Vacation Exit Checklist on page 249 before you leave the house.

9. Bring along music and audiobooks the whole family will enjoy. Also bring joke and brainteaser books.

10. Play Look for the License Plates. Make a photocopy of a United States map. Glue the map to a piece of cardboard, and cover it with clear contact paper. Every time you spot a license plate from a different state, color in the state with an erasable marker. When you arrive at your destination, count the number of states you marked. Wipe off the board and play the game again on the way home.

11. Have the driver and the front-seat passenger share responsibilities. If possible, let each parent be relieved of his or her duties at regular intervals. Interstate traffic may be a delightful change for one parent, whereas the other might have a fresh supply of patience for the backseat. When both parents are tired or a backseat catastrophe occurs, it might be a good time to stop for a snack, air out the car, change the seating arrangement, and then resume the trip as you play that great CD you've been saving for an hour of desperation.

12. Require a 5- to 10-minute period of silence each hour. (This can be a real sanity saver.)

13. Stop every two hours. Let each person have a turn deciding when to stop. For example, an eight-year-old might dictate that at 2:17 you'll stop for ice cream. When that time comes, go to the first place that offers ice cream. Dad might determine that at 5:54 he wants to stop at the first bait store you see after that time.

14. Carry a small notebook to keep pertinent trip information. For future reference, take notes along the way about the places you enjoyed or that gave you good service, such as gas stations, motels, and restaurants. Make note of negative experiences too so you won't make the same mistake twice.

15. Diversity keeps kids content—let them exchange toys, snacks, and seats during the trip.

16. Comfort is everything. Let kids visit restrooms frequently and keep them well fed: Bagels and fruit are good car snacks.

17. Offer kids water while traveling rather than pop or juice. They like water less, so they'll drink less, and you'll visit restrooms less!

18. Stop at points of interest along the way to your final destination. This makes the trip pass more quickly.

CHAPTER 7

MANAGING YOURSELF

If you've made it this far into the book, you and I probably have something very important in common: We want to be great mothers and Family Managers. We understand the far-reaching influence we have on those whose lives we touch. It is part of the fabric from which we're cut to care for, nurture, and sacrifice for the good of those we love.

Sacrifice may be the word with which we most identify. A friend of mine put it like this: "When the platter of fried chicken is passed around, I always choose the wing or the back. I say those are my favorite pieces—but really they're not. I just want my kids to have the best parts."

This is good and bad news. Mothering is a wonder-filled, satisfying, and challenging job. I wouldn't give it up for anything. But the bad news is that mothers typically suffer from neglect. It's true: The caregiver receives the least care.

One of my favorite parts of my work is traveling around the country and meeting the thousands of women who attend my seminars. I love listening to their stories and offering advice about the problems and issues with which they are dealing. I hear one complaint again and again, from coast to coast and border to border: Women are so busy caring for everyone else's needs, they don't have time to care for themselves. They're drained, sucked dry of emotional, physical, and spiritual energy. They know they can't just quit caring for their children and fulfilling their Family Manager responsibilities—but they wonder if they'll make it.

Women are often so busy caring for everyone else's needs, they don't have time to care for themselves.

Sound familiar? If your children are young, their constant demands can be exhausting. Even those of us with older kids can feel strained because our kids still need us, although in different ways. Unless we nourish ourselves, we won't have the emotional, physical, and spiritual stamina it takes to manage the other six Family Manager departments.

When filling out your Daily Hit List, please do not think that the Self-Management column is less important than the other departments. The truth is, listing what you will do to care for your body, sharpen your mind, and nourish your spirit may be more important— because if Mom breaks down, everything else suffers. When you feel overwhelmed, you find little pleasure in life. You have no buffer against the relentless everyday pressures. Something's got to give, and it's usually you.

The buffer every mom needs comes from *self-care*. When you take time to rejuvenate, it pays off in many ways, including being a better wife, mom, daughter, sister, and friend. When you don't, it exacts a high cost. When you're exhausted, you're not much good to anyone.

When you make caring for yourself a priority, you're better equipped to care for everyone else. It's the ultimate cure for impending madness as well as the ultimate gift you can give yourself and those around you.

This may sound strange, but as Bill and I have renovated houses over the years, I've seen a direct correlation between the work we do on those houses and the work each of us needs to do on ourselves. Buying a house with the intention of working on it and then reselling it at a profit is a big risk and commitment. First, a house is never done. By the time you get the kitchen redecorated, the bathrooms functioning, and the living room painted, you may need a new roof. Then it's time to paint the bedrooms and wallpaper the dining room, and lo and behold, the living room needs to be painted again. Then there's always ongoing maintenance—on the furnace, the appliances, the windows, the exterior.

> **When you're exhausted, you're not much good to anyone.**

Second, when you renovate a house, it's important to make changes that add value to the house. Not every enhancement you make to a house adds value to it, and some things you do can lessen its value. (Installing a trickling waterfall in the master bedroom may remind you of your honeymoon in Maui, but it probably won't increase the equity.) When Bill and I buy a house, we try to be as careful as we can to make the kinds of improvements that add value to the house.

So it is with you (and me)—on both counts. First, you will never be done. All the things you want to change for the better are not going to happen today or tomorrow. And even when a lot of the changes have been made, there will always be something else you need to work on.

Second, you will always be a project in progress, hopefully getting better and better. When you make nurturing your body, mind, and spirit a priority, you are creating an enhanced version of yourself, better equipped to handle the inevitable pressures, challenges, and surprises of motherhood. And you'll be on track for becoming the woman God created you to be.

Remember: Most women unconsciously and automatically put the needs of others—spouse, kids, friends—before their own. Our sleep, phone calls, meals, and even bathroom time are all fair game. That means we must be intentional about taking time to replenish our own bodies, minds, and spirits.

One simple way to begin doing this is to schedule a "quiet time" every day, and say no to interruptions. Establish a set quiet time each day—for example, between 2:30 and 3:00 p.m.—during which no one can ask for anything, barring an emergency. If you retreat to the bathroom to soak in the tub, put a "Do Not Disturb" sign on the door. Young children who don't take naps can be taught that even if they don't go to sleep, they must have quiet time in their rooms, looking at books, listening to music or audiobooks quietly, or playing with quiet toys.

As you read this section, look for other solutions you can incorporate into your life right away. And come back to the section when you need quick inspiration or a reminder that taking care of yourself is as essential as taking care of all the other blessings in your life.

The Most Important Things to Remember

1. You have to be in good shape to give good shape to the rest of your life.

2. When your own needs go unmet, your body gets stressed and starts reacting. Your mind races in turmoil, your emotions are erratic, and your spirit becomes discouraged. You are in no condition to nurture anyone else.

3. The next time you're tempted to put your own needs on the back burner, try to remember that your children do not need a cranky, tired, and resentful mother.

4. Making fitness a priority isn't just about looking great. It's about caring for your one and only body in a way that promotes and increases health, energy, and longevity.

5. You make decisions, then your decisions make you.

6. When you work in harmony with the way God created you—instead of trying to be like someone else—you can better manage your home and personal life.

7. No matter how out of control you feel, your life can change in significant, positive ways.

8. Little changes can make a big difference.

9. If you aim at nothing, you'll likely hit it.

10. God created you with incredible potential and wants to help you reach it.

Strategies and Solutions for Managing Yourself

CREATING SELF-CARE HABITS

No-Cost Ways to Build Rest into Your Life
Whatever your circumstances in your life, you can always work on building important self-care habits into your life.

- Create buffer zones in your schedule. Giving yourself even a 10-minute break between tasks can defuse your tension.
- Spend time regularly with people who inspire you and whose company you enjoy.
- Carve out time to help others. Their stresses will help you put yours in proportion, and you'll find that life takes on a new hue when you have a thankful heart.
- Be smart about your monthly cycle. Keep a calendar of emotions for a month or two. See if you can pinpoint when you're likely to be dealing with PMS, and be careful about what you schedule during that time. When you're experiencing PMS, do whatever it takes to get plenty of rest, don't eat sweets, exercise as much as possible, and cut back on caffeine.
- Spend some time outdoors each day—exercising, eating lunch, even reading a book on your back porch. Breathe some fresh air and feel the sunshine, even if it's only for 10 or 15 minutes at a time.
- Look your best for yourself. Getting into the rut of being sloppy in your appearance can drag you down and add to your stress.
- Start working on a project or putter at a hobby you enjoy.
- Find a special place that refreshes and inspires you, whether it's a park bench, a mountain trail, the beach, or the woods. Schedule time to go there as a brief retreat to get away from the craziness of life and read or reflect. Trade babysitting with a friend who would like to do the same.
- Plan ahead for times of extra stress, such as the holiday season or before a big project you're in charge of.

  Sleep a little extra ahead of time.
  Cut back on any activities you can.

Make sure you do your morning quiet time faithfully.
Plan your time as efficiently as possible.
Restrict the demands others impose on you.
Don't add anything unnecessary to your schedule. Wait until the crunch is over to get your teeth cleaned.

- Stick to your priorities. Taking time to care for yourself must be high on your list of what's important or it won't happen. Delete activities and commitments that are not fulfilling. Don't let other people "guilt" you into saying yes to things that aren't priorities to you. Don't feel guilty about not doing what other people want you to do. Remember, when you say yes to something, you're saying no to something else. Don't let it be yourself.
- Learn to relax. Consciously relax your brow. Drop your lower jaw. Avoid clenching your fists or holding tightly to objects; consciously relax your hands, especially when holding a pen, driving a car, or watching TV. Relax your stomach muscles. Breathe deeply.
- Count the blessings in your life, just from last week. If none come to mind, answer some questions: Has your car been running smoothly? Do you have hot water for a shower? Has someone told you that he or she cares? Have you been able to make progress on a project? Has your child come home with a good grade? Attitude colors everything in our lives. Choosing to look for the good instead of focusing on what's bad or missing will make a huge difference in your happiness.
- Plan for free time. Block it out on your calendar just as you would an important appointment.
- Start an informal "support group." Seek out women who have similar interests or are in the same life stage as you. Agree to be there for each other when life gets tough.
- Create a morning ritual. Begin each day with prayer, reading the Bible or an inspirational book, or journaling.
- Exercise. When we exercise, our bodies produce endorphins, a morphinelike substance that can deliver a feeling of peacefulness. Endorphins are the body's natural painkillers. Exercise also serves as an outlet for pent-up stress.
- Give someone else a mental and emotional lift. Showing appreciation and praising someone else is a good way to lift your own spirits.
- Take a vacation. Whether it's a getaway with your husband or a fun group of girlfriends, put this high on your to-do list. But

it's important to realize that a vacation can be just as stressful as what you left back home if you don't follow some simple rules. Here are some tips for how to take a relaxing, refreshing vacation.

Have realistic expectations. A vacation won't change your life in a week, but it can and will be refreshing if you let it be.

Evaluate past vacations. Without being too critical, think of what could be improved.

Give yourself permission to relax. Don't fall prey to free-floating guilt that says you should be working or doing something more useful, or that you shouldn't be having such a good time.

Laugh at obstacles and mishaps. Don't let things like long lines or flat tires flatten your fun.

Decide on a vacation eating plan. Overeating can ruin a vacation. Resistance is usually a little lower during vacations. Fatigue, frustration, and even boredom can stimulate indulgence.

Get regular exercise on your trip. Aim for a good balance between rest and activity.

- Take a vacation from something. If you can't take a vacation to someplace, taking a vacation from something can be restoring, even if it's only for 24 hours. For example, as a family or in your office, decide that you're going to take a vacation from complaining or making any negative comments for 24 hours. A vacation from television and radio can help clear your mind. A vacation from the phone also helps.

Choosing Self-Care Strategies That Work for You

I have a friend who heads to the bathtub with a book to relax. She has a shelf that fits across her tub so she can prop it up and read without the pages getting wet. Her children know that, barring serious injury—and it better be serious—Mom is not to be disturbed for 30 minutes. Another friend gets rejuvenated by "airing herself out," as she puts it. She takes a brisk walk while listening to her favorite music on her iPod.

The point is, we all get refreshed in different ways. Identifying what reenergizes you and carving out time to make it happen will pay big dividends to your entire family. Read the following questions and note which ideas appeal to you or bring to mind times when you've been refreshed.

☆
SMART MOVE

When you give yourself permission to take a class to learn something new, join a women's Bible study, take time regularly to exercise, or get together with friends who inspire you, you are setting a good example of self-care for your children.

GOOD TO KNOW

Medical studies suggest that the ideal amount of time for adults to sleep is seven hours a night.

- Do you notice that a certain style of music in the background steadies your nerves?
- Do you give yourself facials and take care of your skin with good products?
- Do you make it a point to spend time with stimulating, upbeat people?
- What forms of exercise bring a smile to your face?
- When you read a book, do you feel as if you've escaped to another world?
- Are you allowing yourself to pursue a new hobby or interest just for the fun of it?
- Do you allow yourself to take mini midweek retreats—like to a museum or a park?
- Do you collect ideas and quotes that stimulate your thinking or enhance your life?
- Do you attend services or studies that stimulate your spiritual growth and understanding?
- Do you buy or cut fresh flowers to enjoy at home or on your desk at the office?
- Do you make some quiet time to think about where you are in life, about your goals and aspirations?
- Do you keep a journal of your thoughts and prayers?
- Do you keep a dream file of brochures and articles about faraway places you'd like to visit?
- Do you buy or check out audiobooks from a bookstore or public library for listening to and learning from in your car?
- Do you splurge a little every now and then to do or buy something special for yourself?
- Do you allow yourself to get a massage every so often?
- Do you reward yourself with something enjoyable when you've finished a big chore or project?
- Do you look forward to spending time regularly with a group, like a writing club, a tennis league, or a church choir?

Pick one thing from this list that resonated with you, and try it this week to begin building a new habit of self-nurturance.

TAKING CARE OF YOUR BODY

Making fitness a priority isn't just about looking great. It's about caring for your one and only body in a way that promotes and increases health, energy, and longevity. Fitness also builds stamina. You can go more easily with less sleep for brief periods, your body bounces back from minor illnesses more quickly, you set a great lifelong example for your kids, you feel better about yourself, and you can cope with the inevitable setbacks of life more easily. In this section you'll learn some simple ways to be healthy and feel your best.

Get Moving! Building Exercise into Your Life

Think of the tortoise and the hare. For beginning exercisers, this is especially important. Slow and steady wins the race. Doing too much too fast eventually earns us the hare's booby prize—or a pulled tendon, a strained muscle, or a bad back (not to mention the discouragement that follows). So set modest goals in the beginning.

Before you pay for a gym membership or sign up for a 6 a.m. strength-training class, see if the center offers a guest pass for one visit or session so you can see how you like it. You might also consider adding a 30-minute walk around your neighborhood or a favorite exercise DVD into your daily routine. The Centers for Disease Control and Prevention also offers some great tips for people who want to become more physically active (see http://www.cdc.gov/physicalactivity). The following tips will also help you stick to your resolve to become more fit.

1. At the beginning of each week, schedule in brief blocks of time as "appointments" with yourself to exercise. Treat them like any other appointment—break them only if absolutely necessary.

2. If you miss a day, forgive yourself and get back to your routine as soon as possible. Beating yourself up accomplishes nothing.

3. Find a role model.

4. Listen to fast-paced music on your iPod.

5. If you'll be exercising at home, set out your exercise clothes at night so you'll put them on first thing. If you're going outside the home to work, put your workout clothes by the exit door to prompt yourself to go to the gym at lunchtime.

6. Make appointments to exercise with friends.

7. Try a variety of programs to avoid boredom. Cross-training is the name of the game.

8. Don't push yourself too hard.

9. Set up a reward system for yourself.

⭐

SMART MOVE

Walking is the easiest exercise to start. It strengthens your body and relaxes your mind. It requires no expensive equipment (only a good pair of walking shoes), no training, and no expensive facilities.

10. Keep a log of the times you've exercised.

11. Seek out information on health and fitness.

12. Begin to see and talk about yourself as someone who is pursuing health. Even though extra weight takes a while to come off, you're working on it. Give yourself credit!

Good reasons to exercise

In addition to increasing your metabolism and helping with weight loss, regular exercise:

- builds strong muscles and bones
- strengthens your heart
- reduces your risk of chronic diseases, including heart disease, osteoporosis, and high blood pressure
- helps control your weight
- reduces your risk of many types of cancers
- slows the aging process
- reduces symptoms of PMS
- relieves menstrual pain
- improves your self-image
- relieves depression
- improves the quality of your sleep
- improves your posture
- improves the quality of your life, particularly as you age
- increases your metabolism and decreases your appetite
- releases stress
- reduces the severity of varicose veins
- gives you more energy
- increases your resistance to fatigue
- helps you to be more productive at work
- builds stamina for other physical activities
- increases your feeling of well-being
- sets a good example for your children

21 simple ways to sneak exercise into your life

When we get overly busy, exercise is often the first thing we drop from our schedules. During the times when you can't work out at the gym or make it to strength-training class, you can easily make exercise part of your everyday life.

1. Turn the playground into a gym and get fit while your tot is busy having fun. Work the equipment. Giving your child a ride on the merry-go-round will rev up your heart,

firm your arms, and strengthen your legs. Pushing her on a swing is great for toning your arms. You can also grab a pole and do some leg lifts while she's playing in the sandbox.

2. Park in a far-off spot and take the opportunity to walk when you're running errands.

3. Invest in an exercise DVD and work out at home.

4. Don't sit to chat with a friend; schedule a time to walk and talk instead.

5. Get off the bus before your stop and walk the rest of the way.

6. Schedule active fun for weekends: hiking, bowling, tennis, swimming.

7. Take the stairs instead of the elevator.

8. While drying your hair, do some leg lunges.

9. Store a pair of athletic shoes at the office so you can take advantage of a sunny lunch hour.

10. While watching TV, do some crunches.

11. If you don't have a long block of time available to exercise, do brief stints of exercise instead: three 10-minute activities instead of 30 continuous minutes.

12. While you drive, tighten your thighs, buttocks, and tummy.

13. Pick up a two- or three-pound weight and work your biceps while you chat on the phone.

14. Wash your car yourself.

15. When working at the kitchen counter, do calf raises.

16. Make those waits work: walk in the hall by the doctor's office until he or she is ready for you; stroll around the block if you're told there's a 30-minute wait for a table at a restaurant.

17. Swing your arms when you walk.

18. Do leg lifts while dinner is cooking.

19. Wear weights on each ankle while puttering around the house: walking to and from the laundry room, getting the mail, putting towels away upstairs.

20. Do housework briskly.

21. Go ahead—swim, walk, dance, skate—now, not 20 pounds from now.

Smart Eating Tips

Moms are often the last ones seated at dinnertime and the first to jump up when the bread basket needs to be refilled. We also are typically on the run from morning until late at night. While we may carefully monitor our kids' lunches and snacks, it's easy to rationalize that we have to eat expeditiously—whatever we can grab on the fly, if we take time to eat at all.

Yet if you don't give your body good fuel in the form of healthy foods, you won't have the stamina you need to keep up with the daily demands for your time and energy. Eating more wisely doesn't have to be complicated or time consuming. Here are some simple tips to help you get the nutrition you need:

- Stock your pantry and refrigerator with healthy foods that are ready to eat or quickly and easily prepared.
- Avoid refined sugar and high-carbohydrate foods.
- Eat when you are hungry. Stop when you are full.
- Begin a habit of never eating while you're standing up. Let your kids fine you if they catch you doing this.
- Put less food on your fork or spoon, and take smaller bites. Consider using smaller plates; studies have shown that doing so keeps people from eating larger portions.
- Wait 10 minutes when you have an urge to snack. The urge might pass.
- Pack your own snacks when you're traveling.
- Don't buy foods that tempt you. If you know you "can't eat just one," leave them at the store!
- Plan menus that call for baking, broiling, or roasting rather than frying.
- Allow yourself only three taste samples of whatever you're cooking. (By the way, this is the one time it might be best to eat while you're standing up!)
- Eat slowly and play calm background music while you eat. Research shows we eat faster when we listen to fast music while eating.
- Brush your teeth after every meal. You'll be less inclined to continue nibbling.
- If you know your day's plans include a stop at a fast-food restaurant, decide ahead of time what healthy menu choice

you can make. Trying to make a wise choice when it's time to place your order almost never works. If you're not sure what menu items are healthiest, check the restaurant's Web site—or pick up a nutritional information brochure the next time you're there.

- When eating out at a more upscale restaurant, choose an appetizer instead of a main dish. Avoid foods that are buttered, fried, creamed, or scalloped; come with gravy or cheese sauce; or are served au gratin, in a pastry, or cooked in oil.
- Order a low-fat fish such as cod, halibut, sole, snapper, swordfish, or shark.
- Stop eating when you are full, and ask the server to wrap up the extra to take home. If you're served a larger portion than you expected or can eat, consider asking the server for a takeout box right away so you can pack the extra to take home before you're tempted to eat it.
- Look for fruit on the dessert menu. If you don't see it, ask your server if you could order a small plate of fruit. Or order a light, low-fat dessert such as sherbet, sorbet, or angel food cake.
- Have a cup of coffee, tea, or cappuccino made with skim milk. If you have a hankering for something sweet, a teaspoon of sugar in coffee has many fewer calories than a piece of chocolate cake.

Turn Energy Zappers into Energy Boosters
Eating right makes a big difference in your energy level. Eating low-fat, low-carb foods rather than high-fat ones will help you avoid lethargy. And remember, protein is brain food—and brainpower is something we can all use more of!

Slowly working exercise and healthy eating habits into your life can help revitalize you. But if you often feel sluggish, consider whether any of the following factors could help you become more energized.

Quench thirst. You lose the equivalent of 10 cups of water each day through normal activities. And you replace only about four through eating. Hidden dehydration robs you of energy and makes you feel lethargic. Drink water all day, every day.

Get enough rest. If you don't sleep consistently at the same time for at least seven to eight hours, you are probably throwing your body out of whack. Inconsistent sleep patterns will leave you lethargic. Sleep isn't an indulgence; it's a necessity.

⚠ CAUTION!

Ask your doctor to test your vitamin D level. Vitamin D deficiency has become a major health problem, according to Mayo Clinic. Vitamin D aids in the absorption of calcium, helping to form and maintain strong bones. Vitamin D deficiency can lead to osteoporosis, muscle weakness, fractures, common cancers (including breast cancer), infectious diseases, and several autoimmune diseases.

Let there be light. When it's dark, your body says, "Sleep." When it's light, your body says, "Get up and move!" When you get up in the morning, throw open the curtains immediately. Get as much light as you can, and you'll feel more energetic.

Turn off the TV. When you feed your mind with television, you are encouraging your body to be passive. Even "smart" shows like the evening news can zap energy because they put your body into a sedentary mode. So take television in moderation, and make sure you're being active the rest of the time. Make activity, not TV, the highlight of your day. And keep an exercise mat nearby, so that when you do watch TV, you can get in some exercise at the same time.

Take vitamins. Ask your physician about what's right for you. At the very least, you should take a multivitamin. Be good to your body so it will be good to you.

Identify Hidden Stressors

Stress is the reaction we have when small irritations or big catastrophes enter our lives. When we have too much stress for too long, it can result in such physical damage as high blood pressure, a weak immune system, ulcers, headaches, heart disease, and arthritis. Our bodies give us clear warning signs when we're nearing stress overload. Little things that once didn't faze us now set us off. We may have trouble relaxing or feel like human pressure cookers—always ready to blow our tops.

We all have hidden stressors in our lives, and identifying them is the first step to eliminating them. Go through the following list and ask yourself if any of these things are giving you a stress signal.

- cartoons blaring from the family TV
- your teenager's stereo system
- living near a noisy freeway, railroad, or airport
- bad lighting
- an uncomfortable desk chair
- dogs barking
- violence on the evening news
- a drawer that comes off the track every time you open it
- clutter
- a never-diminishing pile of ironing
- the mail
- ill-fitting clothes
- uncomfortable shoes
- a spouse who won't talk

- remodeling or construction
- a messy house
- a decrease in pay or an increase in hours
- problems with your car
- difficulty sleeping
- illness in the family
- houseguests
- debt
- sexual difficulty
- anger toward your spouse
- anger toward your children
- trouble with your in-laws
- weather conditions

You can control some of the stressors above—by turning off the evening news, wearing another pair of shoes, and buying brighter lightbulbs, for example. But if you feel helpless to address your stressors, particularly if you feel near—or past—the boiling point, consider consulting a counselor. Give yourself the freedom to treat stress as you would any other chronic condition. If you had persistent back pain, you'd seek a doctor and get treatment. Pain like this—personal, relational, and situational stress—deserves the same focused attention.

SHARPENING YOUR MIND

When my kids were young, I heard someone say, "You don't grow old. You get old by not growing." At that point in my life I realized that I could recite many of Bert and Ernie's lines, and I'd memorized the names of most of Richard Scarry's characters, but I feared the shelf life of my brain might expire if I didn't make a conscious effort to pursue a higher level of learning. I decided to give myself permission and time to learn new things each day. Today, I feel more confident about attempting new tasks, making decisions, and carrying on conversations with people whose intellects I admire. I am also more open to new ideas and different ways of accomplishing everyday tasks. I truly believe that a commitment to lifelong learning causes you and me to get continually better as we get older.

A lifetime commitment to making our days count, rather than merely counting our days, starts now—wherever we are. How we spend our time in our 20s, 30s, 40s, and 50s will determine what we'll be like in our 60s, 70s, 80s, and 90s. Sometimes it's hard to remember this when you have a baby pulling at your pant leg, a

GOOD TO KNOW

As people age, their ability to remember details about their experiences and manipulate multiple bits of information at the same time decreases. Recent research, says Mayo Clinic, indicates that keeping your mind engaged in new and challenging activities can help prevent or reverse this normal cognitive decline.

grade schooler participating in every activity available, a teenager fighting peer pressure, or a boss who expects you to say, "How high?" when he says, "Jump." I remind you, as I keep reminding myself, that you have immeasurably more to offer to those who need you when you take time to develop yourself.

Why Bother? The Benefits of Continuing to Learn

1. You'll discover interests you didn't know you had. Learning begets learning.

2. The sense of accomplishment you gain from learning bolsters your self-esteem and makes you sturdier in tough times.

3. When problems arise and need solving, you'll have more brain data to draw from.

4. You'll be more fun to be around—for yourself and others. You'll be an agile conversationalist.

5. You'll teach your children the value of learning.

Continuing self-education

1. Keep a list of things you want to learn about.

2. Keep a list of books you want to read, and continue adding to it.

3. Read with a highlighter pen so you can mark thoughts and ideas you like and find them again later.

4. When you encounter something you want to learn about, jot it down so you can look it up later.

5. Create bookmarks on your computer of favorite Web sites.

6. Listen to audiobooks.

7. Research classes at a local college.

8. Watch the newspaper for lectures or events you'd like to attend.

9. Tell your friends when you're trying to learn about a particular subject; this will make them sensitive to information they hear about the topic that they can pass on to you.

10. Set aside time each day for reading.

11. Work crossword puzzles.

12. Play chess or other strategy games.

13. Play word games, such as Scrabble.

14. If you and your spouse like to read aloud, set aside some time each week to do so.

15. Learn a fact or new word a day from a daily calendar; share it over breakfast.

16. Learn more about English by studying a Latin-based language such as French, Spanish, or Italian.

17. Look up any word you hear that you don't know; keep a list of new words you learn.

18. Set up a writing corner in which you can write in your journal about what you're learning.

19. Try your hand at writing poetry or music.

20. Keep a few art supplies on hand in case you feel creative.

21. Start a book club with friends or coworkers.

NURTURING YOUR SPIRIT

Faith-Building Exercises

None of us has a perfect life. We all deal with sickness, pain, loneliness, disappointment, insecurity, failure, and death. How we face the storms of trouble in our lives and how they affect us for the rest of our lives depend on our faith and spirituality. Consider these ways to develop your spiritual self in ways that make you stronger, happier, and more at peace.

1. Remind yourself to be conscious of God's presence—in quiet moments at home, in sleepless moments in the middle of the night.

2. Keep a prayer journal. Write down your requests and record the answers. This will help you clarify your thoughts, be alert to answered prayers, and build your awareness of God at work in your life.

3. Make a point to sign up for a church or citywide women's conference or retreat. If you desire more personal time for reflection, look into attending a silent retreat.

GOOD TO KNOW

About 77 percent of women say that their faith is very important to them, according to a 2007 Barna poll.

4. When you face a dilemma, say to God, "If You are who You say You are, please give me guidance and help." After you ask, be quiet and listen with your heart and mind. He promised, "Call to me and I will answer you and tell you great and unsearchable things you do not know" (Jeremiah 33:3, NIV).

5. When you read a book by an author who speaks to you, try to read more of his or her writings.

6. Jot down ideas, prayers, verses, and quotes from books that give you insight and wisdom.

7. If you wonder, "How do I know that there is a God?" perhaps a more pertinent question to ask is, "If there is in fact a God, how can I find Him?"

8. Practice Sabbath rest. Someone once said, "God rested—and He wasn't tired." Rest is an opportunity for contemplation, reflection, and remembering who's at the center of the universe.

9. Collect inspirational music—music is the language of the soul.

10. Read a portion of the Bible every day. If you've always wanted to read through the Bible, One Year Bibles are arranged to guide you as you read through the Bible in a year (and there's no rule that says you *must* finish it in a year).

11. Take a walk in the park with a small child, adopting his or her sense of wonder. See what the child sees and give yourself permission to express the same awe of nature and the Creator.

12. On your way home from work or the store, pause to remark on the beauty of the sky or terrain.

13. When you eat something today, really taste it—and be thankful for the taste buds that let you enjoy it.

14. Note the different textures you brush up against today. Celebrate the unfathomable complexities of the world.

15. In a difficult situation, look for at least one thing you can be grateful for. The old adage about silver linings is very often true.

16. Write a thank-you note to someone who has had a positive impact on your life.

The Source

Every principle, strategy, and tip I have learned about living a well-managed, satisfying life—from taking care of my body to dealing with anger in healthy ways to running my home smoothly to balancing competing demands for my time and attention—has come from years of studying and applying principles from the Bible to everyday life.

If we had the chance to spend some time together, I would share with you how a quest for peace, satisfaction, and meaning in my own life led me to examine whether the Bible was just a book of stories with nice morals or a book of truth about the universe, men and women, and the Creator. I would tell you that through my failures, successes, questions, doubts, and subsequent search, I found the peace, satisfaction, and meaning I was looking for through a personal relationship with Christ. I would tell you how my faith affects my attitudes and actions on a daily basis, how it has carried me through painful life passages such as breast cancer and gives me the ability to face the future with courage and confidence. I would tell you that God is the center of my life, and He is in the process of helping me become the best wife, mother, friend, and professional I can be—and He will do that for you, too.

17. Practice spontaneous gratitude. When something positive happens to you or someone you love, pause to savor the experience.

18. Give thanks before meals. Thank God for all the people who worked to get it on your table: the farmer, the trucker, the grocer.

19. When you get into an ungrateful state of mind and begin to gripe and complain, try to see yourself in the future—how you'll want to have responded to the situation.

20. Celebrate something good that happens to you by doing something good for someone else. You'll find that your joy is doubled.

21. Make a list of the ways you've fallen short and want to be forgiven. Turn what you write down into a prayer of confession and thanksgiving for forgiveness.

22. When you act in a way that is hurtful to yourself or others, ask for forgiveness.

23. Forgive others in your life as you would like to be forgiven.

24. Share spiritual ideas with a friend. We can deepen our spiritual lives both by hearing others' beliefs and by saying our own out loud.

25. Join a study group with others who want to grow spiritually.

26. Worship regularly.

27. Take time to reflect on important spiritual ideas—the ones you want your life to emulate. As you turn them over in your mind, you'll find yourself living out the principles that have become a part of you.

28. Take the time to get to know an older woman whose faith you respect, who may be lonely and who has a lot to teach.

29. Practice self-control—let your husband wear his ratty sweatshirt in peace; hug your moody teenager; plan extra spots at your family's holiday table and fill them with people who would otherwise be left alone.

Affirmations
Positive truths about you

You are what you think. If you think of yourself as stupid, lazy, and uncreative, your life will express those beliefs. Many of us play criticisms over and over in our minds, and perhaps some of the people around us affirm them. The wonderful thing is, we aren't tied irrevocably to the negative thoughts we think—we can change them. And by changing our thoughts, we can change ourselves.

Following are affirmations from the Bible you can use to adjust your self-image. Read through them, choose the ones that speak to you most powerfully, and write them on an index card. Then post the card somewhere you'll see it every day—the bathroom mirror, inside your daily planner, by the kitchen sink—and say the passage out loud at least once each day. When you do this, you are writing over your mind's computer file—erasing negative statements and replacing them with positive ones.

You made all the delicate, inner parts of my body and knit me together in my mother's womb. Thank you for making me so wonderfully complex! Your workmanship is marvelous—how well I know it. . . . You saw me before I was born. Every day of my life was recorded in your book. *(Psalm 139:13-14, 16)*

Blessed are those who trust in the LORD and have made the LORD their hope and confidence. *(Jeremiah 17:7)*

Charm is deceptive, and beauty does not last; but a woman who fears the LORD will be greatly praised. *(Proverbs 31:30)*

If God cares so wonderfully for wildflowers that are here today and thrown into the fire tomorrow, he will certainly care for you. *(Matthew 6:30)*

Not a single sparrow can fall to the ground without your Father knowing it. And the very hairs on your head are all numbered. So don't be afraid; you are more valuable to God than a whole flock of sparrows. *(Matthew 10:29-31)*

Nothing can ever separate us from God's love. *(Romans 8:38)*

We are God's masterpiece. *(Ephesians 2:10)*

Dear brothers and sisters, I have not achieved it, but I focus on this one thing: Forgetting the past and looking forward to what lies ahead. *(Philippians 3:13)*

Positive truths about God

Even more remarkable than how the Lord looks at us are the characteristics of God Himself. Whenever your life becomes too overwhelming and you tell yourself, *I can't*, remember that God is greater than your circumstances—and His grace and strength never run out.

Who is like you among the gods, O LORD—glorious in holiness, awesome in splendor, performing great wonders? *(Exodus 15:11)*

You bless the godly, O LORD; you surround them with your shield of love. *(Psalm 5:12)*

I cling to you; your strong right hand holds me securely. *(Psalm 63:8)*

The LORD is compassionate and merciful, slow to get angry and filled with unfailing love. *(Psalm 103:8)*

The LORD is close to all who call on him, yes, to all who call on him in truth. *(Psalm 145:18)*

The LORD is the everlasting God, the Creator of all the earth. He never grows weak or weary. No one can measure the depths of his understanding. He gives power to the weak and strength to the powerless. Even youths will become weak and tired, and young men will fall in exhaustion. But those who trust in the LORD will find new strength. They will soar high on wings like eagles. They will run and not grow weary. They will walk and not faint. *(Isaiah 40:28-31)*

We are hunted down, but never abandoned by God. We get knocked down, but we are not destroyed. *(2 Corinthians 4:9)*

Give all your worries and cares to God, for he cares about you. *(1 Peter 5:7)*

WEB RESOURCES

These sites were last accessed in May 2008. While all these sites contain helpful information, inclusion does not imply endorsement by the author or publisher of all the content on any of the Web sites.

Appliances

http://www.appliance411.com
Appliance411.com offers general home-appliance information for consumers, including money-saving purchasing and servicing tips, information about getting repair parts, and many links to merchants and helpful Web sites.

http://www.appliance.com
Appliance.com provides descriptions of household appliances and selected lawn and garden equipment, as well as product reviews and tips on appliance maintenance. It also offers links to dealers, manufacturers, and buyer's guides.

http://appliancehelp.com
Appliance Help allows you to order replacement parts for various types of appliances.

http://www.aceee.org/consumerguide/index.htm
Consumer Guide to Home Energy Savings provides a checklist to help consumers conserve energy and reduce costs. It also gives tips on choosing energy-efficient appliances and lists the best ones based on product directories and manufacturer's data. It only includes models widely distributed in the United States.

http://www.consumerreports.org/cro/appliances.htm
ConsumerReports: Appliances provides reviews, information, and buying advice for appliances. Paid subscription required for full access.

http://www.eere.energy.gov/consumer
A Consumer's Guide to Energy Efficiency and Renewable Energy is a comprehensive U.S. Department of Energy site, including a glossary, fact sheets, and energy-conservation tips for several home systems and appliances.

http://doityourself.com
DoItYourself.com has more than 36 topics, covering everything from appliances and energy savings to concrete and woodworking.

http://www.pcappliancerepair.com
Point & Click Appliance Repair has a diagnostic chart on washers, dryers, refrigerators, dishwashers, and ranges. The difficulty index takes into account the ability of the average person, any special tools required, the time required to fix the appliance, and the danger associated with the repair. This site also allows you to purchase parts, manuals, and accessories.

http://www.repairclinic.com
RepairClinic.com gives troubleshooting and repair advice for most home appliances. It also sells parts and repair tools.

Autos

http://autos.aol.com
AOL Autos provides new- and used-car reviews, tips on buying and selling cars, insurance advice, financing information, and Kelley Blue Book values.

http://www.autodirectory.com
Autodirectory.com provides links to sites related to automobile pricing and buying, vehicle trends and innovations, insurance information, and warranty tips.

http://www.automobiles.com
Automobiles.com gives information pertaining to automobiles, including insurance information; suggestions on buying, leasing, and renting; and the rights of owners.

http://www.autoobserver.com
Edmunds AutoObserver provides information on the automotive industry, including analysis of auto-company events and strategies.

http://www.carspace.com
Edmunds CarSpace allows consumers to participate in forums about automobile issues, as well as write reviews of car dealers.

http://www.edmunds.com
Edmunds.com provides automobile pricing information, car reviews, ratings, and advice about purchasing a car.

http://www.edmunds.com/insideline
Edmunds Inside Line is a site for automotive enthusiasts that highlights auto shows, concept cars, and new automotive trends.

http://www.familycar.com
The Family Car gives tips on selecting a car, caring for it, and handling repair problems. The site also covers safe driving and styling trends.

http://www.fueleconomy.gov
Fueleconomy.gov gives side-by-side comparisons of up to three vehicles at a time and provides information on advanced and alternative-fueled vehicles such as hybrid vehicles. It also supplies information about gas prices and your car's energy impact.

http://www.nadaguides.com
NADA Guides is an online database of the National Automobile Dealers Association and provides price information, reviews, and comparisons for new and used cars, trucks, boats, recreational vehicles, and motorcycles.

http://www.newcarbuyingguide.com
NewCarBuyingGuide.com is an Internet magazine that provides pricing information, reviews, and guides for buying, leasing, and maintaining new and used vehicles. It also supplies information on auto insurance.

http://www.vehix.com
Vehix.com is an online solution for buying, selling, and researching new and used vehicles.

Babies

http://www.aap.org
American Academy of Pediatrics has articles, general health topics, professional-education resources, and a parenting corner.

http://www.americanbaby.com
American Baby offers information about conception, adoption, pregnancy, and parenthood. Read advice from an ob-gyn, a pediatrician, a midwife, and a nutritionist. It also has a fetal-development timeline, a due-date predictor, a baby-name search, a recipe center, and much more.

http://www.babycenter.com
BabyCenter offers info and advice about pregnancy and babies, including adoption, breast-feeding, child care, family finances, postpartum health, and sleep.

http://www.thebabycorner.com
BabyCorner includes baby-care information, pregnancy and baby forums (find others due when you are or with children the same age as yours), tips on preparing for the baby, and more.

http://www.baby-place.com
Baby-Place.com has over 100,000 pages of content. Includes reviews of high chairs, car seats, booster seats, strollers, safety gates, monitors, and more by price categories, and info on free stuff for parents.

http://www.babyzone.com
BabyZone provides parenting advice, chat and message boards, information on childbirth choices, fetal-development timelines, and pregnancy updates.

http://parenting.ivillage.com
iVillage: Pregnancy and Parenting site includes information on fertility, infertility, pregnancy loss, pregnancy, breast-feeding, health, safety, feeding, and much more.

http://www.lamaze.org
Lamaze International provides resources for expectant and new parents, and helps you locate classes in your area.

http://www.mops.org
Mothers of Preschoolers (MOPS) exists to meet the needs of every mother of preschoolers (birth to kindergarten) through relationships established in the context of local groups. MOPS encourages and supports moms through resources such as books, articles, magazines, online forums, and MOPS membership.

http://www.mrdad.com
Mr. Dad offers resources for fathers, including sections for expectant dads, first-year dads, toddler dads, lifetime dads, and single dads. It also includes an Ask Mr. Dad advice column, written by Armin A. Brott, a leading expert on fatherhood.

http://www.newbuyer.com/babyguide
NewBuyer Baby Product Buying Guide has advice for consumers about purchasing gear for pregnancy and babies. It also provides product reviews.

http://www.parenttime.com
ParentTime is designed for expectant families and parents of infants and newborns. This site offers a wealth of information on baby care and pregnancy.

Coupons

http://www.bargainist.com

The Bargainist displays the latest deals found across a wide range of product types and stores. Get coupon codes ready to be used on merchants' Web sites, and register for the "daily deals" e-mail newsletter.

https://www.centsoff.com

CentsOff has a large selection of brand-name coupons to choose from, delivered to you by mail.

http://www.coolsavings.com

CoolSavings offers money-saving coupons, helpful tips and articles, free samples, and more.

http://www.couponcabin.com

Coupon Cabin monitors discounts to more than 875 online stores, sorts through 2,000 weekly e-mails, and updates their coupon directory daily so consumers can take advantage of these great online savings.

http://www.couponmom.com

The Coupon Mom provides free grocery coupons for 36 different grocery chains, as well as restaurant coupons, free-sample offers, an online coupon organizer, and more.

http://www.coupons.com

Coupons, Inc. is the leading U.S. provider of consumer-printed coupons. You can also personalize your coupon lists based on zip code.

http://www.couponsurfer.com

CouponSurfer enables consumers to click or print to redeem personalized coupons from leading online merchants and national brands. Shoppers are notified by e-mail when selected products offer new savings.

http://www.dazzling-deals.com

Dazzling Deals helps online shoppers save money using the most recent coupons, coupon codes, rebates, discounts, promotional codes, special deals, and comparison-shopping at all their favorite stores with over 2,000 online coupons.

http://www.dealcatcher.com
DealCatcher is an online community that helps shoppers save money and make educated purchases. On this site you will find online coupons, products, sales, reviews, and rebates.

http://www.hotcoupons.com
H.O.T! Coupons is a leading online coupon source for consumers, offering local coupons and promotions on products and services for home, office, or travel.

http://www.mommysavers.com
Mommysavers has money-saving tips for families. The site includes forums, recipes, family-finance advice, coupons to print, and more.

http://www.mycoupons.com
MyCoupons provides searchable coupons and promotion codes.

http://www.resource4mom.com
Resource4Mom.com finds the best grocery and store coupons. It also includes the latest articles on health and nutrition, education, safety, entertainment, work-at-home opportunities, budgets, and finances.

http://www.valpak.com/coupons
Valpak online coupons are just like the ones you get in the blue envelope from the mail. Print coupons specifically selected for you based on your zip code.

Decorating

http://interiordec.about.com
About.com: Interior Decorating gives decorating ideas, articles, and tips, plus categorized links about kitchens, baths, home offices, furniture, flooring, and more.

http://www.bejane.com
Be Jane is a women's home-improvement resource and online community that gives ideas on do-it-yourself projects, home repair, painting, plumbing, electrical work, and more.

http://www.decorating4less.com
Decorating for Less has a free page giving step-by-step instructions for many decorating projects. It also has many articles about decorating and remodeling.

http://www.diyideas.com
Do It Yourself provides ideas for quick weekend projects, has articles offering interesting solutions to everyday decor and organization problems, and gives crafty tips to turn any home decor from drab to fab. This site also hosts forums and contains a definition list of do-it-yourself terms.

http://www.getdecorating.com
Getdecorating.com has thousands of photos of interior and exterior home designs to help inspire you. Membership required for some sections.

Emergency Preparedness

http://www.redcross.org/services/disaster/beprepared
American Red Cross: Be Prepared gives predisaster preparation checklists and advice for individuals and businesses on what to do in case of disaster.

http://www.fema.gov/kids
FEMA for Kids is a resource for kids to learn about disaster preparedness. In addition to informative articles, it contains stories and games about preparing for disaster. Includes information for parents and teachers too.

http://www.ready.gov
Ready.gov provides emergency-preparedness guidance from the U.S. Department of Homeland Security. It offers multiple publications and checklists to help you prepare for emergencies. It also contains links to related government and private organizations. There is a special section for kids.

http://www.fema.gov/library/viewRecord.do?id=1536
Taking Shelter from the Storm is a booklet that provides advice and instructions for building a shelter from tornadoes, hurricanes, and other natural disasters. It includes construction plans and cost estimates. On the Web page listed above, you can download or print the various sections of the booklet.

Gardening

http://www.birdsandblooms.com
Birds & Blooms offers easy-to-understand advice and ideas for bird-watchers and gardeners.

http://www.gardenguides.com
GardenGuides provides a collection of top-quality gardening information, including gardening how-tos by top garden writers, plant fact sheets and guide sheets, seasonal tips and garden techniques, garden recipes, and much more.

http://www.gardenideas.com
Garden Ideas helps you find gardening advice, see garden designs, or just get started on a project with a how-to gardening section.

http://www.gardenterms.com
Garden Terms is a gardening dictionary with brief definitions of a large number of terms, arranged both alphabetically and by category.

http://garden.lovetoknow.com
LoveToKnow: Garden has short informational articles on gardening topics, such as vegetable gardens, ornamental plants, indoor plant care, and garden pests. Articles are contributed and edited by users.

http://www.yardener.com
Yardener offers lawn and garden resources for home owners whose garden is not their hobby. Includes information and care data for many plants, shrubs, and trees, as well as help for dealing with pests and other plant problems.

Health

http://www.aap.org
American Academy of Pediatrics provides information about children's health issues, arranged by topic, such as diseases and conditions, child development, and child safety.

http://www.cancer.org
American Cancer Society provides up-to-date information about different types of cancer. It also offers resources for patients, their families, and their friends, supplying information about making treatment decisions and coping with the realities of treatment.

http://www.acog.org/publications/patient_education
The American College of Obstetricians and Gynecologists (ACOG) offers pamphlets on numerous women's health issues, including pregnancy; labor, delivery, and postpartum care; breast health; menopause; contraception; and more.

http://www.americanheart.org
American Heart Association offers practical advice for heart health, warning signs of heart trouble, information on diseases and conditions, healthy lifestyle tips, information on children's heart health, and more.

http://www.cdc.gov/vaccines
Centers for Disease Control and Prevention lists information about vaccines and immunizations, including scheduling and guidelines.

http://www.cmda.org/customcontent/drSearch/Default.aspx
Christian Medical & Dental Associations provides an automated doctor-search service that will locate Christian physicians or dentists in your area.

http://www.firstsigns.org
First Signs provides information about developmental milestones and screening tools to detect early indications of social, emotional, communication, behavioral, and developmental delays and disorders.

http://www.healthatoz.com
HealthAtoZ is a comprehensive, well-integrated health and medical resource developed by health-care professionals. It aims to improve health care by empowering consumers with online tools such as a target heart-rate calculator, an index of health conditions, a prescription-drug index, and a private personal health record where you can store vital medical information.

http://www.healthfinder.gov
Healthfinder.gov is a U.S. government site with a database of health-news articles arranged alphabetically by topic, a provider finder, and more.

http://www.healthywomen.org
HealthyWomen.org provides an alphabetical list of health topics as well as extensive lists of organizations and care providers that offer women-friendly health services.

http://www.kidshealth.org
KidsHealth provides doctor-approved health information about children from before birth through adolescence, with separate areas for kids, teens, and parents offering hundreds of in-depth articles and features. It provides current information about child development, nutrition and fitness, preventive health care, and diseases and conditions. Information is available in English and Spanish.

**http://mayoclinic.com/health/healthylivingindex/
healthylivingindex** *Mayo Clinic: Healthy Living* provides useful and up-to-date information and tools on various topics, such as fitness, sleep, stress, and women's health.

http://www.medicinenet.com
MedicineNet.com provides up-to-date health news, an alphabetical index of diseases and conditions, an interactive tool to help you diagnose the possible cause of health symptoms, a database of procedures and tests, and more.

http://www.mypyramid.gov
MyPyramid.gov includes a tool to estimate what and how much you should eat from the different food groups by entering your age, gender, and activity level. Provides information on your diet quality and physical activity status by comparing a day's worth of foods eaten with current nutrition guidance. This site also offers games, posters, and art projects for kids.

http://www.webmd.com
WebMD offers current health news, an alphabetical index of health topics, and an index of prescription drugs and treatments.

Home Maintenance

http://www.askthebuilder.com
Ask the Builder provides a glossary of home-improvement terms, videos showing how to complete common do-it-yourself tasks, an online store where you can buy e-books on various topics, and even an e-mail link through which you can contact Tim Carter, a nationally syndicated newspaper columnist, with your home-maintenance question. (He will respond personally.)

http://www.clickit.com/bizwiz/homepage/plumber.htm
Ask the Master Plumber allows you to e-mail your plumbing questions to an experienced plumber, who will respond personally. (Freewill donation to a charitable organization requested.)

http://www.bhg.com/bhg/category.jhtml?catref=cat10002
Better Homes and Gardens: Home Improvement Encyclopedia provides articles on topics such as tile work, lighting, shelves, storage, and flooring.

http://doityourself.com

DoItYourself.com includes more than 36 topics, covering everything from appliances and energy savings to concrete and woodworking.

http://doyourownpestcontrol.com

Do-It-Yourself Pest Control contains links to insect identification, insect help pages, rodent identification, recommended measures, professional equipment, and information about professional-strength products you can use yourself. The site also sells various pest-control products.

http://www.thefamilyhandyman.com

The Family Handyman Web site is the online version of *The Family Handyman* magazine. The site contains articles on topics such as simple ways to cut utility bills.

http://hammerzone.com

HammerZone.com provides do-it-yourself home-improvement how-tos.

http://www.homedepot.com

The Home Depot Know-How site (click "Know-How" tab on the home page) provides illustrated, step-by-step instructions for various home-improvement projects.

http://www.thehomefixitpage.com

The Home Fix It Page supplies you with lists of highly recommended service providers in your area who deal with specific home-maintenance issues. The site also lists weekly tips on basic home repair and provides a link through which consumers can send their questions to Dave Baker (of *The Home Fix It Show* on news/talk radio) by e-mail.

http://www.homeimprove.com

HomeImprove.com provides articles, photos, and plans for home-improvement projects, among other resources.

http://www.nettips.com/homepage.html

Home Improvement NetTips gives you up-to-date information about products and services to help you maintain and upgrade the value of your home. It also offers how-to brochures and more detailed information you can order directly from your computer.

http://homeimprover.com
HomeImprover Magazine provides current home-improvement articles, as well as an archive of past topics.

http://www.thehomeshow.com/pages/home_improve_high.html
Thehomeshow.com's Home Improvement Highway offers instructions for home repair and home-improvement projects. The site also provides an e-mail link through which you can send your home-maintenance question to an expert and receive free advice.

http://www.hometime.com
Hometime.com is the Web site of *Hometime*, a PBS home-improvement television show. On the site, you will find instructions for various home-improvement projects.

http://www.howstuffworks.com
HowStuffWorks: Home & Garden provides explanations, reviews, opinions, and prices on cooking, appliances, home improvement, lawn care, and more.

http://www.naturalhandyman.com
The Natural Handyman contains thousands of pages of home-repair tips and articles from some of the best home-repair authors and professionals.

http://www.remodeling.hw.net
RemodelingOnline: where the smart remodelers turn for how-to, design, and business advice.

http://www.repairclinic.com
RepairClinic.com offers free personalized help for appliance repair and also helps consumers identify, locate, and purchase needed replacement parts.

http://www.thisoldhouse.com/toh
This Old House provides advice on planning home-improvement projects and also supplies do-it-yourselfers with photo and video instructions on completing various projects. In addition, it offers an illustrated guide to home-improvement tools.

http://www.toiletology.com/index.shtml
Toiletology 101 offers a complete course in toilet repairs and maintenance. Learn how to save water and money by keeping plumbing fixtures in good repair.

Menu Planning

http://allrecipes.com

Allrecipes is a site that exists mostly as a community to share and review recipes. The site offers excellent search capabilities as well as several printing formats for the recipes. There is a free version of the site, but some of the recipe collections are only available by paid subscription.

http://www.eatright.org/cps/rde/xchg/ada/hs.xsl/index.html

American Dietetic Association is a link to reliable, objective information about food, nutrition, and healthy lifestyles.

http://www.bhg.com/recipes

Better Homes and Gardens: Food & Recipes provides meal ideas and 15,000 free recipes.

http://www.diabetesdiet.com

Diabetes Diet offers reliable articles explaining diabetes and providing nutrition information, advice on diabetic diet plans, and other tips.

http://www.thefrugalshopper.com/tips/grshopping.shtml

Grocery Shopping Tips gives advice on things to consider before, during, and after shopping. The site's main page also offers health and beauty tips, cleaning and laundry ideas, and much more.

http://www.kraftfoods.com/kf

Kraft has great recipes and even grocery lists and corresponding menus for the week.

http://www.mealsmatter.org

Meals Matter is a large site with several great functions. If you want to plan your own meals but like to try new recipes, this would be a good site for you. You can create a personal start page, and once you have a free account with the site, you can plan your menus and create grocery lists. This site includes some health and nutrition features, as well as ways to contribute your own recipes.

http://menus4moms.com

Menus 4 Moms offers free weekly dinner menus, grocery-list software, organizers and planners, home-organization and kitchen articles, recipes, and more.

http://www.nutritiondata.com
Nutrition Data provides complete nutritional information for any food or recipe and helps you select foods that best match your dietary needs.

http://www.healthykids.com
Parents.com: Healthy Kids includes not only health-related information but also food and recipe ideas, craft projects, and game ideas.

http://www.recipezaar.com
Recipezaar is similar to Allrecipes in that it offers a place to share and review recipes and also has both free and paid accounts. It also allows you to search for recipes by course, ingredient, type of cuisine, preparation time, and more.

Parenting

http://www.christianitytoday.com/parenting
Christianity Today: Parenting is a great resource with articles on parenting kids from preschoolers through teens. A weekly e-mail newsletter features articles designed to encourage Christian parents.

http://www.crosswalk.com/parenting
Crosswalk.com: Parenting is a great resource for articles about Christian parenting and faith, as well as resources for the family on marriage, divorce, finances, and homeschooling. The site also hosts community forums devoted to various aspects of Christian life.

http://www.familycorner.com
FamilyCorner.com experts offer advice on important childhood issues, from teething to talking to your preteen about difficult topics. There are also recipes, craft ideas, games, and message boards.

http://www.familyeducation.com
Family Education provides parents with practical guidance, age-specific info about issues kids face, strategies and materials to help you get involved with your children's learning, free e-mail newsletters, and much more.

http://familyfun.go.com/parenting
The *FamilyFun* parenting area is a comprehensive online source for expert advice and ideas on the early stages of parenting, from pregnancy and newborns to preschoolers and kindergartners.

http://www.familylife.com
FamilyLife offers a "Better Parenting" tab with articles and
audio from Dennis and Barbara Rainey, free newsletters and
publications, tips on manners and more, and a Christian parenting forum.

http://www.focusonthefamily.com
The *Focus on the Family* Web site has a parenting section that
offers guides on child development, health and safety, discipline,
and parenting stages.

http://www.mops.org
Mothers of Preschoolers (MOPS) exists to meet the needs of
every mother of preschoolers (birth to kindergarten) through
relationships established in the context of local groups.
MOPS encourages and supports moms through resources
such as books, articles, magazines, online forums, and MOPS
membership.

http://parenting.ivillage.com
iVillage: Pregnancy and Parenting offers information about fertility, pregnancy, and parenting as well as opportunities to participate in discussion and support groups.

http://www.parenthood.com
Parenthood.com provides articles to help you raise a happy,
healthy child from conception to graduation. It also offers recipes, forums, and a tool to help you calculate the cost of raising
a child.

Safety

http://www.redcross.org
American Red Cross provides information about first aid and
safety, domestic disaster relief, community services for the
needy, support and comfort for military members and their
families, and blood donation.

http://www.redcross.org/services/hss/tips/healthtips/
safetywater.html *American Red Cross: Water Safety Tips*
lists general water-safety tips, specific safety information for
a variety of water sports, and advice on keeping children safe
around water.

http://www.aap.org/family/carseatguide.htm
Car Safety Seats: A Guide for Families includes a summary of types of car seats, safe use, latches and tethers, and a list of models and manufacturers including weight restrictions and prices.

http://www.isafe.org
iSAFE teaches kids and teens how to be safe on the Internet by avoiding dangerous, inappropriate, or unlawful online behavior.

http://www.kidshealth.org/kid/watch/out/summer_safety.html
KidsHealth: How to Be Safe When You're in the Sun helps you learn about safety in the heat and sun. Includes information about how sunburns happen, what SPF means, how much water to drink, and heat exhaustion.

http://www.lidsonkids.org
Lids on Kids talks about snow-sports safety and answers questions about helmet use while skiing and snowboarding. Includes games and puzzles, articles, and information about how to get started in snow sports.

http://www.madd.org
Mothers Against Drunk Driving (MADD) provides numerous resources for parents and content for teens to prevent drunk driving, support the victims of this violent crime, and prevent underage drinking.

http://www.nsc.org/issues/index.htm
National Safety Council: Safety Issues offers information on first aid, emergency preparedness, poison prevention, and more.

http://www.drugfree.org
The Partnership for a Drug-Free America includes information about drugs, their effects, and treatments. Shows paraphernalia associated with different drugs and includes personal stories. The site also has a section specifically for teens.

http://www.safekids.org
Safe Kids Worldwide provides information about product recalls, as well as tips on car-seat safety, toy safety, and more.

http://www.seatcheck.org
SeatCheck.org finds car-seat inspection stations by state or zip code. Also provides a recall list, tips, and brochures.

http://www.sparky.org
Sparky the Fire Dog is aimed at children ages five to nine. The site includes articles about child safety, games, and a section where kids can ask Sparky questions as well as learn all about dalmatians and fire trucks.

http://www.cpsc.gov
U.S. Consumer Product Safety Commission (CPSC) provides information about consumer goods and issues recalls on unsafe or dangerous products.

http://www.usfa.dhs.gov/kids/flash.shtm
U.S. Fire Administration for Kids provides short lessons about fire escape planning, smoke alarms, and general home fire safety. The site also offers games and coloring pages.

http://www.cdc.gov/ncipc/factsheets/drown.htm
Water-Related Injuries: Fact Sheet provides information on drowning and prevention.

Schooling

Homeschooling

http://homeschooling.about.com
About.com: Homeschooling provides unit studies, games, a forum, local resources, and a weekly newsletter.

http://www.christianhomelibrary.org
Christian Home Library is a lending library including carefully selected materials that provide customers with thousands of Christian-education options. CHL will mail items directly to patrons' homes.

http://www.eclectichomeschool.org
Eclectic Homeschool Online is an online homeschool portal with extensive resources and support for creative homeschoolers, including state laws and regulations, curriculum reviews, articles, and a bookstore.

http://school.familyeducation.com/home-schooling/educational issues/34389.html *FamilyEducation: Homeschooling* offers tips on how to homeschool and how to stay within your budget, as well as lesson ideas, expert help, and discussion groups.

http://www.homeeddirectory.com
Home Educators Resource Directory provides a comprehensive list of homeschool resources, state homeschool directories, homeschool suppliers, support groups, and more.

http://homeschoolcentral.com
Homeschool Central provides advice for new and veteran homeschoolers, links to sites offering specific curriculum materials, links to support groups organized by state, and more.

http://www.homeschool.com
Homeschool.com offers tips on starting a homeschool program, as well as links to curriculum providers, lists of homeschool field trips organized by state, a homeschooling resource guide, and more.

http://www.homeschoolernetwork.fen.com
HomeSchooler Network provides lessons, activities, and articles to help homeschoolers in the education and parenting aspects of their lives.

http://www.homeschoolinginamerica.com
Homeschooling in America helps parents who are considering homeschooling, those who are ready to get started, and those who have been homeschooling for years. Find information on state laws, support groups, styles, local resources, and support for homeschooling in every state in America.

http://www.home-school.com
Homeschool World is the online home of *Practical Homeschooling* magazine. It contains a large number of articles and current news stories about homeschooling, online experts, an up-to-date events list, support groups listed by state, a list of contests for homeschoolers, a forum, and more.

http://www.learningbygrace.org
Learning By Grace is a provider of online Christian homeschooling curriculum and is the parent organization for several online homeschooling academies, including Jubilee, MorningStar, and Grace.

Private, Christian, and Charter Schools

http://privateschool.about.com
About.com: Private Schools offers information about private
schools throughout the United States and Canada, the admission
process, and tips for choosing the right school for your child.

http://www.greatschools.net
GreatSchools provides information about the differences
between private, public, and charter schools and gives parents
a chance to compare schools in their area. A parent community
forum is also available.

http://www.asd.com
American School Directory offers a searchable database of
schools in the United States and includes maps and directions.
There is a subscription fee.

http://www.aacs.org
American Association of Christian Schools helps parents find
Christian schools in their state.

Public Schools

http://www.ed.gov/
U.S. Department of Education has a section for parents with
tips for helping children succeed in school, options for parents
within the public school system, and the latest educational news
and research.

http://www.schoolmatters.com
SchoolMatters is a site for parents who want to research information about public schools in their area. You can find reviews
from other parents about your child's school or write one
yourself.

http://www.schoolmatch.com
SchoolMatch collects and publishes data such as test scores,
student-teacher ratios, and spending patterns in schools.

http://nces.ed.gov
National Center for Education Statistics provides facts about
schools at all levels as well as a searchable database to find
information about a particular school.

Travel

http://www.camping.com
Camping.com helps you find a campground or RV park, make online camping reservations, view travel guides, buy camping gear, and connect with other campers.

http://www.cnn.com/travel
CNN.com/travel offers tips on travel planning, getaway ideas, and top destinations around the world.

http://www.fodors.com
Fodor's Web site supplements content from Fodor's guidebooks with up-to-the-minute travel advice; user ratings of thousands of sights, hotels, and restaurants; and lively discussion forums where travelers exchange information and ideas.

http://gorp.com
GORP is a site with information on every aspect of outdoor activities and traveling, from destination guides and adventure-vacation packages to information about camping and paddling.

http://outside.away.com
Outside Online has articles from the world's best travel writers, advice on equipment, fitness regimens, expedition coverage, and true stories about outdoor enthusiasts and expeditions.

INDEX

C

cake
    baking tips   123–125
    decorating tips   123–125
calendar   8
canned goods, storing   38
car
    gasoline tips   105
    leakage   104
    maintenance   103, 105
    saving for   199
    warning signs   103–104
    Web resources   276–277
carbon monoxide detectors   80
carpet
    beetles   34
    deep–cleaning   70
    eliminating odors   57
    loose threads   70
    padding   81
    purchasing   77
car pool   184–185
catalogs   45–46
cheese, shopping tips   131
Cheesy Potato Boats   116
children
    activity overload   186–187
    age-appropriate chores   57,
        61–63
    allowances   214–215
    anger management
        for   155–157
    artwork   47
    assigning chores   19
    bedroom organizing   33
    bedtime and   188–189
    book storage   33
    chores and   145–147
    clutter control   46–47
    disciplining   154–155
    faith building   157
    finicky eaters   115–118
    grandparents and   159–160
    home alone   185–186
    homework   182–183
    honesty in   153–154
    Internet and   162–163
    manners and   160–161
    physical fitness and   157–159
    sex education and   163–164

teaching about
    money   213–215
teaching values   151–152
test-taking skills   183–184
TV and   161–162
chimney cleaning   82
choices. *See* decision making
chores
    age-appropriate tasks   57,
        61–63
    benefit to kids   178
    delegating   11, 145–147
    kitchen   113–115
Christmas   240–242
circuit breaker   94
clean, family definition of   146
cleaning
    10-minute tasks   48–50
    abrasive cleaners   81
    five-minute   18
    one-day clean sweep
        plan   51–52
    one-hour tasks   50
    shortcuts   52–56
    treating stains   70, 71
    while you sleep   50–51
    Closet Cleaning Day   33
closets
    cedar   34
    children's   33
    master bedroom   34–35
clothing
    attic or basement
        storage   31–32
    caring for   71
    closet storage   34–35
    drawer storage   35
    shopping tips   202–204
clutter
    attic   29–31
    basement   29–32
    bedroom   34–35
    children's room   33
    conquering   43–47
    contest   47
    controlling children's   46–47
    control plans   43–47
    declutter in a day   43–44
    garage   41–43
    home office   35–38

S

ACKNOWLEDGMENTS

For many years I dreamed of writing a helpful reference book for busy moms. I am exceedingly thankful for all the people who have worked to make my dream come true:

Dan Johnson, president of The Idea Agency; Jan Long Harris, Doug Knox, Kim Miller, Nancy Clausen, Sarah Atkinson, Yolanda Sidney, Maggie Rowe, Sharon Leavitt, and Mike Morrison from Tyndale; and Tyra Damm, Mary Darr, and Ann Matturro, who provided expert editorial and research assistance.

Most of all, I thank my husband, Bill, for his love and commitment to help me fulfill my calling.

ABOUT KATHY PEEL

Kathy Peel is called America's Family Manager by the media and by millions of women. She is the author of twenty books (over 2 million sold), including *Desperate Households*.

She is founder and CEO of Family Manager. Her company provides training and resources for women and families through a national network of certified Family Manager Coaches trained through the Family Manager University online campus.

Kathy serves as AOL's Family Coach and is a contributing editor to Scholastic.com, *American Profile*, and *HomeLife*. Her articles and ideas have appeared in *Family Circle, Ladies' Home Journal, Redbook, Woman's Day, Reader's Digest, Parents, Parenting, Child, Woman's World, FamilyFun, Cooking with Paula Deen, Cooking Light,* and many other magazines.

Each year Kathy is a guest on many TV and radio programs, including repeat appearances on *Oprah, The Early Show, Good Morning America, The Today Show,* CNN, MSNBC, WGN, HGTV, Lifetime, the Fine Living Network, the Discovery Channel, and *Focus on the Family*.

She speaks frequently—nationally and internationally—at conferences, corporate programs, colleges, and churches about life and family management, work-life balance, parenting, entrepreneurship, leadership, and women's issues.

A graduate of Southern Methodist University, she and her husband, Bill, have three grown sons. They live in Dallas.

Her Web site is www.familymanager.com.

Restore order & harmony to your life & home... starting today!

Feeling overwhelmed? It's time to turn to Kathy Peel, America's Family Manager, for help. In *Desperate Households*, Kathy offers realistic, do-it-today ways to complete your own life-changing household makeover and bring calm to your chaotic days. You'll learn about common scenarios that cause women the most stress; pinpoint what's driving your own anxiety; and discover personal, lasting solutions that will work for your family.

Make home your favorite place to be— and sweep desperation out the door!

desperate households

Features
10 LIFE-CHANGING FAMILY MANAGEMENT MAKEOVERS

kathy PEEL